You Don't Have to Go It Alone

Passing on Wisdom about Motherhood to the Next Generation

Katharine Wistar Block

PRESS

Katharine Block

to Kimberly —

May God Bless you !

§

"Kitty Block's new book promises to be a "**block**-buster" in the Christian arena! She has masterfully woven reality with truth from the Scriptures to make a heart-rending story that's hard to put down. Godly principles are modeled and explained in such simplicity that seekers and young Christians alike can understand and apply them to their own lives. It's an awesome story of love and joy in the Lord. A *must-read* for all young women, mothers or not!"

Joyce J. Ashley
Founder of JoyJoy Ministries
Author and Speaker

"This book offers hope and encouragement not only to young mothers, but also to Christian families and leaders who value and promote a strong family unit and connectedness. It is a realistic Christian approach to healthy family living and community support without legalism."

Brigitte Ranae
Certified Life Coach,
Empowered Living

"I have known Kitty Block for over thirty years. The positive impact that she and her husband have had on me and my wife in our marriage—and especially in raising our kids—is inestimable."

Tom Kraeuter
Author and Speaker

"God designed the family as a place where we can grow in our relationships with Him and with one another. This book is a *treasure* of God's wisdom to build healthy families—rare items in today's society! Together, Frank and Kitty Block have discovered some of the 'treasures of wisdom and knowledge' in Christ mentioned in **Col. 2:3** for building a strong family *His* way. I highly recommend this book as an important resource for all Christians seeking to learn and apply key principles from God's Word about victorious family living through Christ!"

Mary Jo Starkey
Senior Pastor's wife
Victory Church, Pevely, MO

"In an era of single parenting and broken homes, this book shines as an "easy read"—full of simple, Godly wisdom for how to keep ourselves or our families on track. None of us have perfect role models and nobody gets things right every time but the characters in the book show us how we too can triumph over issues that face each of us in our roles as daughters, single women, wives, parents, and believers in God. I came away from the book challenged to grow with a pocket full of new ideas to help me along the way."

Abby Schwartz
Mother of two boys

"Kitty has a mother's heart and a friend's words of encouragement and consolation. Reading this book is like having a chat with her in her living room. It's full of hope and wisdom."

Becky Powell
Mother of four

But as for you, speak the things which are proper
for sound doctrine;
that the older men be sober,
reverent, temperate, sound in faith, in love, in patience;
the older women likewise,
that they be reverent in behavior, not slanderers, not given to much
wine, teachers of good things—
that they admonish the young women to love their husbands, to
love their children,
to be discreet, chaste, homemakers, good, obedient
to their own husbands,
that the word of God may not be blasphemed (**Titus 2:1-5**).

Table of Contents

§

Author's preface

§

The book you are about to read is what I'd say to you if you came to me looking for help and we could sit down together, have a cup of coffee and talk about motherhood, marriage, raising children and creating a family that works. It is wisdom gleaned from the years of raising six children, with the accompanying trials, tears and triumphs.

Women have passed down motherly wisdom to one another through the ages and this book continues that tradition, answering the age-old question: how *do* you raise healthy, happy and god-fearing children? It is particularly geared toward the young woman who may have missed out on being mothered well herself and feels shaky and insecure as she approaches motherhood or who is already in the midst of it and finds it overwhelming.

The story is fiction, but everything I discuss I have put into practice in the real-life crucible of our own family of eight. And please know, our family was as real as they come, complete with strife, noise, squabbles, love, loyalty, laughter, teasing, anger, hurt: the whole bit. I count our children among my best friends now, but it took a while to get there!

My husband and I started out as hippie college students—he an atheistic Jew and I a faintly believing Quaker—with no clue as to who Jesus really was. Oh, we'd heard of Him, the way most people in America have heard of Him but neither of us had ever read the Bible. We were lost, disillusioned, rebellious and going nowhere fast until God reached down and beckoned. Inexplicably, we followed.

We married as brand-new believers, and quickly realized our own ways weren't sufficient to withstand the strain of living together on a daily basis. In desperation, we began reading the Bible, trying to understand and follow what it says about husbands and wives and raising children. The pages that follow are the result of those years of trial and error, study, failure, success and grace.

For it's God's grace that follows us wherever we go; it's that same grace that underlines all we do; it's that same grace that forgives our errors and sins and encourages us onward. I pray you will get whiffs of that grace as you read on.

I hope Katie comes across as real and fallible, since she's loosely based on me, and I am utterly real and utterly fallible. Our family has had its share of trials, some of them due to my ineptitude or inattention, and I know how frail and human I am. That's where that grace comes in.

Families are where we are nurtured and raised, for better or for worse. As parents, and specifically as mothers, we have the responsibility to make those families as strong, healthy and loving as we can make them for they truly form the foundation for the rest of our children's lives. God promises to bless our families, but we have to fight for them. They don't just happen. His wisdom is there, available to each one of us, to guide, heal and strengthen our families, but we have to dig for it.

I trust this book will be a gold mine where your digging will be fruitful.

I need to say a word or two about the experiences I included that did not actually happen to me. I mentor women in our church, mostly listening and encouraging as they talk their way through their problems, and much of the material related to Theresa's character comes from things they've told me. I salute these women for their courage and determination to find healing and wholeness.

And a word of deep admiration for the people who have made up the bulk of the material for this book: my family. I love you all passionately and am grateful for the love and forbearance you've all shown me over the years, especially when I've failed you. Thank you for all you've taught me about being a mom. (I'm actually still learning, as I watch you now with your own families!)

And to my husband: favorite man, best friend and dear companion, the one who makes me laugh, the one who has guided our family with wisdom and humor for over forty years now: my love forever.

One last thought: This is a second version of the original book. The chapter on discipline has been completely re-worked and the name of the man of the family has been changed to honor my husband, who never liked the first name I chose. Other than that, and a few minor grammatical changes, the book is essentially the same.

Katharine W. Block
November, 2012

Tossing the knife on the cutting board and rinsing my hands, I grabbed the phone.

"Hel-*lo?*" I bit off the word. Whichever kid this was had better make it quick.

"*He-e-y* there, *Ka*-tie, it's me, Jean-*nyne!*" If enthusiasm had a name, it was Jeannyne. I could just see her full, open-mouthed smile, red painted lips and deep dimples—her best feature, she often said. I could almost smell her strong perfume.

Oh. . .wonderful. . .just what I need. I closed my eyes and felt my whole body droop. This would not be a quick conversation.

Breathe, Katie. Take a cleansing breath. Relax. I quietly breathed, a deep one in through the nose and out through the mouth.

"*Gir-rl*friend! You *the-ere*?! I'm *tal*-king to you! *You* hoo! *Smile,* honey, it makes you look *so-o-o* much better!" Her loud, singsong voice collided with my headache and I winced.

Put a smile on your face, girl, even if she can't see it. I put a feeble smile on my face. Good thing she couldn't see it.

"Yep, I'm here. What's up?" I picked up my knife again.

"Hey, I have a favor to ask! A hu-*mong*-ous favor!" she burbled. Surely I was thrilled?

I can hardly wait.

"Is this a good time? I *know* you're busy, but this is the only time *I* could find and—"

I'm nowhere near as busy as you, right? So don't worry about it.

"My sister, Theresa," Jeannyne went on without drawing a breath, "I've told you about her and her problems a ga-*zil*-lion times, well, she just called, *cry*-ing for pity's sake, saying she's in a crisis, a-*gain!* I mean, when has that girl *not* been in a crisis? She flunked out of *community college,* can you believe that, I mean, really, *community college?* Puh-*lease!* She diddled around so much, only going when she felt like it that she lost her scholarship, not that it was that much, but *still!* She could have done better if she'd applied herself, but *no-o,* she couldn't do that. And would she listen to sister Jeannyne who was valedictorian of her class of 456 students at the state uni-*versity* and who *might* have some good ad-*vice* now and then? Not on your life! To add to her problems, she and Mom are in a huge fight. All Theresa wants to do is laze around, so Mom kicked her out of the house, and now baby sis has nowhere to live, surprise, surprise. She's just *couch* surfing, hanging out at other peoples houses. Can you buh-*lieve* that? I mean, we *nev*-er, and I mean *nev-er*, no matter how poor we were, we *never* just *mooched* off people. Moochers, the *low*-est beings on the social ladder. And I mean *the* lowest!"

Jeannyne sounded as though she was removing something distasteful from her mouth.

I sighed, quietly, through flared nostrils.

I thought it was 465 students...at least that's what you said last time...or was that the time before?

Taking a quick breath, she swept on.

"So, anyway, girlfriend, she *never* calls me until she's a complete mess and *then* she calls, crying, expecting *me* to bail her out. I mean, if she'd called earlier, maybe I could have done something, but *now?* Katie, she needs help, *your* help. I am *not* the one to help her, buh-*lieve* you me, since I have tried, and *tried*. I have told her a million times to get her act together, but our talks always ends in a dis-*as*-ter—I'm talking about a screaming and yelling disaster—so now *once* again, her life's a *mess*, but will she listen to *me* about getting it in order? No, sir-ee bob*!* Don't listen to old Jean-*nyne*—*she* doesn't know what she's talking about, even though *she* has a house in the 'burbs, a husband with a job and two kids making straight A's, but *no*, don't listen to *her!* What does *she* know about life?"

I threw the chicken pieces into a casserole dish and shoved it into the microwave. Jeannyne was on a roll now and stormed on.

"And she used to be a smart girl, too. Won the state spelling bee in third grade. And *now* look at her! What a mess! But *you're* the mothery type, Katie, and I bet you'll be able to talk some sense into her head and anyway, don't you have a spare bedroom in your basement? So, did you say yes, she can come stay with you guys until she can get her act together again? I'll owe you big time, I mean for-*ever*, and I *so* appreciate—"

I don't recall being able to get a word in edgewise, much less saying yes.

"I'll have to talk it over with Craig. How long does she need a place to stay?" I ran hot water into the sink, gave it a good squirt of soap and began scrubbing the cutting board.

"Girlfriend, I *hon*-estly don't know, could be a week, two weeks, a *month* even! Who *knows?* She's just *moping* around, has *no* sense of responsibility, *no* motivation, *no* initiative, *no* *gump*-tion! Can you buh-*lieve* it? I mean, she's an a-*dult*, so who does she think she is? The queen of *She*-ba or something? She needs someone like *you*, girl-friend, to help her get *Off. The. Couch*!!!"

I could hear her banging something in her immaculate kitchen on each syllable.

"She needs someone like you to tell her to shape *up* and get *moving*! What is *with* her, I have *no* idea! I mean, look at me, *I* made it through school okay, I mean I'd say more than just okay, on the dean's list for three out of four semesters at OSU for pity's sake, so for the love of *mer*-cy, why can't *she*? You know, sometimes I lose my *pa*-tience with her, just the *tiniest* little bit. Honestly, I'd help her in a flash if I could..."

"Mmmm hmmm..." holding the phone to my ear with my shoulder, I scrubbed my hands in the soapy water, dried them and began getting out ingredients for a salad.

"But you know as well as I do that *that's* out of the question."

Yes, I figured that out a long time ago.

"I mean, come *on*, I have a family to take care of and I volunteer three mornings a week. . .*you* know how it goes when you're busy. Well, maybe you don't since you're just home all the time and don't work but anyway, can *you* help her? Seriously, girlfriend, she *needs* your help. I mean, if you can believe it, this could be her *last chance*." She made this last pronouncement as if she were already thinking up her sister's obituary.

Closing the fridge, I laid the phone on the counter for a moment and closed my eyes, rubbing my aching temples. Yeah, I could believe it. I was there once.

Jeannyne picked up again before I could think of a thing to say. "She *says* she's a Christian, but girlfriend, I sure don't see her *living* like one. I *think* she loves God, in a weird way, and if you can believe that I have a bridge to sell you in Arizona, but she doesn't have a *clue* how to live a Christian life, hel-*lo-o*, with marriage, family, kids, job—all that stuff *you're* so good at! So what do you think, when can you and Craig—"

I swept the vegetable peels into the disposal and rubbed my tem-ples again. Jeannyne's voice was not designed to soothe headaches.

"I'd love to help if I can, Jeanie. We'll have to see how the live-in thing will work—"

I glanced at the calendar on the wall. Also at the clock.

Jeannyne barreled on; did she even hear me?

"—pick her up? I know you'll be just *mar*-velous for her, you're so good at family stuff. Thanks, Katie, thanks a *bil*-lion, I *knew* you would, you're a *doll*, you have no i-*dea* how much this means to me since I care about the kid, I really do, even if she does drive me *wild, if* you can believe it. I mean ab-so-*lute*-ly *wi*-ild! You *know* if *I* could teach her anything, I would, in a New York minute, you know I would, don't you? I'm sure you know that since really, we're close, I mean, after all, she's my only sister, but she says I have my life so together that it's *sickening*—can you believe that? Sickening? That was the very word she used—and she says there's no way she can relate to anything *I* tell her. Can you just buh-*lieve* that!"

I could almost see her proudly surveying her designer kitchen.

Well, yeah, I could believe it. I'd never seen so much as a speck of dust in her house. An art deco rooster standing on a wrought iron table amongst the decorations on her front porch held a pump of hand sanitizer for guests to use *before* they entered the house—without shoes, please—while inside, plastic covers protected every chair from human contact and slippers were provided for those wishing to walk on the white carpet. From what I'd heard of Theresa, yeah, I could understand her problems relating to Jeannyne. Our house would be a much better place for her.

"She won't have to worry about being perfect here! There's junk on the floor and dust behind the couch. We mostly just muddle through."

"Yeah, I know, but your *mudd*-ling seems to work! Don't know for the life of me what your *se*-cret is, but your kids seem so respectful, and I've never even *heard* you and Craig raise your voices at each other, and Katie, sometimes *I* wish I could come over and live with you for a just a few days. . ."

Was that a touch of vulnerability I just heard?

"Get out! You wouldn't last a minute in this house! All the noise and commotion and kids? Ha! It'd drive you crazy in a minute."

"You are *so* right, girlfriend!! I'd just curl up and *die*! I *don't* know how you do it, Katie! All those kids. . .all that noise. . .no *thanks*." She laughed. Whatever else drove me crazy about Jeannyne, her laugh made up for it: full-throated and warm, it seemed to say we were both in on the joke and that, despite her hyper personality, she was a good friend. To me, anyway.

"But *seriously*, girlfriend, I've told you our story a *jil*-lion times: dad, the jerk, left mom—and her with only a tenth grade education for pity's sake—with us two little girls to fend for ourselves while he skips off with Wife Number Two, with her blond hair, bronze skin and all, and then, *after* mom's done all the hard work of raising us—or *ruin*-ing us, I can never tell which—he reappears with *Trophy* Wife, that's what I call her, *Trophy Wife, Troph for* short, I'm like, hi *Troph, so* good to see you, *not!*—and her two *perfect* little blond-headed clones who I can't *stand!* The *jerk*!! Mom was so busy working three jobs trying to make ends meet, *she* didn't have time to teach us how to be good wives or mothers. I've just been *wing*-ing it for the past nine years, an' I sure wish someone had given *me* some guidance along the way, so when do you think you could—"

"Let me talk to Craig and I'll get back to you soon as possible. Couple days okay?"

"Sooner the better, girlfriend, sooner the better. I don't know how much longer these people she's hanging out with are going to put *up* with her, but another few days won't kill her, so just let me know, and I'll pray Craig says yes, and you'll call me as soon as–"

"Yep. I'll call you. Craig's walking in the door, gotta run. Love you."

"You too, girlfriend, you too, and you're a doll, just a plain *doll,* and I just *know* you're gonna be *so* good for her–"

"Gotta run, Jeanie, bye. I'll be in touch soon."

Click.

I don't think I'd ever heard Jeannyne actually say good-bye.

*   *   *   *   *

I stood there looking out the window for a minute after she hung up. A slow crawl of anticipation stirred down in my gut somewhere.

God, please give me wisdom. There are so many young women like Theresa, who've never been taught how to have a happy marriage and family life. Show me how I can help.

*   *   *   *   *

I called Jeannyne back a few days later.

"Jeanie? It's Katie. Craig and I've prayed about it and we'd love to help Theresa. Jason had just moved down to the basement bedroom, but he and Jocelyn say they'll be willing to share a bedroom again for a while."

"That is *so-o* amazing, Katie," she gushed, "your kids are *so-o* cool. Mine would never in a million *years* give up their bedrooms for some total *strang-*er, so tell them *thanks* from me, will you—double, triple, quad-*ruple* thanks—and tell them their aunt Jeanie loves them and thinks they're *won-*derful, and I'll make it all worth their while in the *very* near future, I *pro-*mise, and Katie, uh. . .there's one thing I didn't tell you. . . uh. . .Theresa's pregnant and there's no dad in the picture, but I'm sure that will be no big deal for the two of you, you're so wonderful about stuff like that that I just *know–* "

Gulp.

"Wow. Glad you told me. Doesn't change anything on this end, but it's good to know. How far along is she?"

"Maybe four or five months, but *really*, how should *I* know, she never tells me *any-*thing, but I'm sure it won't be a problem for you and Craig, since you guys–"

"Nope, it won't. Tell her she can come over this weekend. That'll give us a few days to change the kids' rooms around. We're looking forward to meeting her."

"Don't get *too* excited, now, girlfriend, she's kind of a *pain*, you know, not at all re-*spons-*ible or anything—"

Yikes, God. A pregnancy too?

*   *   *   *   *

I helped Jason take down all fifty paper airplanes he'd thumb tacked to the ceiling of his basement bedroom. We moved them, his huge Lego collection, his beanbag chair, and his Star Wars posters back upstairs to the room he'd shared with his twin sister Jocelyn since babyhood, re-tacking all the planes onto the ceiling of his half of the room.

I knew I was pushing it; at ten, the twins were almost too old to share a room, but they were willing to give it a try again for a while. At thirteen and fifteen, Molly and Liz had shared a room all their lives, and the older boys, Rob and Jeff, had small bedrooms out in the addi-tion we'd built after the twins' arrival. That was their territory where they could listen to their own music and clean their own bathroom. I rarely stepped foot out there.

Jocelyn had divided the room with a line of masking tape across the ceiling, down the wall and across the floor. She'd pushed her book-shelf right up to the line, the shelves facing her side. Her Barbies sat across the top, their grotesquely long legs waving out into Jason's air-space. She'd taped off for herself a generous easement so she could reach the closet, and a piece of tape divided the closet bar into thirds; two for her and one for her brother. When I pointed out this discrep-ancy, she replied that boys hardly have *anything* they need to hang up. For *real*, Mom!

Jason shoved his much smaller bookshelf against hers, facing his side, and filled it with his Lego creations. He carefully tilted each Barbie onto her back so her legs didn't touch his bookshelf.

Hmmm. . .should be an interesting few weeks.

*   *   *   *   *

"Okay, guys," Craig said, at the supper table that night, "if any of you has a problem with Miss Jeannyne's sister living with us, let Mom or me know. We don't know how long her visit will last but we want to make her feel welcome for as long as she stays. Jase and Jossie, thanks for being willing to share a room again."

"Just as long as Jossie doesn't leave her girly stuff all over the room, I'm cool with it." Jason said around a mouthful of spaghetti.

"You, Joss?"

"Just as long as Jason doesn't act like a hotshot, we'll be fine. If he does, I'll put my Barbies down in his bed." She tossed her head, running her hand through her hair as she'd seen the big girls do.

"Gross!" Jason about choked on his spaghetti.

"I don't think we'll need to go that far, Princess. You older kids?"

"I think it's awesome we can help Miss Jeannyne's sister! I'm gonna get our youth group to pray for her."

"Let's not spread her problems all over church just yet, Lizzie. I appreciate your eagerness to help, though.

"Is she gonna stay here until she has the baby?" Molly wanted to know, "'Cause maybe I can help her with it. We're studying parenting in Life Skills class and next month we have to carry a doll around for a week that cries and wets for real. It'd be cool if I get to practice on a real baby." She cradled her flat chest as if a real baby already lay there.

"Quit snickering, Jason! It's okay if I like babies! If Mom hadn't liked babies, you wouldn't even *be* here. So *there!*" She stuck the tip of her tongue out at her brother.

"Does it wet and go wanh-wanh? Do you get to feed it a bottle? Do you get to cawwy it awound?"

"Jase, quit bugging your sister!" Craig gave Jason 'the look' and turned back to Molly. Jason mimicked his sister rocking a baby.

"Mo-om," Jocelyn hissed at me, "Jase is–"

"Shh! Dad's talking."

"We don't know how long she'll be here, honey. We'll just take it a week at a time. Guys, any thoughts?"

"Just make sure she doesn't smoke because of my asthma. Otherwise, she can do what she wants. I'll be busy with my job and school and stuff." Serious and focused, Jeff was looking ahead to high school graduation and college in the fall.

"Rob?"

"I'm cool with it. Just as long as she doesn't mess up our family too much. Like, are we going on vacation with her? I sure don't want to spend two weeks in the camper with some strange chick and her baby."

"We'll deal with that when the time comes. We've got a while yet. So, everybody's okay with this idea? Go for it, guys. I know you'll do a good job."

A loud belch rang out.

Rob looked at his father in wide-eyed innocence.

"That'll be twenty-five push-ups."

"Aw, Dad, I couldn't help it. It just came out!"

"That'll be thirty. You know the rules; on the floor!"

Rob leapt to the floor and did thirty push-ups in perfect form, fast and hard. Red-faced, he slid back into his seat, glancing at Jeff for approval.

"Great meal, sweetheart, thanks. Kids, make sure to thank your mom for the meals she puts on the table night after night. Who's on dishes tonight?"

Groans all around. The schedule for dish duty was often hotly contested, but I let them figure it out on their own. That was one problem I didn't need to mess with. Tonight I had other things on my mind.

CHAPTER 1

Jeannyne Asks Me a Favor

Questions for Discussion

§

1) What would you do if you were in Katie's place and a friend asked if her sister could live with you for a while?

2) Would you put time limits on the stay, or keep it open-ended? Would you feel free to say no to a request like that?

3) If you have children, would you ask them to give up their bedrooms, as Jason did, so a stranger could use their bedroom for an indefinite period of time?

4) Have you ever been in a situation similar to Katie's where you took someone in to live with your family for a while? How did it go?

5) Have you ever been on the opposite end, like Theresa, needing a place to live for a while? How did that go?

6) Do you think it's easier to be on the giving or the receiving end of help of this sort?

7) Discuss your thoughts about our responsibility—or lack thereof—to mentor and help others who may be in need. How far does this responsibility extend? When is it okay to say no to a request of this nature? Or do you feel it is ever okay to say no to someone in need?

CHAPTER 2

Theresa Comes to Our House

§

The following Saturday Craig, Jason and Jocelyn went to pick Theresa up. I puttered around, straightening an afghan here, a picture there, wondering what we were getting ourselves into. Going outside, I picked a bunch of daffodils from my weedy garden and took it down to her room in the basement.

I straightened the lace doily on her bedside table, placing the vase of flowers next to the reading lamp. I smoothed the old red bedspread I'd dug out of the closet and fluffed the pillow in its red and white flowered sham. Light slanted in from the high window. I turned on the bedside lamp to make the place look a little more cheery.

Upstairs, the front door banged open.

Gotta put a doorstop behind that door before it makes a hole in the wall.

I hurried up the stairs.

That or just train the kids not to bang it open like that.

"Mo-om! We're home!" Bang again.

Think I'll just try a doorstop.

"She's here!" Jocelyn announced, dragging Theresa into the family room.

"I can see that, sweetheart. Theresa, hi, we're glad you're here. I'm Katie. You've met Craig and the twins. Here's Molly, our thirteen year old. Molly, meet Theresa. Lizzie, our older daughter, is babysitting, but she'll be back early this afternoon. Our two older sons are working today, but they'll be back in time for supper. You know, food draws boys like a magnet." I smiled widely.

Why was I babbling on so?

"Nice to meet you, Mrs. Tucker." Theresa murmured, barely audible. Head down, she stood in the middle of the family room where Jossie had parked her. A dingy pink gym bag hung off one shoulder and an oversized, fake black leather purse kept sliding off the other. She hitched it up, keeping her eyes on the floor. She wore short shorts and a faded red tank top under an old grey sweatshirt that hung loosely over her bony shoulders. Her shorts and tank top didn't quite meet over her little bulge, showing a belly button ring. Worn flip-flops on grimy feet completed her outfit. She tucked a strand of lank hair behind her ear and clutched her sweatshirt around her, keeping her eyes on the floor.

"Oh heavens, please call me Katie! Everyone else does. Except these guys, of course. To them, I'm just plain old Mom!"

Theresa smiled ever so faintly, flicking her eyes at me for just a second.

"Let me show you to your room." I said, heading downstairs. "Towels are on the bed, the closet's over there, bathroom's just down the hall. You look tired, would you like to lie down for a while?"

"Thanks, ma'm, er, Katie. I am kind of tired. I guess Jeanie told you I'm pregnant? I seem to be tired all the time these days. Tired and kind of sick. 'Specially in the mornings."

"That's no fun, I know. I spent my share of days hovering around the toilet, trying to decide if I was going to throw up. It'll pass, I promise."

"A nap sounds good about now." She dropped both the gym bag and the purse on the floor and flopped onto the bed facedown.

"Okay, everybody, clear out! Theresa needs a nap. We'll call you for lunch, honey. Rest well and don't hesitate to ask if you need anything." I shooed the gang upstairs and closed the door softly behind me.

*   *   *   *   *

Theresa slept through lunch and into the afternoon. I didn't have the heart to wake her.

After lunch, I started folding a huge pile of laundry on the dining room table, the only place big enough to hold all the laundry these kids generated. The house was quiet: Craig had gone on an errand; the big kids were working; Jason was playing basketball with some buddies down the street, and Jocelyn was in another world, lying on her bed reading. I wondered how Theresa was doing.

Half an hour later, she wandered up the stairs, a little dazed.

"Hi, there! You sure slept a while! Feeling better? Bet you're hungry. Want a snack?"

"Actually, I could eat a horse. But don't bother fixing anything. Just show me the way to the kitchen, and I'll grab some chips or something." She stood at the door, hugging her sweatshirt around her middle, barely looking at me.

"Honey, if you're going to have a healthy baby, you need to eat well. I'm not going to preach to you, but if I was your mama, that's what I'd tell you." I led the way into my sun-filled kitchen. It was the one room we had remodeled and I loved the sky lights, hickory cabinets and green and white marbled wallpaper bordered with ivy.

"Yeah, well, my mama didn't teach me much, so whatever you want to teach me is okay with me. I sure don't want to be a bother to you folks. I appreciate you taking me in for a while to get my feet under me again, but don't feel like you have to keep me forever." She murmured all this so quietly I had to strain to hear her.

I pulled out a stool at the breakfast bar for her but she remained standing.

"I guess Jeannyne's told you about me. . .?" Her voice faded out as if even talking about Jeannyne was painful. She twisted her hands on the counter in front of her. Her fingernails were painted black, chipped, bitten to the quick.

"Not a whole lot. Just that you're pregnant and need some place to live for the moment."

"Yeah. Well, I don't know how long this 'moment' is gonna be. I'm at my wits' end, if you really wanna know."

She leaned against the bar stool, pulling her sweatshirt tight, trying to be invisible.

"I don't know what to do since I got pregnant. It was unexpected.. . .I mean, the father and I aren't even dating. He was just some guy one night at a party. . .When I told him I was pregnant, he just said, 'You sure I'm the dad?' As if I slept around! I told him to get out of my life. I didn't want any jerk like that being the father to my child. So here I am, left holding the bag. As usual. Pretty much the story of my life." She hitched herself heavily up onto the stool, as if already feeling the weight of her unborn child.

"I mean, what am I going to do?" She mumbled more to the counter than to me.

"I flunked out of my first semester of community college. I lost my scholarship because I missed too many classes 'cause of morning sickness. My folks are no help. My mom's not speaking to me; she's got her hands full just getting food on the table—she's never been much help to me anyway, and certainly not after I went and got myself pregnant—and my dad," she ducked her head, letting her hair cover her face, "now that he's been sober for a while and has turned his life around, well, he has a new family. . .a glamorous wife, two little girls who get anything they want. . .and they sure don't need *me* messing up their perfect life. Anyway, he lives in California.

"Jeannyne's a pain. Her house is so perfect, I'm afraid to sit down. Besides, she nags all the time. Are you gonna tell her everything about me?"

She looked at me with pleading eyes. Mousey hair fell limp over the side of her face, half covering a strawberry birthmark that ran from her jaw into her neck. She tucked her hair behind her ear and restlessly pulled it out again, playing with a strand. The sweatshirt, old and saggy, slipped off her shoulder, revealing a twisted and grimy bra strap peeking out from under her tank top.

"Honey, whatever you say here stays here. Whatever you and I talk about will be between us, unless you tell me I can share it. It's up to you." I poured her a glass of milk and got out some graham crackers and continued talking.

"Now, about us.

"The whole family eats dinner together every night, and you're invited to join us. You're part of the family for as long as you're here, with all the rights and responsibilities attached thereunto," I finished cheerfully.

Could I elicit a smile?

Theresa drooped on the counter, leaning her head on her hand, looking at me doubtfully.

Maybe not.

I rattled on. "Supper is whenever we're all here, usually around six-thirty or seven. The boys don't get home from their jobs until then. If that's too late for you, feel free to have a snack earlier, but we'd really like you to eat with us."

And that's *not* a suggestion, I almost added.

"Wow. I don't know if I've ever eaten a family dinner around a table. You guys do this every night?"

"We do. It's the only time we can talk and see how our days have gone, so we make sure we're all there. Occasionally one of the girls has a babysitting job but eating together is an important way for us to keep our family together." I leaned against the bar across from her, munching on a cracker, studying her.

Has she ever had a family dinner in her life?

"Wish my parents had thought of that." She murmured in a barely audible voice, letting her hair fall in front of her face again.

"One of our sons has asthma, so no smoking in the house."

"Don't smoke. That's one thing I've never tried."

"Good. It's terrible for a baby in the womb, not to mention a newborn. The other thing is the TV. There's not much worth watching in my opinion, maybe the news, the Olympics, the World Series, or the elections, but not much else. I encourage the kids to do things other than sit and watch TV. You watch it much?"

"I kind of like my soaps. . ." She smiled, a brief flicker and it was out.

"They're on during school, aren't they? Maybe we can work something out. I don't want you to feel like you've entered boot camp or anything!" I smiled, held it for a beat, hoped she'd smile back.

Again that wan smile flickered on and off.

"Got any questions for me?"

"I'm in kind of a daze right now. Don't know what to think. But thanks. Thanks for the milk and crackers. Don't know when I've had milk and crackers for a snack before." She pushed her hair behind her ear again, pulling it out and twisting it.

"Well, make yourself at home. We're glad you're here." I smiled again, trying unsuccessfully to catch her eye.

Leaving her at the bar, I went back into the dining room, placed the piles of folded clothes into the basket, and holding the towering pile down with my chin, headed through the kitchen for the back stairs. Placing the basket on the first landing for the next person, probably me, to carry up, I called over my shoulder,

"Gotta start dinner. Want to help?"

"Sure. Don't really know how to cook, though." She muttered, licking her fingers and using them to pick up the graham cracker crumbs.

"Just keep me company. We can talk." I put on a garish red and blue plaid apron with yellow rickrack and uneven ruffles the twins had made for me two Christmases ago. It was the ugliest apron I'd ever seen but they made it for me so I wore it.

"So, tell me about yourself. What are your plans and dreams?"

"Well, I *was* in college. I was hoping to be a nurse. That's pretty unrealistic right now, though, since I've been bouncing around from place to place. I can't find any anchor, if you know what I mean. You probably don't, though. You've got your life all organized, just like my sister's. Everything's going your way."

"Just like the song, 'Everything's going my way'?" Trying to elicit a smile, I sang the line from the old musical. Theresa looked at me strangely.

"Sorry, showing my age. That's from *Oklahoma*—the musical."

"Oh. We never saw musicals or anything like that. My folks divorced when I was three, and after that I lived with my mother. She didn't have time or money to take us to fun stuff. I think she was pretty depressed and resented us girls. Especially me." She traced a pattern on the counter top.

"I'm sorry to hear that. Raising children is hard enough with two parents; I can't imagine doing it as a single mom." I ran a pan of water for the potatoes.

"Yeah, well, don't praise her too much. She didn't do that great a job, with me especially. Jeanyne was older when everything began to fall apart, so seemed to turn out all right, but I'm just bumbling along, barely making it."

She leaned one arm out along the counter and laid her head on it.

30

Lord, help me teach Theresa what she needs to know before she leaves our house.

Katie, just love her. Let Me do the teaching.

CHAPTER 2

Theresa Comes to our House

Questions for Discussion

§

1) Why did Katie emphasize that they all ate around the table each night for dinner? Why was it so important to her that Theresa join them there each night?

2) How do you think Theresa was feeling as she heard Katie discuss their family life? What emotions do you think Theresa was feeling as she entered this totally new environment?

3) If you had a similar live-in guest, how would you handle meal times?

4) How do the evening mealtimes go in your home? Is eating together important in your family?

5) What did you think of Katie's remarks about TV?

6) Discuss the things that you think bring a family together. What things can cause families to drift apart, even while living in the same house?

CHAPTER 3

Forgiveness

§

T he next morning, Theresa didn't show up for breakfast. Craig could tell I was irritated.

"Give the girl a break, Katie. She just got here, probably doesn't feel well and maybe she's not in the habit of eating breakfast. Not everybody's a rise and shine girl like you, lovie."

I clamped my mouth shut, smiled sweetly at the kids and ate my oatmeal.

A few hours later, Theresa moseyed into the kitchen. She obviously hadn't showered in a couple of days; her hair lay lank and greasy with a rat's nest in the back, and she had terrible morning breath. She wore the same tattered sweat shorts she'd been wearing since she arrived and a stained grey tank top. The shorts and top didn't meet in the middle, exposing a tattoo in the small of her back of a rose with the word *beautiful* arched over it.

She only had that small gym bag with her when she arrived yesterday. I wonder how many clothes she has with her or even owns?

"Morning, sleepy-head! Hungry yet? I've just finished cleaning up after breakfast, and usually I don't cook again until the next meal, but I'll make you something today."

I hoped she caught the word *today*. If she did, she didn't comment.

I'm sorry, God, but I'm not going make a meal every time she decides to show up!

"What'll it be? Eggs, cereal, toast?" I asked brightly, whipping the red and blue plaid apron back on.

"You have any coffee? I usually drink that and have a few crackers in the morning since I feel so sick. I don't usually do breakfast, but I'm trying for the baby's sake. Just show me where they're at, and I'll get them myself. I don't want to put you out," she mumbled in a monotone, as she slouched in the doorway, one foot tucked behind her leg.

"It's no problem, honey. Why don't I show you around the kitchen anyway? I'm hoping you'll give me a hand with meals sometimes. The girls are so busy with school and sports and their babysitting jobs that they're not as much help as I'd like."

"Yeah, well, I'm not sure I'll be much help, but I can try. You folks are nice enough to take me in, the least I can do is to help a little. Just show me what to do." She parked herself at the kitchen bar and began pushing her hair behind her ears and pulling it out again, twirling a strand between her fingers, looking distinctly ill at ease.

*   *   *   *   *

For the first two weeks, I put up with Theresa's tardy arrival for breakfast dressed in her slovenly sleepwear with as much grace as I could muster. Which wasn't much.

At least I put a smile on my face each day, thinking that would suffice. It seemed that we were all on our best behavior, at least for a while.

Theresa consistently slept in until eleven or twelve. Sleeping in was something I didn't have much patience for even with my own children. I figured everyone should get up in the morning and get on with the day unless they were on vacation.

I reminded myself that she didn't feel well, that this was all a new lifestyle for her, and that my job was to love her, not correct her.

One morning, however, I'd had enough. I don't know if I was having PMS or what, but I lost patience with her as she moseyed upstairs yet another morning around 11:30, smelly, sleepy and unattractive. I couldn't tell when or if she'd showered, and I'm not big on body odor, not even my husband's. Leaning my elbows on the counter where she sat at the bar stirring her fourth spoonful of sugar into her

34

coffee, I peered up into her face behind that veil of hair, trying my best to keep my voice gentle and kind.

"Theresa, I'm going to level with you. I've asked you to join us for breakfast several times now. This is not a hotel where people can come and go as they please and eat at whatever time of day suits them. I make meals at mealtimes, not all hours of the day. You're welcome to have a snack any time you want, but please show up for meals. If you need to go back to bed after breakfast because you're not feeling well, that's okay. I do expect you to abide by the house rules, though. Do you understand?"

Normally I hated confrontation, but I was on a roll now.

"And while I'm at it, please make sure to come to the breakfast table decently dressed. We have teenage boys in the house, and I don't want them to see you like this." I waved my hand at her outfit, the same smelly shorts and tank top she wore every morning. I didn't recollect having seen her do any laundry, and it showed.

Without a word, she turned around and went downstairs again. I heard her bedroom door close softly.

I didn't see her for the rest of the morning, and I sure didn't feel like going down there to check on her.

Eventually I went grocery shopping. After that, I picked up the twins from school. A teacher workday meant noon dismissal, giving me time to spend with just the two of them, something we didn't often have. I took a cooler to put the groceries in just in case we decided to go to a park on the way home and hang out for a bit.

As I drove, I talked to God, something I often do. I'm not good at having a formal prayer time every day, but I do talk to Him a lot about the everyday things in my life, and this was one of those times.

Lord, I'm getting a little tired of this. Can't she help out a little? I don't like having a slovenly character exuding bad breath and body odor drift upstairs any time she feels like it! Can't she conform to our household rules just a little? *I'm not a* saint, *you know!*

Did I hear a faint heavenly chuckle at that statement of fact?

Okay, okay, so You and I both know I'm no saint. So I need Your help, Father. Please give me the patience and wisdom I need to help Theresa. She really is kind of like a motherless lamb, wandering around.

Just like you used to be.

35

You're right, God. I was lost until I found You. The things I did in college before I knew You. . . .

I shook my head.

No point in going there now. Someday, maybe, I'll tell Theresa. Maybe it would help her relate to me better?

It surely might.

*   *   *   *   *

The twins and I decided to pick up some hamburgers and go to the park down by the creek to eat them. We'd gone there since they were little and even now they liked to sail leaf boats under the bridge and wade in the water, looking for crawdads. I pulled my jeans above my knees to give my white skin some sun and, seated at a picnic table, stretched my legs out in front of me. I leaned my elbows back on the table and watched the two of them gingerly wading out into the water. That is, Jossie waded gingerly; Jason splashed on ahead.

Lord, they're growing up so fast. Before I know it, they'll be teenagers like the rest of the kids. When they turn thirteen, we'll have five teenagers in the house. Dear God, help us.

I remembered something my pastor's wife had told me years ago as we were stepping into the teen years and I was apprehensive, big time. "Just enjoy them," she'd told me. "They may be going through all kinds of changes—these years are a wild ride for parents and kids both—but they're fun years, too. Enjoy them."

At the time, I'd been a bit skeptical and worried what the teen years would be like but I was finding out that she was right; it was fun. I almost didn't want Jeff to fly out the top of the nest. He'd be turning nineteen just before leaving for college next fall and I knew our family was about to change forever.

*   *   *   *   *

We arrived home just in time to start dinner.

No time to check on Theresa now. She'll be up when she smells food, I'm sure.

I pulled out the leftover casserole from the night before. It looked a little crusty and dry, and there wasn't as much as I had planned on. My head felt heavy; I couldn't think.

Why can't I think straight? Let's see, we'll have this with some broccoli and salad. . .no, that's what we had last night. Okay, we'll have. . .

I held my head in my hands with my elbows propped on the counter. Nothing seemed to come to mind. My brain felt fuzzy.

God, I can't think!

Isn't there something you should be doing?

Yes. Make supper. I just can't think what to have!

Katie. . .

Don't bug me about her, God. She's the one who stormed off!

Silence.

God, I need your help planning supper here; give me some inspiration, please! I'm tired and I can't think straight and I need to feed my family.

Katie. . .

What?!!

First things first.

Okay, God. I'll go check on her. You happy?

Untying my apron and flinging it on the counter, I stormed down the stairs.

God, give me patience because I really need it right about now. Please give me your love for this girl 'cause I sure don't have any of my own!

I jerked open the door to her room. It was empty. A piece of paper lay on the bed. With a sinking heart, I picked it up and read: "If you folks don't want me here, just say so. I don't want to be a bother to nobody. Call Jeannyne. Bye."

Oh God, I moaned, sinking down on the bed. *When will I ever learn to curb my tongue? What have I done to this poor girl? Why can't I learn to be more patient?*

Keep going. Everything's under My control.

I'm glad it is, because I'm not doing that hot of a job here. What do I do now?

Call Jeannyne.

Well, I guess I could have figured that out on my own!

God, I do want to help Theresa, but I'm not getting anywhere, *so would you please be in charge here?*

I am.

*   *   *   *   *

I dialed Craig's number and cradled the phone between my shoulder and ear as I gazed out the back window, tapping impatient fingers on the counter. It looked like a storm was brewing.

How appropriate.

"Honey, dinner's gonna be late tonight. I have to go over to Jeannyne's to get Theresa."

"What's she doing over there? I thought the two of them didn't get along."

"Yeah, well, it's kind of a long story. I read her the riot act this morning about functioning more as a member of the family—you know, not wandering upstairs at 11:30 in her stinky night clothes every morning—and she split. Fortunately she's just over at Jeannyne's because otherwise I wouldn't have a clue as to where to start looking for her."

I rested my head in my hand.

Did I really want to do this?

"You gonna be able to handle this, honey? The last thing any of us need in this family is to have a stressed-out, grouchy mother. You're the hub of the household, you know. You get out of whack, we're all out of whack."

"I know. I think I can handle it. I *want* to handle it. I *want* to help her, Craig, I really do. I just need more patience, that's all."

Thunder grumbled in the distance.

"Well, if you think you've blown it, you know what to do. I'll bring home some pizza for supper. I'm willing to give this a try for a couple more weeks, but if it's gonna send you spinning, it's not worth it to me."

"Just pray for me, will you?"

"I will and I am. Love you, babe."

"I love you too, sweetheart. I can't do this without your support."

"I know. Now you go find her and make things right between the two of you."

"I'm going, I'm going."

Blowing an exasperated sigh out from between tight lips and hanging the cordless back on its stand, I trudged out the door.

God, this is kind of a pain, You know!

*　　*　　*　　*　　*

Twenty minutes later, after stepping into Jeannyne's magazine-perfect house, greeting my friend and promising we'd talk later, I scuffed down the hall in her slippers and pushed open the door to her guest room, done in Blue American Country. Theresa lay on the crisp white eyelet bedspread, scrunched into the fetal position, her hair over her face, still wearing the same clothes she'd worn that morning. I thought she was asleep. I hated to wake her, but we had to get home to our family.

"Theresa?"

I tip-toed across the deep pile cream carpet to the bed and gently shook her shoulder. Jerking her head up, she looked around, dazed. I sat down on the edge of the bed.

I wonder how long she'd been asleep.

"Hey, girl," I said softly.

"Look, you don't have to keep me if you don't want to, you know. I'm not a charity case or nothin'." Her eyes looked unnaturally bright and for a brief moment, I wondered if she was high.

God, I hope not. I'm not sure I could handle that along with every-thing else.

"No, honey. Listen to me. I'm sorry I hurt your feelings this morning. I got mad and said things in a way that was not kind or loving. That was wrong of me and I am sorry. I know I've offended you. Can you find it in your heart to forgive me?"

She sat up and stared at me, brushing the hair out of her face.

Had anyone had ever said those words to her before?

"Me, forgive you? I don't get it."

"I was sharp and nasty to you and hurt your feelings, and that was wrong of me. As a follower of Christ, when you hurt someone's feelings, you need to repent to them and ask their forgiveness. That's what I'm doing now. Will you please forgive me for hurting you? I was wrong to be so snippy."

"Yeah, I forgive you, whatever that means. But you don't have to do this, you know. I mean come after me an' all an' say you're sorry. You don't owe me nothin'."

"Well, really I do. If I'm going to follow Jesus with all my heart, I have to apologize when I blow it. Even if it *is* a little embarrassing!" I tried a smile. She didn't smile back. Mostly, she just seemed dumbstruck.

"We do want you back. Will you come? We'd love to have you and you're not a charity case, you know!" I tugged gently on her toe.

That seemed to clear her head because she suddenly focused on me and said firmly, "Yes, I forgive you and yes, I will come back. Thanks." She pushed her hair out of her eyes and swung her feet over the edge of the bed.

I gave her a hand up.

* * * * *

Supper was unusually subdued that night with everyone either tired or walking on eggshells. Afterwards, Theresa helped with the dishes and quietly slipped down to her room. The older kids did their homework; Rob and Molly sprawling on the family room floor amidst books and papers and Liz at the dining room table, working on her math. Jeff was out in his room, listening to music, no doubt. Craig lay on the couch, reading the paper. I played a few rounds of War with the twins, eventually sending them off to brush teeth and get ready for bed. After I'd followed them upstairs a few minutes later for prayers and good-night kisses, I thought of Theresa lying down in the basement bedroom by herself. On my way back through the family room, I mumbled something to Craig about going down to check on her and tiptoed downstairs. I sure didn't want to wake her if she was already asleep.

She was lying on the bed, staring at the ceiling.

Good grief, there's nothing for her to do down here. She should come upstairs with the rest of us.

You sure she feels comfortable doing that?

Ok, God, I'll try to make sure.

"Hey, Theresa." She sat up, startled. I started again. "Hey, I just thought you might like to come upstairs for a before-bed cup of tea or something. You don't have to stay down here, you know. For as long as you're here, you're part of the family."

"I've just been thinking about you asking for my forgiveness. No one's ever done that to me before. Amazing. . ." she shook her head. "You were the one who was angry with me, and then you come to me all soft and gentle and ask *me* to forgive *you?* I thought I was the one who was wrong."

Help me say the right thing here, Lord.

I sat down on the bed by her feet, and taking a foot between my hands, rubbed it gently. It was cold and rough, with calluses and chipped toenails.

"Well, perhaps you were, but that's between you and God. My responsibility is to take care of my part. Nothing frees a person up like asking forgiveness when they've blown it, or, on the other hand, forgiving someone who's hurt them."

"Well, I've never had anyone ask my forgiveness before–though there sure has been plenty of opportunity! So this is all new to me. You *did* hurt my feelings, and I *was* mad at you—and now I'm not. That's amazing! I don't even feel mad. Wow." Pushing herself up on her elbows, she smiled a real smile at me for the first time, a small one, pushing the hair out of her face.

"You know, honey, this is part of what it means to be family. We get mad at each other; we hurt each others' feelings; we make mistakes, but we can make it right with each other again by asking the person we've hurt to forgive us. It's forgiveness that keeps mountains

41

of anger and resentment from building up. All *they* do is to separate us from one another!"

"Tell me about it! That's the story of my life."

She sat up, making sure to leave her foot in my hands.

"The only way we can forgive, or ask forgiveness which is sometimes harder, is through the power of Jesus. He's the one who gives us the grace to humble ourselves enough to ask forgiveness."

I put that foot down and picked up the other, continuing to rub.

Next time, I'll have to use lotion.

"Could you, like, teach me how you do this stuff? I mean, I see your family, and you actually seem to be happy with each other. . .I've never seen that before. . .I don't know. . .can you help me be that way, too?"

"Theresa, I'd love nothing better. Let's go get a cup of tea, and we can talk. I'll be happy to tell you whatever you want to know." I gave her a hand off the bed and asked, "Mind if I give you a hug?"

Head down, hair falling over her face, she gave a quick shake no.

Her shoulders felt bony beneath my arms, but I felt her relax just a tad as I gave her a squeeze.

As I turned to go upstairs, I heard her mutter, "Can't remember when I was last hugged...my mom sure never did."

CHAPTER 3

Forgiveness

Questions for Discussion

§

1) How were anger and hurt feelings handled in your family of origin? What about your current family?

2) Did your parents model forgiveness and repentance when they blew it (which every parent does), or were ugly outbursts and hurt feelings "swept under the carpet" and not dealt with?

3) What were the results of the ways your family of origin solved (or ignored) hurt feelings and anger?

4) There seems to be a turning point in Theresa's heart during this chapter. When does it occur and why do you suppose a change begins?

5) What do you think about parents repenting to their children for their mistakes? Do you think that kind of humility and honesty makes the child think less of their mom or dad, since he or she is admitting his or her mistakes? Or does it create respect for that parent?

6) Discuss the difference between just saying, "I'm sorry," instead of, "I was wrong for (name the specific offense), will you please forgive me?" Is there a difference and if so, is that difference important?

CHAPTER 4

What Are Salvation and Grace, Anyway?

§

A few minutes later, each holding a cup of tea, we curled up on either end of the sage green couch in the formal living room. The room had white walls and white carpet and we'd never gotten around to replacing either with something more kid-friendly. We didn't use the room much, but at a time like this it was a quiet place to talk. A large picture of a seascape filled the wall behind the couch, the blue-green and lavender of the ocean echoing the lavender-blue of an afghan on the back of the sofa.

I got up and laid the afghan around her shoulders.

She looks like she wishes she could just crawl up on somebody's lap.

"Okay," I said, settling myself back with my cup of tea, "the only source I know of hope and direction for our lives is God. He's the one that's made all the difference in my life."

"How's that?" she murmured from behind teacup and hair.

"I became a believer in Jesus in college. Up 'til then, I had no idea what a believer in Christ was. I had no idea about sin or salvation. No one had ever told me about Jesus. I'd never opened a Bible. I didn't even know the Lord's Prayer!"

Theresa shook her head, incredulous. "You? Can hardly imagine it," she murmured, sipping her tea and looking at me over the top of her cup. "So what happened?"

"'Well, to that point, I'd had little moral guidance in my life, and I was wandering down the wrong paths, searching for the masculine love I wasn't getting at home, giving myself to male after male, not knowing that there was any other way. I despised myself. I used to look in the mirror and sneer at my reflection, saying, 'your name *Katharine* means pure. Ha! You're anything *but*. You're filthy!'

"I'd dropped out of college once because of depression, and after a year out, was trying it again, but it wasn't going well. I could feel myself spiraling down into another depression. I could find no meaning to my life. I was looking, searching, in one relationship after another, having sex; the whole bit. In fact, I remember saying to myself, 'If I end up having a baby, I'll just keep it here in my dorm room in the closet and feed it between my classes.' How's *that* for both stupid and dumb? But that's how I was until I met these girls. . ."

I stared off into space for a moment, musing on my life back then. *What if you hadn't found me, God?*

"Yeah? Go on. Don't leave me hanging there." Theresa snuggled into her corner, hands wrapped around her tea cup, watching me intently.

"I met two girls in my dorm who were excited about life, and who believed God was excited about their lives, too. They were so different from me and all the other depressed college students around us that I had to know what made them tick.

"One day, they invited me to a prayer meeting. By then, I was so desperate for the peace they had that I would have crawled to church if I'd thought it would've helped! After the prayer meeting, I walked home in the rain and with tears and raindrops mingling on my face, I cried, 'Whatever this is, God, I want more of it! I want all You have for me!'"

"So what happened? Did God appear to you in a blaze of light or something?"

"No. Little by little He convinced me that not only was He God, but that the Bible is true and that Jesus is the lover of my whole being Who took the punishment for my sins so I wouldn't have to." I took a sip of tea, watching her. Did she get the significance of what I'd just said?

"Wow, you don't know how much this is helping me. . . Just to know that you started out as ignorant and messed up as I am, maybe even making some of the dumb mistakes I've made. . . . I feel better already."

"But now that you've heard about how I started on this journey, let's talk about you. Where do you stand? Are you interested in knowing more about God and Jesus and what They want to do in your life?"

"Well...I *say* I'm a Christian, but I don't live like one. I know about sin and that Jesus died for us to take the punishment for our sins that we deserved—my grandparents taught me about that when I was a kid—but I don't believe it for myself. I just feel like a failure and don't think that God could love me after all I've done." She twisted a strand of hair and briefly looked up at me. Hope and despair struggled for preeminence on her face and she hid both by ducking her head.

"Well, let's start there. God doesn't care where you've been or what you've done. There's nothing you could do to make Him stop loving you. Nothing. He loves you with a never-ending, exuberant love. If you were the only person on earth, He still would have sent Jesus to die for you; that's how much He loves you."

"I sure don't feel that way."

She twirled her hair around her finger, restlessly tucking it behind her ear and pulling it out again.

"I understand, believe me. I've spent much of my life believing lies too: God couldn't possibly love me; I'm no good; I'm useless; I'm a failure, etc, etc. Blah, blah, *blah*!

"I think many of us women feel that way, for too many reasons to count. Can you take it on faith that it's true—God does love you with all His heart?" I sipped my tea, waiting, looking at her.

"I can try. I don't really know how to, but I can try." She answered, head down, voice barely audible.

"Do you want to experience God's love in your life? Do you want to be in a relationship with Him?"

"I think so. I went to church as a kid with my grandparents, and I remember walking down the aisle holding my grandma's hand to get saved when I was about five. I haven't thought about it much since then, though."

"Well, want to talk to Him again, and tell Him how you feel now? Do you want His help with your life? Do you want to exchange your messes and mistakes for the peace and joy He offers?"

"Yeah, I think so. Nothing I'm doing is making my life go right. And it's sure not peaceful or happy!"

"If you're sure, and you're not just doing it because I say so, we can pray right here."

"I'm sure. Will you pray? I'm not really used to talking to God." She dropped her head, and once again hid her face behind the curtain of her hair. It was still lank and greasy, but somehow I didn't mind so much.

"Absolutely.

"Dear God, You can see us down here and You've known Theresa since she was born. You know all about her life and You're familiar with her heart. You know her struggles, Jesus, and You know the plans You have for her. You've heard her say that what she's doing isn't working, and that she wants to invite You into her heart to be part of her life from now on. Come into her heart, Jesus. Tear down the barrier of sin between her and the Father, and let her know she's clean in Your sight, and precious in the Father's. Please guide her on the path You have for her. In Your name I pray. Amen."

Wiping her nose with the back of her hand and pushing her hair behind both ears, she smiled a wobbly smile up at me. Digging in the pocket of her shorts, she pulled out a wadded tissue, dabbed her eyes and blew her nose.

"I'm sorry to cry. It's just that no one has ever taken the time before to pray with me like that. And to think that God really loves *me*. . .I just want to cry forever. With gratitude? Relief? I don't know. Or maybe I just want to laugh. I'm just not as used to laughing as I am to crying." She wiped her nose and dabbed again at her smudged mascara.

"Oh, honey, I remember what it feels like! Cry all you want. God offers us such an amazing deal! He sees us struggling with anger, hurt, pride, greed and a host of other sins separating us from Him, so He says, 'I want you back, my beloved child. I'll make a way for you to get back into the relationship I created for us in the first place. I'll send My Son to *become* a man, one of you, and He'll take the punishment you deserve for all your foolish choices. He'll die instead of you. Just accept what He's done for you and come back to Me. No questions asked.' When you begin to grasp what He's done for us, it *is* a little overwhelming.

"Here's a clean tissue." I pulled one from the box on the end table and handed it to her. She took it with a watery smile.

Sniff. "Thanks." Wipe.

"So, did you pray like that back in college?"

"No, not specifically like this that I can remember. I just kind of fell into this whole God-thing backward without knowing what steps I was supposed to take. God knew how desperate I was to have His peace in my life, so He reached out and gave me a hand. He's that way, if He sees we want to love Him and live with Him, He'll make it happen."

"That's comforting, because I know I can't make it happen on my own. I'm too weak to do the right thing all the time. I just know I'm gonna mess up."

She ran the back of her hand under her nose again.

"I know how you feel. Some days all I do is make a mess of things! But, you know, because we're humans we mess up repeatedly. We get discouraged, prideful, and envious of what other people have; we lie to make ourselves look good; we're selfish. The list goes on and on. But God never gets tired of helping us get back up. I can imagine Him reaching His big hand down to me—or you—and helping me stand up again. And again. And again. To me, that's the definition of grace."

"I've never really understood what grace is all about. I used to hear my grandparents use that word all the time, and then there's that song, 'Amazing Grace'. What does grace really mean? What's the big deal about grace?"

Was there a hint of hope in her eyes?

I took a sip of tea to give myself time to think, tucking my legs under me on the couch.

God, how do I explain this?

"You know what grace is like? Have you ever watched a baby learn to walk? He takes a step, and his parents cheer and hold out their hands for him. At first, he takes a step or two, and then he falls down and crawls. Eventually, he toddles a few steps more, and then he lunges the rest of the way into his parents' hands, staggering like a baby drunkard. The parents catch their baby and cheer him on like he's just done the greatest thing in the world.

"The next day, they do the same thing all over again. They pick their baby up when he falls, they give him a kiss, and they clap when he totters another few steps. They keep at it until their baby learns how to walk, one wobbly little step at a time. They're so proud of him, and they keep encouraging him to do more each day. That's how God is with us, and that's how I understand grace. I just keep imagining God cheering me on when I fall, picking me up, dusting me off and setting me on my way again."

"Wow. I never thought of it that way. If that's what grace is, well, maybe I can try this Christian life after all."

"It's getting late, girl. You look sleepy, and although I could stay up all night talking about this, morning comes early around here. I have to get to bed or I'm going to be a zombie all day tomorrow."

Theresa jumped up, a stricken look on her face. "Oh jeesh, I'm sorry! I had no idea it was so late. You go on to bed; I'll take the cups to the kitchen. And, thanks for the talk," she mumbled over her shoulder. "Can we talk like this again? You might actually have some answers for me."

"I'd love to, honey. Let's just start a little earlier, okay?"

I blew her a kiss and turned to go upstairs. As I passed the old wall clock hanging in the front hall, I noticed that it was almost midnight.

*　　*　　*　　*　　*

The next morning at six-thirty I was groggily making breakfast when I heard someone come into the kitchen. Normally the kids didn't come down 'til the last minute and I'd given up asking them to help this early in the morning so I threw a quick glance over my shoulder to see who it was. My eyebrows shot up and my mouth fell open as I stared at Theresa standing there, dressed in jeans and a clean tee shirt with shiny hair and a clean face. I even smelled a whiff of floral body spray.

"Well, good morning, sunshine!" I croaked, not knowing what else to say.

"I know. You're shocked out of your mind. I don't blame you. I'm pretty shocked myself. I haven't been up this early in I don't know how long. It actually feels kind of good. Can I help you?"

Now I thought I really would fall on the floor, but that didn't seem to be the right response at the moment, so I smiled and handed her the forks and knives I was about to put around the table. "Want some tea?"

"Sure, but I'll fix it. You're busy with the waffles. Wow, I've never seen so many waffles at one time before."

"The kids love 'em. They're easy to make and this morning I couldn't think of anything else."

"I've never had homemade waffles before. I think I might actually like one."

"With butter and syrup? Or we have something we call 'blana mash': bananas mashed up with orange juice that we eat on our waffles with powdered sugar."

"I'll stick with butter and syrup for now. But thanks. Just having breakfast is enough of a shock to my system." She pulled a tiny butterfly clip out of her shiny hair, and twisting the strand that usually fell in her face, clipped it up on the top of her head. I kept my eyes on the waffle maker so I wouldn't stare.

Wow, Lord. What happened?

"Right, best not to overdo at first," I answered. "Mind pouring the orange juice?" I glanced at the clock. "Yikes, it's late. I'm slow this morning, but it looks as if everyone else is too." I dashed to the back stairs and yelled up, "Breakfast is ready! Hurry up, guys, or you'll be late to school!"

*   *   *   *   *

The next time I drew a peaceful breath, it was close to ten o'clock. After getting the kids off, putting the second load of laundry in the dryer and cleaning up the kitchen, I sat down for a moment in the family room to look over last night's paper. This was my time of day to catch my breath.

Theresa appeared at the kitchen door with an armful of dirty clothes. "Mind if I do my laundry?" she asked.

"Go right ahead. My last load's in the dryer. You know how to use the machine?"

"It doesn't look that complicated. I think I can manage. Would you have time to talk again after I put my load in?"

"Absolutely," I smiled, pushing my mental to-do list back an hour or so.

Please help me fit it all in, Lord.

I will. Just do your part.

CHAPTER 4

What Are Salvation and Grace, Anyway?

Questions for Discussion

§

1) Do you know, down to your toenails, that God is crazy in love with you? If not, why not? What are some of the things that can get in the way of us knowing, feeling, and believing that fact?

2) Do you have the kind of relationship with God where you can talk to Him like a person? Or is He more of a distant figure, somewhere far away? Or don't you know Him at all?

3) Believers in Christ often use "Christian-ese", using words like sin, salvation, redemption, forgiveness of sins, even the word "Christian". These words are often used as if everybody knows what they mean but they may be loaded with confusing or negative connotations for many people. Can you explain the concept of salvation in your own words without using "Christian-ese"?

4) If you are a follower of Christ, what was your experience like when you first believed in Jesus?

5) If you have been a follower of Christ for a while, can tell someone else in 100 words or less what you were like before asking Him into your life, what caused you to turn to Him, and what your life has been life since then? (Try it; it's harder than you might think.)

6) Discuss what grace means to you, and how it affects how you treat yourself and others. Did Theresa's taking a shower and washing her clothes have anything to do with grace, in your opinion?

CHAPTER 5

Developing a Relationship with God

§

Theresa appeared back in the family room fifteen minutes later carrying a tray with two cups of tea and graham crackers on a plate. I smiled, remembering the first snack I'd offered her some weeks ago.

"Mind if we sit in the formal living room again? It's so peaceful; I feel like we can talk better there."

I rolled my eyes at the clutter in the family room as I walked through, stepping over Craig's shoes, Rob's science book and Molly's history papers scattered across the floor. "I'm with you on that one. It's nice to have one room in the house that stays clean. I tell the kids they either have to be quiet or adult to be in this room."

"Well, maybe I'll qualify on one of those scores," Theresa remarked drily, setting the tray on the coffee table and handing me a cup of tea.

"I even put honey in, the way you like it."

Lord, I can't believe the changes in this girl. . .

"So," she began, settling her increasingly ungainly self down on the end of the couch and curling her legs under her. "What comes next? How do I stay in touch with God? What's going to keep me from straying again? I don't trust myself to stay on the straight and narrow yet, if you know what I mean."

"Well," I munched a graham cracker to give myself a moment to think, curling up on the opposite end.

What do I say, Lord?

Tell her what you've learned.

"It's all about developing your relationship with God. We need to feed this relationship just like we'd feed any living thing. You like plants, don't you?"

I had no idea where that question came from; I just had a hunch she might.

"I love flowers. What's that have to do with it?" She wrinkled her forehead at me.

"You have to water flowers, and weed them, and make sure they get plenty of sunshine, right?"

"Yeah. . ."

"So, in the same way, you have to feed your relationship with God; water it, keep it alive."

"Okay, but how? I haven't had the best success with relationships," she looked at me wryly, "as you might have figured." I smiled, enjoying her sense of humor, and continued.

"God speaks to us in different ways; most importantly through the Bible. It's His love letter and instruction manual."

"I've tried reading it a couple of times, but it's so dry! I can barely understand it, especially with all that 'thee and thou' stuff, and the begats—who can wade through all those?"

"Get a version you understand. We might have one around here you can borrow. And then start with some of the familiar passages like the Psalms or the Gospels."

"Thanks. But it's still hard to understand. I mean, the thoughts and ideas. . .they're way beyond me!" She pulled her butterfly clip out, twisted the strand of hair it held and re-fastened it.

I tried not to stare, so I looked at my hands. This was a new person I was talking to.

"Well, no one said it would read like a novel. God says that His thoughts are not our thoughts and His ways are not our ways, but the more we read it, the more He opens it up to us. Ask God's Spirit to help you understand it. After all, He's called our Counselor and Helper for a reason. And remember, He's with us always."

"So, like, am I supposed to read it every day? A chapter a day or something?"

"Reading the Bible is like eating; we do it for survival. If we go without food too long, we start running on empty and lose our strength and vitality. Likewise, if we go too long without reading the Bible, our spirits will start running on empty. We feed our spirits by listening to God speak to us through the Bible. Every word in the Bible is saturated with God's Presence, so we benefit from it no matter how we get it into our minds and hearts. But, like exercising or eating right, it's easier said than done."

"So how do I do it?" She pulled the afghan off the back of the couch. The early April morning was brisk and the room a bit chilly.

"What works best for you? Especially after the baby comes, you may not have much time for yourself. When my babies started arriving, I hardly had time for a shower, let alone for reading the Bible, so I had to figure out what worked for me.

"The important thing is staying attuned to God throughout the day. I've never read that Jesus prayed for an hour each morning. Instead, He went away to pray whenever He needed to be alone with His father. We can do the same. Maybe you can have some time with Him when the baby is asleep, or when you're out walking and she's tucked into her stroller. Maybe the rare hot bath you get to take by yourself will be your time to talk to God.

"Actually, I don't think God is as interested in us checking devotions off our schedule—devotions, done; now I can go on to other things—as He is about the condition of our hearts. Do we *want* to spend time with Him? Are we turning to Him when we're folding laundry or nursing a baby or getting ready for work? Do we keep His ways before us as we go through life, like a road map showing us the way to go?"

"Kind of like a flower turning its face toward the sun? Just soaking it all in?"

I looked across at her, amazed at what I was beginning to see under the surface. "You should be a poet, Theresa. That's a beautiful way to put it. Exactly. Just turn your heart toward Him, no matter where you are or what you're doing. Sometimes listening to praise music helps, or listening to the Bible on a CD or an iPod; anything to get the God's word into our hearts. The more we read it or hear it, the more it sinks in."

"Okay. Reading the Bible. That's one thing. Now, what about prayer? Doesn't that fit in there somewhere? I used to hear my grandparents praying out loud with each other every night before they went to bed."

"We'll get to that in a minute. There are other reasons to spend time with God."

"Like?"

"Like keeping short accounts, with yourself, with God and with other people, to make sure anger or hurts from the past don't fester. Time alone with God is a good time to think through your relationships and your feelings. Are you mad at anybody? Is anyone mad at you? Do you need to ask forgiveness of anyone?"

"You mean the way you did the other day?"

"Exactly. If I hadn't done that, resentment would have grown in my heart, and hurt feelings in yours. Soon neither of us would remember the cause of the argument, just the bad feelings between us. And, like mold, bad feelings grow. They don't just disappear by themselves."

"Tell me about it. That's the story of my life."

"It is for a lot of people. Asking forgiveness isn't easy—we have to swallow our pride and that's always hard—but it wipes away the resentment and anger and allows us to move on in love. On the other hand, if we don't keep short accounts, bitterness takes root in our hearts, and it gets harder and harder to dig it out."

"Wow, do I wish my family had known this while I was growing up! I might not be the basket case I am now." She shook her head, staring out the window, eyes bright.

Were those tears?

"Pretty cool that you get a fresh start with your baby," I said, reaching over and patting her leg.

"Believe me, I'm looking forward to being a different kind of mother than my mom was, even if I do end up being a single parent."

She looked down at her belly as if she could already see the baby lying there.

"You go, girl! That's the spirit.

"Okay, another reason to spend time with God is to counteract all the junk that floods into our minds every day—from TV, radio, newspapers, magazines, e-mail, internet, videos, you name it. Our minds and hearts become clogged with what the world is screaming at us. No wonder it's easy to get depressed and off-track. Keeping our mind focused on God and reading the Bible is a good way to counteract all that garbage. It helps us to rearrange our thinking into what I call a God-pattern."

"What's that supposed to mean?" She asked, pushing the hair out of her face.

"When you're sewing a dress, you cut around a paper pattern to get the correct shape for your pieces of cloth. In the same way, we have to use the Bible as a pattern to shape our thoughts and actions around in order to get it right."

"We had a semester of sewing in life skills class in school; I remember doing that."

"And if our relationship with God is genuine, it shapes every area of our lives, not just Sunday morning. It needs to affect how we treat other people, make decisions, or use our time or money. We have to live our whole lives by God's pattern."

"I thought that was a given. If I'm going to follow Jesus, I want to do it in all areas of my life. That's why I'm asking you all these questions; to find out how it all works. Up until now, the choices I've made on my own without God have led me down some pretty dumb paths." She pulled her hair out from behind her ear and twisted it around her finger. "To tell you the truth, I was almost suicidal before I came here. There just didn't seem to be any way out, the direction I was going."

She looked down, still flipping her hair back and forth, her voice fading away.

"Without God, there aren't any ways out. We just flounder around, trying to make it through life the best we can, hit-or-miss," I agreed.

Oh God, I remember those days. What an awful, hopeless feeling.

"Yeah, that's me all right!" She tucked her hair behind her ear and pulled it out again. "Just hit or miss. Mostly miss."

"But the fantastic thing is that by reading the Scriptures we begin to understand God's ways of doing things. The more we understand how God works, and how He's set up this world to work, the more we can fit into *His* ways, and the more peaceful and happy our lives will be. For example," I held out my teaspoon, "you know that if I drop this spoon, it will always fall to the floor because of the law of gravity, but did you know that spiritual laws are just as unbreakable?"

I dropped the spoon. Unsurprisingly, it landed on the floor. Theresa looked at me quizzically.

"God's spiritual laws," I said, leaning over to pick it up, "are as unchanging as His physical laws. We can conform to them or not, but the laws don't change."

"Makes sense to me. So how do you begin to dig into the Bible to find out these laws? "

"It's not always easy, I'll admit. Sometimes I skip around, reading here and there, thinking about the verses I read for that day. Other times I'll read through a whole book, maybe outlining it as I go, which helps me to understand it as I put it in my own words. Or I'll get a Bible study book and work my way through that.

"One of the best ways I've found to keep myself on track is to keep a spiritual journal that I write in every couple of days."

"Oh great!" she groaned. "I'm horrible at writing! What do you write?"

"Whatever comes to mind: my thoughts on the verses I've read; my complaints to God; my struggles; my prayers and hopes for my family—just stuff between God and me. Nothing very interesting for anyone else to read."

I finished my cup of tea, lukewarm by now. Ugh.

No wonder you hate lukewarmness, God.

"Try me," she said, twirling her strand of hair back and forth, back and forth, brushing against her ear.

"You'd be bored to tears in five minutes, I'm sure. It's just a record of how I'm progressing spiritually; a record of God working in my life. I can look back and see what He's done with the prayers I wrote down in the past. It builds my faith.

"For example, a few years ago, I prayed that one of our sons would start to use the brain God gave him and quit floating along in school the way he was doing, barely passing. I wrote the prayer down and forgot about it until just a month ago when I was rereading that old journal and saw it. I had to grin as I thought about that same son now, about to go to college and doing great in his senior year of high school."

"That's awesome to see your prayers answered like that. Do you do that all the time?"

Theresa picked up her teacup, drained it and set it on the floor. She awkwardly pulled her legs up in front of her and wrapped her arms around them, resting her chin on her knees, looking intently at me.

"No, I just write what I want, when I want. For me, it keeps my mind on track when I'm having a prayer time with Jesus. I'm much too easily distracted if I don't write stuff down. I find myself looking out the window, or wondering if the dryer buzzer has gone off, or thinking of what I need to fix for supper. Writing helps to keep me focused."

"Sounds like a lot of effort to me. What if I fail; what if I can't do all this? I know myself: I'll be all gung-ho about something, and then in a few days, my enthusiasm fades and I'm back to my old self. How can I change?" she looked up at me wistfully.

How many times has she tried, and failed to change already?

"Boy, do I know that feeling! Been there, done that, probably a hundred times. First, ask God's Spirit to help you. He's the one who enables you to hear from God. You're right, we *can't* make ourselves grow spiritually, any more than a flower can make itself grow just by trying. It's God who helps us grow, as we turn to Him.

"And second, keep on keepin' on."

"What do you mean by that?"

"We have to keep on keeping on—you know, like that baby that falls down and gets up again fifty times in a day. No matter how many times we fail, get discouraged, or lose our enthusiasm, if we turn back to God He will *always* pick us up and set us on our way again. Our part is not to lose heart, but to keep on keepin' on, to keep on turning back to God."

"Hmmm," she said, stroking her cheek thoughtfully with her strand of hair, "I'm going to have to take some time to absorb all this. Okay; what else?"

"A quiet time is a good time to ask God about any major decisions you might be facing," I went on, hoping all this was making sense to her. "Pray about them. Read the Scriptures and watch for ways in which God may speak to you through them. If you're still not sure which way to go, ask a pastor or a mature follower of Christ their opinion. God never contradicts the Bible, and neither will a godly counselor."

"Up until now, I haven't known too many godly counselors, as you say, Katie."

"I know, and I'm hoping that will change. If and when you start going to church with us, hopefully you'll meet some people you can trust. But back to a quiet time; it's just a good time to be with your heavenly Father: It's a time to bask in His love for a few moments, and a time to slow down from the hectic pace of our lives long enough to hear His voice or simply sense His presence."

"I'm gonna have to start writing this stuff down."

"Good idea. That way you can look it over at your leisure." I smiled at her.

"Actually, just being quiet in the presence of God is wonderful. We have so little *silence* in our lives; it's good just to be quiet once in a while. Besides, as long as we're doing all the talking, we can't hear what God has to say."

She picked up her cup and straightened up, untangling her legs.

"You've given me enough to think about for one day and I know you have work to do. Is there anything I can help you with? I'm here just kind of lounging around all day. What can I do to help?" She heaved herself up and stretched.

"Wow, I don't get *that* kind of question very often! Let me think for a sec; what needs to be done the most?" I contemplated this free offer of help for a moment. "What about washing the windows? Think you could handle that, as big as you're getting?"

"Oh gee, thanks. Rub it in, why don't you?" Theresa grouched, but I could sense a smile underneath there somewhere. "Sure, I can wash windows. Just show me where the stuff is. And when we talk again, could you tell me more about hearing God's voice? I can't seem to hear it no matter how hard I try. There are just too many competing voices in my head for me to make any sense of them."

"Be glad to."

"You know, I'm really kind of glad I ended up here, even though I didn't think I was going to like it at first. At first I thought you all were kind of weird."

"Maybe we are. Who knows?" I grinned, pushing myself up off the couch and stacking the cups on the tray.

"You're getting big, girl. How much longer, do you think?"

"You know, I'm a little foggy on that score. I guess I should find a doctor pretty soon."

"Good idea. I should have thought of that sooner. I can give you the name of my ob-gyn if you'd like."

"I guess you're right. I'm going to have to face the music sometime."

CHAPTER 5

Developing a Relationship with God

Questions for Discussion

§

1) Having a quiet time with God seems to be one of the hardest things for a follower of Christ to do on a regular basis. Have you found this to be true? What ways have you found to have a regular quiet time, especially if you are the mother of young children, or have some other kind of demanding schedule that doesn't leave you much time for yourself?

2) Is God like a friend; can we spend time with Him in the same ways we might spend time with a friend? Why or why not?

3) Have you ever kept a journal, spiritual or otherwise? If you do, do you find signs of change and progress in your life as you look back over it?

4) What are some of the negative effects, spiritual or physical, of letting hurts, bitterness and anger linger in your mind and heart?

5) Do you find yourself being overwhelmed at times by the daily flood of negative news on TV, radio, the internet, magazines and newspapers? Does this make it hard for you to stay focused on God's truths?

6) Do you find yourself in the same situation Theresa mentioned of being gung-ho about something and then losing your enthusiasm? What does Katie's suggestion of "keepin' on keepin' on" have to do with this problem and how might it help?

7) Discuss why your personal time with God is the root of your whole relationship with Him.

CHAPTER 6

The Voices We Listen To

§

A couple of days later, Theresa approached me as I was ironing in the family room.

"It's a beautiful day out today, Katie. When you're done ironing, you think we could take a walk and we could talk some more?"

"I'd love that. While I finish, why don't you do me a favor and straighten up the family room a bit? I only have two more shirts to go."

A soft breeze blew in through the half-open windows, unusually mild for mid April. Theresa puttered around, huffing and puffing as she bent over to retrieve shoes and newspapers off the floor.

"So, last time you said you wanted to know how to hear God's voice, right?" I asked her, gliding the iron around Craig's shirt collar. "That's a good a question, 'cause if we can't distinguish God's voice from all the other voices out there, how are we ever going to know the truth?"

"My thoughts exactly," she said from the corner where she'd found a stash of clutter.

"So how do we tell God's voice from all the other voices out there? I don't know about you, Theresa, but there's chatter that goes on in my head that always sounds like I'm saying the words and it's always negative. And the worst part is that I believe it! It sounds like my voice and I don't stop to ask where it comes from."

"Exactly! It's almost as if there's this tape in my head that keeps playing, on and on, tearing me down." Theresa made a heap of the clutter, plopped on the couch and began to twist a strand of her hair.

"Well, let me tell you a story. See if this sounds familiar to you.

"I was running errands recently and I knew in the next hour I had to make it home, put the groceries away, fix supper for the kids, and dress for the evening since Craig and I had a special date that night. Suddenly it began to pour down rain. I'd been hoping I could beat the clouds but no, of course not. And of course, I had no raincoat or umbrella or hat, or *anything!* I looked for an empty grocery bag, a newspaper, even one of the kids' old school papers to put over my freshly styled hair, but there was nothing.

"I couldn't park in our garage like normal people do when it's raining because it was crammed with bicycles, sports equipment, strollers, camping gear and who knows what else! The doors wouldn't even close all the way. So I parked as close to the house as I could, wriggled out of the car backside first to keep my hair under cover as long as possible and stepped right into a mud puddle! Naturally. Mud stains halfway up to my knee. Great.

"Loading up as many bags as I could carry and trying to hold a cereal box over my head to protect my hair, I waddled to the mailbox on the way to the back door. I sure wasn't coming out into the rain a second time just to get the mail! With the grocery bags cutting into my arms, I yanked the mail, most of it junk, out of the mailbox and stuck it under my elbow. Still trying to hold that cereal box over my head I waddled to the door, trying to dig my keys out of my purse as I went.

"As I fumbled with them, a bunch of those *stupid*, slick ads slid out from under my elbow and scattered onto the wet patio. When I bent down to retrieve them—grunting like an old woman—one of the bags burst open onto the brick patio. Apples bruised, oatmeal spilled, and a jar of mayonnaise shattered, splattering my already muddy pants leg. Then, to top it all off, a breeze sprang up, blowing rain in my face and scattering the soggy junk mail across the moth-eaten lawn, which hadn't been mowed in a couple of weeks.

"Thoughts began running through my head like, '*Why can't I do anything right? What a dummy! All that money spent on a new hairdo, and I ruin it before I even get in the house! Not to mention the apples and the mayonnaise. If I'd just clean the garage once in a while, none of this would have happened. When will I ever learn to do things right?*'

"I gathered up as much of the mess as I could and trudged into the house, aggravated and grumpy. The thoughts continued, masquerading as my own. *'I'm out of shape, too! Disgusting. I can't even bend over without huffing and puffing. Clumsy* and *fat, now that's a lovely combination! Craig's going to get tired of me looking this way. Maybe he already is, and I just don't know it. If I had a* real *job, I wouldn't be out in the middle of the day, in the middle of a rainstorm, without even a hat, (enter mental picture of a neatly coiffed and stylishly dressed career woman in classy rain coat), trying to lug all this stuff in the house by myself. (Insert another mental picture of said career woman carrying two small bags from the WholeGrainEarthBread store over one arm, purse over the other, keys in hand as she stands in freshly painted entryway, out of the rain.)*

The thoughts continued bombarding me, all sounding like the truth to my battered heart.

I'm not good enough for a real *job. . .I'd never make it out there. . .I'm nothing but a homemaker. . .don't have any* real *skills. . .I'm sure not reaching my potential. . .just wasting the gifts God's given me. . .and I'm wearing out-of-style polyester pants with an elastic waistband, too! How out of style can I get? What a loser! Just give it all up. Why don't you?'"*

By this time, both Theresa and I were both laughing as I replayed this onslaught of self- condemnation. Unfortunately, it was all too familiar.

I hung the last shirt over the back of a chair and folded up the ironing board.

"This sound like anything you've ever heard inside your head? Do ideas like those just appear in your mind sometimes?" I asked Theresa, rolling my eyes and shaking my head.

"Every day! That's *all* I hear. Ever. But until you began saying it like that, I thought it was the truth about myself."

"We all do. And that's exactly what Satan, our enemy the devil wants. If he can make it sound like our own voice we will believe it, and we don't realize it's lies from the pit of hell; ugly thoughts dropped into our minds from the chief deceiver himself." I stashed the board in the family room closet.

"C'mon, let's go outside." I hauled her up off the couch and we headed out to the back porch. This was one of my favorite places; a covered porch running the length of the back of the house, overlooking the meadows beyond our yard. We were the last house on a cul-de-sac and I always preferred to look out this way. She settled herself on the porch swing on one end and I took the wicker rocker facing her.

"The trick is to figure out who's saying all this garbage to us. We need to get to know the characters involved in this play called life."

"Hunh? Tell me what you mean." Rocking gently in the swing, Theresa pulled a strand of hair out from her messy ponytail and began to twirl it back and forth, looking at me expectantly.

"Okay, here's the cast of characters." I held up both hands.

"First there's God, Jesus, and the Holy Spirit, on this hand. On the other, there's the devil, or Satan, as he's known, with all his disgusting little followers, commonly known as demons. By the way, there's no gray area between God and the devil. You're either in one camp or the other; there's no third option."

"What do you mean? Explain that," she challenged me.

She kicked the swing back and forth, still twirling her hair.

"Jesus tells us that God's kingdom is made up of those who love God and follow Him with all their hearts. Satan's kingdom, on the other hand, is made up of those who choose not to follow God. There's no middle ground. Many people think there is some sort of neutral territory where they can drift along, neither being a follower of God nor a follower of Satan, but Jesus tells us that if you're not in the kingdom of God, you're in the kingdom of Satan. The Bible calls Satan the prince of this world, meaning that the world is his kingdom. Those that follow Jesus make up the Kingdom of God. There is nothing else."

"I'll have to think about that one. . .okay, go on." She kept rocking.

"We have to get to know the personalities of each of these characters if we're going to tell which voices go with which character. We can't see them, so we have to learn to distinguish them by what they say."

"How do we do that?"

"Let's start with God. We know that He cherishes us beyond our wildest imaginations. We are the apple of His eye. Even when He corrects us, He does it because He wants the best for us. His voice is always loving and encouraging.

"And, on the contrary, Satan is pure hate. His voice will always be condemning."

I leaned my head back for a minute. It felt good to slow down. A soft breeze blew in from the meadow, bringing the scent of earth and grasses.

Ah, God, thank You.

"So where does all this negative talk in my head come from?" Theresa wanted to know, breaking into my reverie.

"In your head, you hear the self-critical babble that I was doing a minute ago, right?"

"Right. Constantly." She tucked her hair behind her ear.

"So when you hear nasty, ugly talk like I was just doing, who do you think is behind it?"

"Well, I never really thought about it. I always took it to be the truth, that I *was* stupid, incompetent, ugly, and all the rest."

"Do you think God would say things like that to you? He who is crazy about you?" I rocked gently, almost feeling God's love like an afghan on my shoulders.

"Now that I think about it, no. So I guess it would be the devil? What about it just being me, telling myself the truth about myself? I have done some pretty dumb things, you know," she said, hanging her head.

I shook my head no, looking at her, just loving her.

"That's just what Satan wants us to think. He doesn't want us to realize that when we hear degrading talk like that in our heads, it's him, the father of lies, talking to us, putting condemning thoughts into our heads, dropping them in like you might drop pebbles into a pond. The Bible tells us that Satan's chief aim is to steal, kill and destroy *(John 10:10)*—and that means us. He wants to destroy us however he can, whether it's by hatred—of self and others—or depression, jealousy, despair or discouragement. He especially loves to kick us when we're down. The more down on ourselves we get, the more he likes it. And his demons follow right along after him.

"So we have to train ourselves to hear God's voice. His voice is always loving and encouraging, and we don't need to listen to any others. The world says that in order to be successful, we have to be rich, skinny, popular, beautiful, intelligent, and have great teeth. The devil tells you all that's impossible, so don't even try. You're worthless; you'll never amount to anything."

I put my feet up on the edge of the swing and began rocking in sync with her.

"Only God tells us the whole truth: that we are born into sin, but we're the apple of His eye anyway. We're the love of His life. He is so in love that He sent His own Son, Jesus, to take the punishment of death that our sins have earned for us. We get to go free.

"Because of Jesus, God sees us through the eyes of love. There is no more need to punish us for our wrongdoings: the selfishness, pride, greed, rebellion, anger—all the things that separate us from him. He has provided Jesus to be a bridge back into a loving relationship with him once again, the way it was at the beginning."

Theresa leaned back, lulled by the rocking, hands folded under her belly.

"Satan, on the other hand, *hates* it that God loves us, so he constantly tells us how bad we are, how unworthy of God's love. He constantly tries to persuade us that God doesn't *really* love us. He knows if he can get us to believe all that garbage about ourselves, we'll turn away from God in discouragement."

Despite being lulled by the rocking, Theresa was listening intently, I could tell. This was new territory for her and she was taking it all in.

"So if I hear negative talk like you were just doing, which I hear *all the time* in my head, I can ignore it and remember that it's the devil talking in my ear and not God?" she asked.

"Exactly! God will never condemn you. He may correct you or even rebuke you, but He will *never* condemn you, *especially* if you've turned your life over to Him."

"This is *so* awesome! You mean I *really* don't have to listen to all that self-condemning talk?" She searched my face intently.

"You really don't. Just learn to recognize it when it starts. All you have to do is face the devil and tell him to get his ugly self out of your life and then ask God to tell you the truth about yourself. And then *believe* it!"

"Why do some people, like me, struggle with this kind of thing so much more than others? I'm always down on myself, but look at someone like Jeannyne; she never seems to be!"

Privately I doubted that, but that seemed like a story for another day.

"I think a lot of it has to do with what was poured into our hearts from an early age on," I answered her, remembering the many books and teachings I'd heard on this same topic.

As we continued to swing in sync there on the porch, Theresa lifted one foot up and tucked it in the rocker, between my thigh and the arm of the chair. I gently rubbed her ankle as we talked.

"Jesus tells a parable about seeds which a farmer scattered on the ground *(Mt 13:3-8)*. The seeds that fell onto fertile soil took root and bore much fruit, some forty, some sixty and some a hundred-fold. We can use the same analogy for the negative words others have dropped into the fertile soil of our hearts as children, weed seeds which bear the fruit of misery and self-condemnation if we don't recognize them and pull them out."

"That describes me to a tee! My mother *never* said anything loving to me that I can remember; nothing but harsh, angry words, all the time. So what do I do about all that junk? My heart is full of weeds of self-hatred, doubt, fear, and inferiority. How do I get rid of all that? Just pasting on a happy face isn't going to work."

She twirled the strand of hair by her ear, flicking it back and forth against her cheek. I rocked gently and kept rubbing her ankle.

"You're right: it's not. You need to get to the root of the problem. Ask God where all this junk comes from. When did it start? Ask God's Spirit to help you remember. Then treat that old thing just like a weed in a garden: pull it up by the root and replace it with God's truth."

"You're losing me. What do you mean?"

"Sorry. Let me give you an example. For the longest time, I couldn't figure out why I never succeeded at the things I tried to do. I've written articles that were rejected, done projects that ended up on the scrap heap, and tried one thing and another, all of which seemed to fail. Worst of all, I never really believed in myself, never believed that I could do any of the things I thought God had called me to do. I was sure I'd always fail."

"You? You don't look like a failure to me," Theresa muttered under her breath.

"To you maybe I don't but I felt that way on the inside much of the time. So, I asked God where the problem was and if there were any words spoken to me that had convinced me that I would never succeed."

"And?"

"I remembered a high school teacher telling me, 'You're a B student with an A personality.' I think it was meant as a compliment but all I heard was 'B student'; in other words, one that will never quite succeed. At that age, not questioning what my teachers told me, I received those words into my heart where they quietly took root and grew into a large and healthy plant of self-doubt."

"So what did you do about it?"

"Once I realized that for most of my adult life I'd believed that I would never fully succeed at anything, I repented of believing it and acknowledged that it was a lie from Satan, who wants nothing but failure and misery for me. God would never tell me something like that. I'm determined to live by what God has to say about me so, like pulling up a weed and planting a flower in its place, I proclaimed that what I'd believed about myself all this time was a lie, and I replaced it with **Proverbs 31:26**: *"She opens her mouth with wisdom, And on her tongue is the law of kindness."* That's what I'm determining to believe about myself now."

"That's pretty cool, 'cause I'd say that was true about you." She flashed a tiny grin.

"Well, thanks, girl," I beamed. "That's one of the nicest things anybody's said to me in a long time!" I took a deep breath, let it out slowly through a small and satisfied smile, and leaned my head back on the wicker rocker, feeling good about myself and our talk for the day.

Maybe Craig could bring home some pizza and give me the night off?

Resting her head against the back of the swing, Theresa asked with half open eyes, "So. . . can we have pie for dessert tonight?"

"You conniving little critter!" I sat up and shook my finger at her.

"Here I thought you were giving me a genuine compliment and all you want is pie!" I flopped her leg onto the porch beside me, and got up out of my chair.

"I'm not being conniving. I meant both things. You are a wise woman and the teaching of kindness is on your tongue, and I do want pie for dessert tonight!"

I grinned at her, shaking my head.

Just like one of my kids.

"And tomorrow can we talk about how to hear *God's* voice better? You know, for guidance and all that? I can never tell if it's God's voice I'm hearing, or just my own desires, wanting my own way. How do you tell?"

"Ah, my dear, that's a story for another time. I have a pie to make before dinner." I leaned over and kissed Theresa on the head. "Why don't you take a nap, sweetie? You look like you could use one."

CHAPTER 6

The Voices We Listen To

Questions for Discussion

§

1) Are you aware of the kind of negative self-talk that Katie described to Theresa? Sometimes we're so accustomed to it that it's like the weather, something that's always there affecting how we feel but we're rarely aware of it.

2) Who or what do we focus on when we are down on ourselves? Where do we focus when we feel confident, happy and secure?

3) Have you ever stopped to question the source of such negative self-talk or, like Theresa, have you just accepted it as the truth without questioning or examining it?

4) Can you imagine a life without such inner criticism? A life that is filled instead, with positive and encouraging talk in your innermost self?

5) What do you think about Katie's statement that there is no middle ground; either we are in God's camp or we are in Satan's camp? Do you think that there is a middle ground, a neutral place where one can be neither for God nor against him?

6) Have you ever thought about Satan as a real being who is out to destroy you? Any thoughts on why he hates you and me and the rest of humankind so much?

7) Why would Satan want to disguise himself so that we wouldn't realize that he is at work, trying to tear us down?

8) What is your response when you look at yourself in the mirror? For years, mine was barely more than a cynical sneer, but lately I've begun to look at myself and say, "Hey, girlfriend, you're looking good today. I sure love you. You're doing a good job with your life." (I know, it sounds a little weird. Nobody has to hear you.) Discuss what might happen in your heart if you started doing that to your reflection.

CHAPTER 7

Hearing God's Voice in Your Life

§

The next week was a busy one for me. Jason and Jocelyn had alternating ball games four out five nights; Molly wanted help with a science project, and Liz needed some girl time with her mom. She had a major crush on a boy who didn't seem to care if she lived or died, and her fragile self-esteem was bruised. A couple of evenings I snuggled in bed with her while she sobbed under the covers in the dark. All I could do was listen to her and love her.

"Mom, I don't think he even knows I exist! He just walks right past me as if I wasn't there! I must be invisible or something." She slammed the pillow over her head, pulling away from me.

Oh, God, it's so hard to feel like you just don't matter!

"Honey, you're not invisible. You're especially not invisible to God. He's got your future all planned out and I'm sure that includes a boyfriend some day."

"I don't want one *some* day; I want one *now*!"

"I know, honey. It's hard to wait; I know."

"Mom, do you think I'll *ever* find a husband who will love me and who loves God? *And* who's handsome?"

"You have a little way to go, sweetie, before you need to be worrying about who you're going to marry."

She pulled the pillow off her tangled hair and stared at me with a wet face and a runny nose.

"Maybe I do," she whimpered, "but how will I know when I get there? How *do* you know how to pick the right man, Mom? What if I meet some great guy and think he's the one for me, and then he turns out to be a schmuck? And what if what I'm looking for in a guy isn't what God wants for me? Do you think He'd make me marry some little nerdy guy with no muscles and thin hair and pimples? Anything but that, please God!" She buried her head under her pillow and collapsed into tears again.

"Sweetie, I'm sure God has a man out there for you somewhere, sometime. He'll let you know when the time comes. Your job right now—and always—is to keep your eyes on Him and let Him lead and guide you."

"But how will I know that it's God guiding me and not just my own feelings?" she wailed into the mattress, pulling the pillow more tightly over her head. "How will I know, Mom? How can I trust that it will be God and not my own silly, yearning heart?"

There it was again; this question: how do we truly know when it is God talking to us and not just our own silly, yearning hearts?

Lord, I'm not sure I know. How do I help these young ladies–Lizzie and Theresa both– figure it out?

Listen to Me. Read my Word. Spend time with Me. Get to know Me.

OK, Lord. I'll try to teach these things to my girls. Please help me. Always.

*   *   *   *   *

A few days later, Theresa walked up behind me in the kitchen and nudged me with her hip as I stood in front of the sink, finishing the last of the breakfast dishes.

"Hey, Katie, I'll finish cleaning up the kitchen if you'll talk to me afterwards about hearing God's voice. Go in the front room and get ready to share your pearls of wisdom."

"Yes, *ma'm!*" Giving her a mock salute, I wiped my hands and dropped my damp apron on a stool. I stepped over last night's newspaper, a sweatshirt and six shoes on the floor of the family room and sank down with a sigh onto the soft couch in the clean and peaceful living room. I leaned my head back and closed my eyes for a moment.

Thank you, God; I love watching her blossom. Please give me Your wisdom for this talk.

A few minutes later, too soon to have cleaned the kitchen thoroughly, I thought, Theresa arrived, wiping her hands on my apron, looking for all the world like an experienced mother. The apron barely stretched over her middle; underneath was a too-tight tee shirt and a pair of blue jeans that barely snapped under her increasingly large belly.

I really should get her some maternity clothes. How could I be so blind?

Taking off the apron and dropping it on the floor, she plopped down on the couch with a sigh. "So tell me; how do I hear the God? How do I know when it's Him and not just my own emotions leading me around by the nose like they've done most of my life?"

"Theresa, if I knew the answer to that and could sell it, I'd be a millionaire! It's hard to know for sure, but there are steps we can take when we're looking for His guidance. As I see it, there are inner steps and outer ones. The inner ones happen in our hearts, where we talk to God, pray, and try to hear His voice. The outer ones include reading the Bible and asking for advice from other wise people who have been following Jesus for a while."

"Have you ever heard God speak out loud to you?" she asked, settling herself on her end of the couch and kicking off her shoes. The day was warm, so she didn't snuggle up in the afghan; rather, she scrunched it up in her lap, holding it close to her chest. Her hair was still flat, but it was clean and shiny and she had that little butterfly clip holding it back from her face.

"No. I never have. All I do is to try to hear him in my heart. If I'm struggling with something, I talk to God about it; I tell Him what I want, and then I tell Him that despite what *I* want, what *He* wants is most important to me. It's just as Jesus said in the garden, ***"Father... not My will, but Yours, be done."*** **(Luke 22:42)**.

"I have to mean it, even if I don't feel like it. Sometimes when I want something *really, really* bad, but I'm not sure it's God's will for me, I hold my hands out palms up and say: 'Lord, You know that I want this thing, but I am determined not to grasp for it, so here are my hands, open to you. If You want to fill them, fine. If You don't, that's fine too.'"

"I like that—open hands. That's an image I can remember." She held her hands out, palms up, and looked at them thoughtfully.

"In order to receive guidance from God, you need to be willing to hear *His* voice and follow *His* will. Only when we quiet our own demanding hearts can we hear His still, small voice. We can't hear Him when our own wishes and opinions drown out everything else."

"You make it sound so easy. Is it?"

"It's one of the hardest parts of my walk with God, because I have to let go of *my* wants, *my* opinions and *my* desires—which is never easy. I call it dying to myself."

"Dying to yourself? That sounds pretty heavy duty; what do you mean?"

"I'm sorry; that's Christian jargon. I hate it when I or anybody else uses that kind of language. Let me try to explain it better."

Theresa settled herself into the corner of the couch, trying, and failing, to bring her knees up in front of her belly so she could wrap her arms around them; instead, she folded them Indian style in front of her and twirled a strand of hair. "I've got all the time in the world. Back up as far as you want. Just explain it so I understand it."

"Okay. I'm sure you've heard that we're made up of three parts: body, soul and spirit?"

"Yeah, that much I have heard about."

"Good. Most of us think of ourselves as a body that has a soul with a spirit out there somewhere; we're not always sure where."

"Well, that's kind of the way I see it. I mean, I can see and feel my body, but the spirit thing is pretty vague. And I'm not even sure I know the difference between soul and spirit."

"Let me give you some definitions. The body's obvious. The soul is our mind, our will and our emotions. For most people, that's as far as they get: they're a body with a mind, a will and emotions. But the spirit is actually the most important part since it's the part that connects us to God, like an umbilical cord between us and God."

"Wow. I never thought of it that way." She reached inside her shirt to pull up a slipping bra strap. Straightening her too-tight tee shirt, she looked up at me. "Go on."

"Our spirit is asleep, or shriveled up like a dry seed until we turn to Jesus and tell Him we love Him and want to live with Him forever. When we receive the gift He gave us by dying in our place to pay for our sins, our spirits start stirring, and we're literally born into a new life, just like an old, shriveled-up seed turns into a plant when it cracks open and starts to put down roots. Jesus calls that being born again. Are you familiar with that term?"

"When I was little, my mom used to drop me off at my grandparents' place in the summer for a couple of weeks at a time and they'd take me to church which is where I first learned anything about Jesus and the Bible. So, yeah, some of these terms are familiar, from way back in the shadows of my mind."

"So, our spirits are like seeds that have lain dormant in the earth until the sun and rain stir them into life. When we admit that we're powerless to make it back to God by our own power, and instead receive the gift that Jesus offers us, our spirits come to life and, just like a seed in the ground putting out roots and shoots, they point our hearts and minds toward God.

"I mean, look at you. It's your spirit that's causing you to want to know more about God and His ways. Would you have believed a month ago that you'd be sitting here listening to me talk about how to hear God's voice?"

"Not in a million years!" she laughed. "I was too busy partying, drinking, having sex, basically destroying my life. I *thought* I was having fun. I *thought* I was taking charge of my own life, but I was sure doing a lousy job of it."

She shook her head, eyes closed, as if even thinking of those days was painful.

"So, when you walked through the door that Jesus opened for you by His death, Theresa, the door to heaven that God's thrown open wide, your whole being turned upside down. Or more accurately, right side up. Your soul is no longer running the show and your life's goal has changed from doing whatever feels good, whether it destroys you or not, to doing what God wants you to do."

"I never thought about it that way. I *am* kind of different from the way I was when I first came here, aren't I?" She hugged the afghan to herself and grinned a little, ducking her head so her hair fell over her face.

"Yes, and that's because you're getting the three parts of yourself in the right order. As long as our bodies or souls are leading us, we're in trouble because that's not the way God made us. He made our spirits to lead us, since our spirits connect us to God. We can't relate to Him with our five senses; we can't figure Him out with our minds; we can't even always relate to Him with our emotions. So until our spirits connect us to God, we float around, unconnected to Him in any meaningful way."

"Kind of like a dog with no leash?"

"Huh? Now you've got *me* puzzled. What do you mean?"

"Well, if a dog's on a leash, he can feel his master tugging him to stop or come back. If there's no leash, the dog can't feel anything and wanders off on his own, checking out garbage and piles of poop. That's what I've been doing all my life: checking out garbage and piles of poop. The leash is like our spirits, connecting us to the Master."

"You know, Therese, some day you're going to be quite a teacher. The things you come up with," I shook my head, "you amaze me."

"Yeah, well. . ." She looked away. For a moment, I thought she might cry. "Anyway, go on."

"You're right. It is like a dog on a leash. The dog can only feel the master guiding him when they're connected. Otherwise, as you say, the dog wanders off to check out garbage and piles of poop. Too many of us are like that dog, wanting to go our own way; not wanting to connect to our Master. Since He's given us free will, He'll never force us to be connected to Him. He wants us to obey Him because we *want* to, not because we have to. Actually, He wants us to go one step further and obey him when we *hear His voice*, not when he tugs on our leash."

"Yeah, I feel like I'm playing tug-of-war with God a lot of the time."

"I know what you mean. I do too. That's our will, tugging against what we think is God's will. When we don't know God well, we think His will is heavy-handed and harsh, but that couldn't be less true. God *always* wants the best for us. Maybe His best isn't easy, maybe it's not what we'd envisioned, but as a loving Father, He'll always help us do whatever He's asked us to do."

"Wow. You mean He doesn't just tell us to do stuff and then leave us to our own devices? I always thought I had to work really hard to please God. That's why I kind of gave up even trying, to tell you the truth."

"I know exactly what you mean. I used to feel the same way. But once I began to understand that God gives us the strength and wisdom to do what He asks us to do, then life with Him became kind of exciting. He tells me what to do and then gives me what I need to do it. Pretty cool, huh?"

She nodded her head slowly. "Yeah, pretty cool. And a whole new idea."

"So," I continued, "when our spirits lead us, we *want* to do God's will. We long to hear His voice in our hearts guiding and directing us. When God sees that honest desire to submit our wills to His will He does guide us in His own mysterious ways. So, this effort to conform our wills to His, that's the part that goes on inside us."

Holding the afghan in a bunch and resting her chin on it, Theresa listened intently, nodding slightly as I continued.

"And then where do we go for guidance outside of ourselves? The first place is the Bible. Do our plans contradict what the Bible teaches, or do they go along with it? God will never tell us to do anything that disagrees with what He's already written."

"Yeah, that would be kind of pointless."

"But there are a lot of things that aren't specifically mentioned in the Bible."

"Like what guy to marry."

"Right. Like what guy to marry. One of the most important decisions we'll ever make, yet it's hard to find specific guidance on it in the Bible. Of course there are principles we can follow, but there's no section marked 'How to Find a Good Husband'."

"I wish there was." She muttered, head down.

"I know, it sure would make things easier, but God has His reasons. So where do we get guidance about specific question like that?" I looked at her, but she remained blank.

"Well, the third step is to get counsel from a godly person in our lives, like a parent, a pastor, or a wise older person."

"Someone like you, you mean," she said, giving me one of her rare grins.

"I'm not a pastor but I am a parent. And to you I am a mentor, so yeah, I guess so. God puts various people in our lives for our benefit. If a person doesn't have godly parents—"

"That would be me."

"—they can always go to a pastor of a church. It's best if it's someone who knows you and your situation so they can pray with you more knowledgeably, but even if they don't, if they love Jesus and revere the Bible, you can't go too wrong."

"So that's it? Pray, tell God you want to do things His way, read the Bible and get advice from a godly person?"

"In a nutshell, yes. But, remember, telling God we want to do things His way—and meaning it—is the most important part. Plenty of people pray like this," I put my hands over my ears, squeezed my eyes tight shut and muttered in one long breath: 'God, I-don't-want-to-hear-You-and-I-don't-want-to-see-You, but-please-answer-my-prayer-the-way-I-want-it-answered!'

I've done it myself." I shook my head sheepishly.

"Yeah, that sounds pretty familiar," Theresa laughed.

"Next time we talk, we can talk about prayer if you'd like."

"That would be great. Thanks."

"Okay, girl, class is over. Time to get back to work! I've got a full afternoon ahead."

"Need some help?"

"You're a dear. Why don't you take a walk? It's a gorgeous spring day, and you look like you could use the exercise."

"I was going to walk with Liz when she came home. She has some things she wants to talk about and I have some good wisdom now." Theresa nodded slowly, smiling at me, looking smug and self-satisfied. I threw a pillow at her. She dodged it and threw it back at me.

"If you're sure you don't need my help, then maybe I'll take a snooze. You don't mind?"

"Be my guest, sweetie."

She stretched out on the couch with a contented sigh, and I covered her up with the afghan.

CHAPTER 7

Hearing God's Voice in Your Life

Questions for Discussion

§

1) Have you ever had trouble figuring out what God is saying to you?

2) It's been said that if it's something you really *don't* want to do, it must be God's will for you. What do you think about this statement and why do you think people think that way?

3) How does knowing the character of God help us to understand what His will for us might be?

4) Where do you first turn for guidance when you have a big decision to make, or simply need guidance in your life? (Not all of us turn to God right away.)

5) Aside from telling God that you want—with all of your heart—to go His way, reading the Bible, and talking to a mature, Bible-believing Christian friend, are there other ways you know to find out God's plan for your life?

6) What do you do when you think you *should* do something, thinking it is God's plan for you, but you don't *want* to do it?

7) Do you think God would ever ask you to do something that could put you in harm's way? As a loving Father, would He do that?

8) Discuss the matter of perspective: God's and yours. Are they always, or ever, the same? Does this discussion change your thoughts about question #7?

CHAPTER 8

What is Sin?

§

A few days later Theresa joined me after lunch as I knelt in the garden, pulling weeds.

"If I help pull weeds, will you talk with me some more?"

"Sure. These are the flowers," I pointed out a tiny marigold just emerging from the ground, "and the rest are weeds. Have at it. I appreciate the help."

"You said you didn't know what sin was when you were growing up. I'm not sure I know what it is either. So tell me about sin." She took the old kitchen knife I offered her and began poking somewhat randomly around in the dirt.

"The best definition I've heard for sin is that it's missing the mark of God's perfection, like an arrow that misses the bull's eye. Even missing it by a hair is still missing it."

"Don't we all miss the mark?" she sat back on her heels to catch her breath. "How can we ever live the Christian life then? If God expects us to be perfect, I'm outta here!"

"Let me tell you a story. Maybe it'll show you what I mean.

"When I was a teenager, I went to a camp in the wilds of northern Minnesota and learned how to find my way through the woods with nothing but a map and a compass. We're talking real wilderness, with no roads or trails."

"I'd die out there, but go on." She put down the knife, giving up all pretense of weeding.

"To do this, you find the direction you want to go with your compass and then you head out in that direction by lining up trees or landmarks and walking from one to the next. It's very simple, providing you keep lining up your landmarks carefully."

"And the analogy is?"

"If the compass is like God's plan for our lives, then the landmarks are like the Bible, telling us how to get to our destination. If we veer off the track to the left or the right, we'll wander off and get lost into the wilderness."

"Gotcha. . .I think."

"I learned this the hard way. Our final test that summer was to find our way ten miles through the woods using our maps and compasses."

I yanked at a particularly tough weed but the root went deep and all I managed to do was to break it off. Frustrated, I dusted my hands off and sat back to take a breather.

"So, we started out early, watching our compasses and lining up our trees but we couldn't seem to make any progress. We didn't know it but iron ore in the ground had thrown our compasses off and we'd been walking in a big circle all day, ending up at 2:00 in the afternoon where we'd started that morning. Giving ourselves a pep talk, we started out again, a bit fearfully this time as dark came on fast in the deep woods. Within a few hours, night fell with us still far from home and we found ourselves trying to find a place to sleep in the pitch-dark woods. All we could think of were bears and how scared we were."

"Man! I would have been scared spitless!"

"We were: believe me!"

"You see, each time we'd lined up our markers, we were a little off due to the iron ore. So each step was just a hair off from the last one, eventually leading us in a circle. That's all it takes in our life with God too, just a little off here and a little off there without correcting ourselves and pretty soon we're off wandering in a scary wilderness of deception and sin."

"So what happened? How long were you out there?"

"We wandered around in the woods for three more days and nights before a search plane found us."

"Three nights out in the woods with bears and hoot owls and who knows what else that crawls around in the dark?! Ugh! I'd die!" She hugged herself and shivered.

Having given up any pretense of weeding, it being too awkward to squat down or bend over, she dragged a lawn chair off the porch and sat down, watching me and listening.

"Believe me; we were scared, hungry, weak and just wanted to go home."

"Kind of sounds like my life."

"Yeah, mine too before I met Jesus. So you see, sin is missing the mark of God's perfection, veering off the trail of His plan, and doing our own thing instead of His. If we wander off like that, eventually we'll be just as lost, spiritually speaking, as we were in those woods."

"What about food? Didn't you starve?"

"Our picnic lunch didn't last long and we got so hungry we ate our toothpaste. That's what happens when we wander away from God; we get so hungry for real satisfaction that we do stupid things to satisfy the yearnings of our hearts. God gave us those yearnings—for love, for a stable home life, for satisfying work, for family—but when we're lost in the world of sin, we can't find real love or happiness to satisfy those yearnings so we fill them with cheap imitations which, like eating toothpaste, don't truly satisfy."

"Tell me about it. How do you think I got this big belly? Not because I was happily married to a good man, that's for sure!" She kicked at the dirt with her foot.

"And then, to make matters worse in our struggle with sin," I said, tugging on an especially tough weed until it let loose with a jerk and I fell on my backside, "we start calling it by pleasant names, persuading ourselves that it's no big deal. Our enemy, Satan, just loves it when we do that." I dusted myself off and sat up. "Okay, that's it; enough gardening for the day."

"What do you mean? What kinds of names?" she asked, laughing at me and giving me a hand up. Collecting my tools, I headed for the porch, dropping them in a bucket by the back door as I stepped into the kitchen. After tying on my old red and blue apron and washing my hands, I stooped in front of the fridge to get out salad ingredients. Theresa followed and parked herself at the bar.

"Well, here's another story to illustrate how we avoid calling our sins by their real names. Years ago, I was attracted to a friend's husband. I was happily married to Craig and wanted to stay that way but

I still struggled with feeling attracted to this man. Eventually I asked a close friend what she thought I should do."

This was embarrassing to remember; I stuck my increasingly warm face further into the fridge and kept rummaging.

"I thought she would sympathize with me—tell me not to worry about it, that it was no big deal, that I was a good person, etc, etc. I sure wasn't prepared for what God spoke through her! She said, 'Katie, that's emotional adultery, and adultery is a sin whether it's emotional or physical. You need to repent of it *now*. Get away from him. Do whatever it takes, but get this sin out of your life *now* because it'll ruin you.'"

"Wow, that's pretty strong."

"You're right, but it was exactly what I needed to hear. If she had said something like, 'Follow your heart,' or, 'It's no big deal,' I could be a miserable mess right now, probably having ruined my marriage and family. His too, for that matter. The point is that I needed to hear, straight out, that what I was getting my heart involved in was emotional adultery. *Adultery.* Suddenly, when I heard that, I realized how wrong it was and how much damage it could do to our family. And I realized I needed to repent of it and turn away from it in a hurry!"

"So what did you do when she said that?" she asked, walking over to where I was trying to hibernate in the fridge. She leaned against the counter, looking down at me.

"At first I was shocked and wanted to slap her and say, 'It is *not* adultery!' I had been trying to label it all sorts of other pleasant things, but certainly not adultery."

Standing up, I shut the door hard, remembering that embarrassing confrontation.

"But I bit my tongue long enough to realize she was right. Then, even though I was embarrassed and ashamed, I admitted that I was lusting after a man not my husband and that it *was* adultery, even if it was only emotional. I told God I now saw how wrong it was and that I was sorry and would He please forgive me of my wrongdoing? I told Him that I wanted nothing more to do with this man and asked Him to help me turn my mind to other things when I thought of him in the future.

"But the first step was to call my sin for what it was: adultery."

"Wow, that's pretty heavy. I never really thought of myself as *sinning*, just maybe doing stupid things."

"You know," I said, laying out the ground beef and salad ingredients on the counter, "one of the hardest things that I struggle with about sin is the fact that we all do it. All of us. Including me. Sometimes, in my heart, I want to cry out, 'Not me, Lord! I'm a good person! Surely you can see that?'"

"And He says?"

"He reminds me that we have *all* sinned and fallen short of the glory of God *(Rom 3:23)*. All. Not just the really bad ones. All of us. Remember, missing the bull's eye by just a hair is still missing it. And believe me, I miss it by more than a hair most days! I exaggerate, which is lying; I say stuff to make people like me even if I don't mean it, which is lying; I want my own way, which is selfishness. . ."

"*That*, I can identify with!" She followed me to the stove where I started to brown the ground beef for spaghetti. When she thought I wasn't looking, she reached into the pan and popped a chunk of cooked meat into her mouth.

I reached out to smack the back of her hand with the spatula, but she was too quick for me. I smacked the counter instead.

"Ha! Missed me," she taunted, dangling her hand in front of my face.

"Oooh, don't temp me, girl!"

"It's nice to know that even *you* miss the mark sometimes! 'Cause I know I miss it all the time."

"Believe me; I miss the mark a lot! From the world's point of view, I may seem to be a pretty good person—I don't kill or steal; I try to be kind and polite—but from God's point of view, I'm just as filthy as the worst sinner. Being nice just isn't enough. It's not perfection."

"Okay, so we sin, pretty much all the time, it looks like. What do we do about it? How do we get free from that heaviness, that guilt, that feeling bad about ourselves?" She dragged a stool over to the counter where I worked and sat down heavily, resting her head in her hands, her momentarily playful mood gone.

"Maybe this story will answer that question. Once when the kids were little, the two older boys got into trouble. Thinking it was Jeff's fault, Craig disciplined him without asking too many questions. But Rob—who'd been trying to slink away without being seen—was actually the culprit. When Craig discovered that, he punished Rob accordingly, both for the original sin and for trying to sneak out of it. Then he went back to Jeff and asked his forgiveness for punishing him when he *didn't* deserve it. He told Jeff he'd been wrong to act so hastily and that he was sorry. Jeff forgave him easily, the way little kids do, and Craig hugged both boys, prayed with them and sent them on their way.

"A few minutes later, still feeling bad about punishing Jeff for something he didn't do, Craig apologized to him again, 'I am so sorry, buddy. Please forgive me. I was wrong to punish you.' Jeff looked up from playing and asked, 'Forgive you for what, Daddy?' He'd already forgotten the matter.

"Craig had asked Jeff to forgive him for his mistake; Jeff had forgiven him and forgotten about it. That's the way it is with God. When we tell Him we did something wrong—that we're sorry for it and will try not to do it again—and we ask Him forgive us for it, He does. Then He reassures us of His love for us, and we move on. He forgets about it and so can we."

"That easy, huh?" She looked up at me hopefully, resting her chin in her hand.

"Easy for us, but not easy for Jesus. It was God's original plan that we–His kids–would live in friendship with Him in the beautiful world He originally created. But once Adam and Eve disobeyed Him and broke the one restriction on their freedom, it was as if the gates opened and sin and ugliness entered the world like a flood, affecting the rest of humanity forever. The Bible tells us that the punishment for sin is death, and since every person born from that time on would be infected with the ugliness of sin, every person from that time on was destined for eternal death, away from God forever *(Rom 6:23)*.

"There was nothing any human could do about this sentence of death. Trying to be good enough wasn't good enough; we could never reach the perfection that God wanted for us. We were permanently infected with sin and permanently condemned to die apart from God. So, out of His love for us, God created a way for us to cross back to Him. He sent His own Son to be the required Sacrifice. In the Old Testament, it was the blood of goats and lambs that cleansed the people from the effects of sin, but the cleansing only lasted for a day at a time. Now it would be the blood of God Himself that would cleanse His people from the effects of sin, forever.

"So Jesus came to earth to live as a Man among us and He gave His own body as a sacrifice to pay for sin so that humanity could find its way back to a life with God. That payment is a free gift and anyone who receives it walks through the door to heaven. God welcomes all His children in, saying: 'Come in! come in! Your sins no longer bring death upon you. My Son has paid the price for them and it's a free gift to you, My child. *Anyone* who receives this gift is welcome to enter in: Jew, Hindu, Muslim, Christian, black, white, brown; *all* are welcome'. Come in!"

Theresa turned around, resting her elbows on the counter behind her and watched me as I moved around the kitchen preparing the meal. I handed her a knife and a loaf of French bread and asked, "Here, slice this up, will you?"

She took the knife in one hand and the bread in the other, still thinking about our conversation.

"Wow. So you mean we don't have to pay for our sins somehow? I mean, I've done a lot of really stupid things in my life—sins, I guess you'd call them—and I can get free of them just by confessing them to God and asking Him to forgive me? That's all it takes? It seems too easy."

"I know. It does seem too easy sometimes. But if you think of the price Jesus paid to obtain that forgiveness for us, suddenly it doesn't seem quite so easy. Here's Jesus, the Son of God, second Person of the Trinity, the One who created the universe, hanging as a naked, helpless Man on that cross, mocked by the jeering crowd, abandoned by His own disciples, suffering, bleeding, thirsting, dying. And as if that wasn't enough, God the Father turned away from Him at the very end, leaving Him to suffer and die alone. He did all that out of his love for us. Can you believe that?"

"Wow...I'm not sure I'll ever really grasp what Jesus did for me on that cross," she said thoughtfully, slowly starting to slice the bread.

"You never will and I never will because we're not Jesus; we don't know what it was like to be Him, living in heaven, equal with God, and then come down to earth to be seen as an ordinary man by most people and a blasphemer by some. We can never fully grasp what it must have felt like to have the Father turn away from Him or what it felt like to have the sins of the whole world on His bleeding shoulders. All we can understand is our response to Jesus' sacrifice."

"And what should that be?"

"The only response I know of that's at all appropriate is adoration and gratitude. And also a desire to follow and serve Him, whatever it takes."

"Which of course is the big question: whatever it takes. What *does* it take to be used by God? Will I ever get to the place where I'll be free enough of my own hang-ups and fears that I can be used by Him? I don't know if He'll ever be able to use me, I'm so messed up." She looked ruefully at her stomach.

"Theresa, that reminds me of one more truth about sin." I put down my spatula, came over to the breakfast bar and taking both her hands in mine, I looked her in the eye.

"Whenever we turn our sin over to Him, He takes it and turns it into something wonderful. Just like this baby you're carrying."

"The ultimate Recycler," she mused, looking up at me, skepticism struggling with hope on her face, "Who takes our junk and turns it into a piece of art? For real? I'm not so sure."

"Theresa, I hope you know how good you are at putting things well. Someday, girl, someday, you'll be teaching all this stuff, better than I ever could."

"I doubt that!" she snorted. "Not this crazy, messed-up girl. But next time we talk, will you tell me how God could possibly turn this piece of junk into a piece of art?"

"Wait 'til I've got about five baskets of laundry to fold and we'll have ourselves a good talk on that topic. Is that a deal?"

"Deal. I'll even help fold."

CHAPTER 8

What Is Sin?

Questions for Discussion

§

1) Have you ever struggled with the idea that we *all* sin? Do you think of yourself, as Katie did, as basically a good person? Do you rank sin in your mind with murder being far worse than telling a white lie? Do you think God ranks sin like that? If not, where do you think that idea come from?

2) Do you have the feeling that as long as you're a good person you'll go to heaven?

3) In this chapter, it is explained how we get to heaven. What is that explanation? Can you put it in your own words?

4) If God loves us so much, why is there a separation between Him and us? What causes this separation? If God loves us so much, why doesn't He take everybody to heaven, no matter what they believe?

5) Why did Jesus to have to die? Couldn't He have paved the way back to God some other way?

6) Why does sin have to be punished?

7) Discuss Theresa's final observation at the end of the chapter about God being "the ultimate Recycler". What did she mean by that?

CHAPTER 9

Who, Me? A Homemaker?

§

Ice grew an inch thick on the shelves and walls of our old upright freezer. I had to clean it and it wasn't one of my favorite jobs. I sighed as I collected my implements of destruction.

Suppose we could get a new freezer one of these days, Father? One that defrosts itself?

It was in the basement so I stuck my head into Theresa's room on my way. She was lying on her bed reading a magazine.

"Hey, you want to help me clean the freezer?"

"Oh, can't wait. The fun things you think up for us to do. . ." she said, rolling her eyes and sitting up.

"I know. I was an entertainment director on a cruise ship in a former life. Ha! I just want your company. All you have to do is watch. Here," I said, offering her a hand up.

"That wouldn't hurt me, I guess. I've never seen anyone clean out a freezer. All these little homemaker things—I don't have a clue. My mom sure never did any of this stuff." She rolled off the bed and followed me down the hall into the freezer area of the basement. My well-used washer and dryer stood on one side of the area with the freezer and a table for sorting and folding laundry along the other wall. A few milk crates were stacked under the table. Two or three coolers of various sizes lined the walls beside the washer and dryer. A bare bulb hung from the ceiling. We'd refinished the other half of the basement, but this half was still plain old cellar.

I slipped on a pair of lined rubber gloves and opened the freezer.

"Yeah, well, defrosting the freezer's not all that exciting, but somebody has to do it. Here, I'll hand you the frozen stuff, you mind packing it in that picnic cooler over there? I'd like to keep all this meat from thawing out."

"You know, Katie, I've been meaning to ask you," she said, taking the first package of meat and stowing it in the cooler, "I've been watching you, and, well. . .okay, here it is: Aren't you bored staying home doing things like folding laundry and cleaning out the freezer? Wouldn't you rather be out in the world doing something a little more challenging? I mean, don't you ever feel like your talents are wasted staying home all day?"

I sat back on my heels for a moment, the freezer door open in front of me, just pouring out expensive cold air. I reached around and unplugged it.

"Yeah, actually I do. Sometimes I struggle with those feelings a lot. I pout to God, and wonder if I'm wasting my time and talents here at home, just as you say. At times like that, I can think of a hundred things that sound more exciting and fulfilling than staying home and cleaning house and making meals.

"But you know, when our kids began arriving one after the other, Craig and I decided that the most important thing I could do for our family was to stay at home and take care of them. So my career, if you will, is being a *homemaker*. I like that term, by the way, better than *housewife*, since I'm making a home, not being a wife to the house! But seriously, I do this out of a sense of conviction, not because I can't think of anything better to do."

"Yeah, but it isn't very satisfying, is it? You do the same things over and over, day after day, and never really get anywhere. It would drive me crazy!" She frowned at me, trying to comprehend why I did what I did.

"I know, a lot of what I do each day *is* pretty repetitive, I admit. And it can get boring. But you know that quilt hanging on the wall in our front entry? That one with the thousands of tiny pieces?"

She nodded, wondering what I was getting at.

"My grandmother made that quilt, by hand, no less. I can hardly *imagine* the number of hours she put into that thing! And talk about boring—I would have gone out of my mind, I'm sure!"

She nodded emphatically. "And this relates to being a homemaker. . . how?"

"As I do the same things over and over again each day, much like the hours she spent sewing those quilt pieces together, I'm building something just as beautiful as she did with her quilt. Only I'm building a family, stitched together with threads of repetitive acts of love. It takes a long time and a lot of small acts all added together to make a family that works. And you don't get to see the full picture until it's all done. I'm still waiting for that day." I handed her a load of frozen green beans. We'd had a bumper crop in our garden last year.

"And you know, Theresa, in the long run, I don't think there's any more important thing a mother can do than raise her children to love and serve God and their fellow man. I believe that good parenting is the number one factor in setting a child on the right path in life. What we do as mothers in our children's early years can affect them for the rest of their lives. I can't tell you how many people I've talked to who are struggling as adults because of the poor parenting they received as children." I tucked my hands in my armpits for a moment to warm them up.

"Well, that I can believe. Just look at me. But why do *you* have to be the servant of the family? Why can't the others do their fair share?" She closed the cooler and sat on it while she waited for me.

"We each do our part. Right now, the kids' job is to go to school and work hard there. The older ones have after school jobs as well. Craig works long hours to provide for our family, and he's tired when he gets home. And, if you've noticed, he does help with the kids and homework in the evenings. He takes care of paying all the bills, something I'd be terrible at, as well as keeping the cars in good shape. When the lawn gets mowed, it's Craig who does it. And I'm sure you've noticed that the kids all have household chores they have to do on Saturdays. Don't worry; I'm no martyr. I took my six least favorite jobs and handed them out to the kids. I haven't cleaned a bathroom in ten years!" I laughed, starting on the next shelf of the freezer. Blueberries this time.

"Yeah, but how'd you decide which work was for which person? How come you ended up with all the drudge work? I mean, here you are, cleaning out this freezer. You'll just have to do it all over again in, what, six months? Or take cooking. Good grief! You cook every night and just have to do it all over again the next night. How frustrating is that?"

"Each woman is different, Theresa. Each one has a different tolerance for staying home, which *can* be boring and monotonous, and each one has a different view of what she wants to do with her life. And each one has a different financial situation. Besides believing that this is the best thing I can do for my family, I'm a homebody; I love being a wife and a mother. Most of the time, doing that is enough career for me. In our case, I'm very grateful that Craig earns enough so that I can stay home and take care of my family."

"I think I'd want to work even if my hypothetical, future, rich husband did make enough money so that I could stay home."

"A lot of women feel that way. There are times when it definitely looks a lot more fulfilling and interesting to work outside the home, I'll grant you that! And for some, that is the best choice. But the way I see it is that the Bible tells us that God made woman to be man's helpmate, or helper *(Gen 2:18)*. I understand that to mean that she comes alongside him and helps him in whatever way she can. That's not to say that women can't have careers, but if the husband and wife are each pulling in opposite directions, putting their own career goals before the family's needs, it can cause a lot of strife and stress in the family, often to the breaking point."

"Hmmm. Never thought of it that way."

"I know women who have full-time careers out of the home and are still able to raise happy and loving children. But most of them have to miss some important moments with their kids and most women I've talked to in that situation wish they could spend more time with their families. Each woman has to assess her own situation and ask God which direction He wants her to go in."

I handed her the last of the blueberries we'd picked earlier in the year.

"But you know, Theresa, Jesus tells us that we should lay down our lives for one another. He says that unless a grain of wheat falls into the ground and dies, it will not bear much fruit *(John 12:24)*. He tells us that we are to do nothing from selfish ambition, but in humility we're to see others as better than ourselves. We're to look out not only for our own interests, but also to the interests of others *(Phil 2:3-4)*. Jesus himself took the form of a servant, laying aside the glory that He had in heaven, and came to earth to give His life for us *(Phil 2:6-8)*. That's my role model, which means that, at this stage of my life, while the kids are still home, I need to lay aside my ambitions and desires and serve my family. Craig serves the family, too, by going to work every day."

"You serve by letting me live here and teaching me all this stuff. Because I *am* learning from you, you know." She gave me a quick sideways glance. I handed her two packages of frozen burritos.

Thank you, God. That makes it all worth it.

"I'm glad you are. In my eyes, that's what being a mother is all about; having the time and energy to talk to and listen to the important people in her life, being able to spend time with them and to pour herself into them."

"Yeah, I've noticed you having long talks with Molly and Lizzie at bedtimes sometimes."

"And that's why I play games with Jason and Jossie in the evenings, too. I want them to remember spending time with me and having fun with me, because for most children, love equals time and attention. I can say I love my family all I want, but if I don't spend time with them and give them the attention they need, my words are pretty empty. Time is our most valuable currency and also the one we hoard the most. We think our time is our own, to do with as we please. Actually, God gave us the time we have here on earth to serve Him and love Him. It's really not ours at all."

"That's a new concept; nobody ever told me that before. I always looked at my life as my own, to do with as I wanted." She closed the full cooler and sat down heavily on it.

"That'll probably change in a hurry when your baby arrives. Nothing like a baby to let us know that our time is not our own! You might as well settle it right now that once you become a mom your life will never be the same. What you think of as *your* time will go out the window; part of your heart will forevermore be tied up in that little person, and the main goal of your life will be to make sure he or she thrives. Raising her'll be the hardest thing you've ever even *thought* of doing, but also the most rewarding." I hacked at the thick layers of ice with my dull table knife. A few chips fell off. I hacked harder.

"So I'm supposed to devote all my time and energy to my baby? That sounds a little scary! What if I get bored? Or fed up? Or restless?

96

Or need to earn a living?" She scooted the cooler closer so we could talk over the noise of my hacking at the ice.

"Honey, I'm not saying you have to devote *all* your time and energy to her. All I'm saying is that as humans we tend to be selfish with our time and energy. You need to be sure her needs are met before your own. That's part of what it means to serve someone else."

"I'm not so sure I'm liking this."

"Look at it this way. My marriage and my family are the most precious things in the world to me after my relationship with God," I said, poking and jabbing. Spits of ice flew in my face. "I will do all I can to see that they not only survive but thrive because when I stand before God after I die, I want to be able to tell Him that I did all I could to take care of the family He gave me. I don't want to have any regrets about how I spent my time. So, if that means I have to clean out the freezer," I caught the tip of the knife under a slab of ice and pried it off, "or fold the laundry, so be it. It's all part of the larger job of taking care of my family."

"So does that mean that all of us women have to stay home and just take care of our kids all day long?"

"Not necessarily. There are plenty of other things you can do in addition to taking care of your children. Especially after they start school, you'll have time for other things. Just don't make the mistake of thinking that once they start school they no longer need you! They'll probably need you more than ever during their school years. Those are tough years." I loosened another slab and it fell with a satisfying shatter.

"And also, I wouldn't say that it is a matter of 'just' taking care of them. Teaching, training and taking care of a child is really teaching and training an eternal soul. You could make the difference in your child's life between spending eternity with God or spending it forever apart from Him in hell.

"And think about this: we're raising children who eventually become adults and adults are the ones who run this world. Everything in the world revolves around people in some way or another, so if we as mothers have the privilege of training and raising those people—giving them a good start in life so they can be healthy, happy contributing members of our society—we've really done the most basic, important work there is." The slabs were falling off faster now. I loosened them all and began sweeping out the melting ice in the bottom of the stand-up freezer.

"Seems like a lot of drudgery to me. Nothing much exciting about it."

She pulled a strand of hair from behind her ear and began flicking it back and forth across her cheek.

"Well, sometimes that's true. Our society doesn't much reward mothers—or nurses or teachers either, for that matter. All three of those professions have immediate, hands-on contact with people, but they're not much recognized for what they do. Those who entertain and amuse us are the ones our society rewards, not those who lay down their lives for us. But where would we be without mothers who love and train their kids and who launch them as healthy human beings into the world?" I turned back to the warming freezer and swept it out fiercely, pushing the icy mess toward the drain hole in the cement floor.

God, it bugs *me, the way our society undervalues motherhood!*

Theresa shoved the cooler even closer so she could see my face as we talked.

"I don't think I was very well launched. In fact, I think my mother did a pretty crappy job with me; excuse the vernacular. I mean, look at me: I'm a mess; I've never had a decent relationship with a man; I failed at college; I'm pregnant and there's no dad in the picture. Worst of all, I have all this anger and bitterness inside of me that I don't know what to do with. There. I said it. That's the main problem. I hate my mother. I'm angry at her for failing me and for making me what I am now. And I don't know how to get past all this. I'm just filled up with hate and anger, and it's all her fault! I hate her!" Theresa buried her face in her hands. I reached over to stroke her back, but she flinched and pulled away.

God, give me wisdom here, please.

Just love her. Speak the truth to her.

Don't let me say the wrong thing, God, please.

"Hey, sweetie, you look like you could use a hug. May I hug you, just a little?" I picked up a strand of her hair and tucked it behind her ear so I could see her better.

"No!" She jerked her head away. "I don't want anybody to hug me! I want to be angry. It's easier that way. Then I don't have to love anybody."

"Theresa, baby, come here." Despite her protests, I kneeled next to her and gathered her resistant body close to me, right there in the midst of the thawing freezer and melting ice. After a minute of stiff resistance, she slumped against me.

"I just hate her so much," she whispered. "She used to do awful things to me. It wasn't just that she was impatient and too busy for us. She was cruel, too. She'd shut me in the closet if I got on her nerves. She'd yell at me when I got whiney. And she never, ever told me she loved me. That's all I wanted; for her to tell me she loved me, and to hold me in her arms. She never did though." Pulling away, she dropped her head in her hands and began rocking herself on the cooler where she sat. After a moment she began to cry; a soft, high-pitched wail like a forlorn baby, the saddest sound I'd ever heard. Getting off my knees, I pulled another cooler next to hers and sat down, putting my arms around her and hugging her awkwardly to me. I began rocking in rhythm with her, not knowing what else to do. Water from the freezer continued to drip.

God, please minister to her. I can't heal the innermost parts of her heart. Only You can.

Just keep rocking.

The water dripped out of the freezer and ran down the drain in the floor. I held Theresa and rocked her gently, back and forth, back and forth. After a long time, her wailing stopped and she lay limp in my arms. I rocked and rocked, trying not to think of all my hamburger thawing out in the picnic cooler. It's hamburger I can buy more of, I told myself.

Rock, rock, rock.

I began to hum softly. It was the tune to Braham's lullaby, but years ago I had put my own words to it. After a while I started to sing:

Good night, sleep tight,
and wake up bright in the morning light,
to do what's ri-i-ght with all your mi-i-ght,
good ni-i-ght, sleep tight.
May God bless you
and keep you

and make His face to shine up-on you,
may He give you His peace forevermore.
Good night.

I must have sung it twelve times before Theresa stirred.

"I've never been held and rocked like that before." She lifted her head and smearing tears across her face with the back of her hand, smiled a watery smile. "Thanks. If you don't mind, I think I'll go back to my room now. I just want to lie down and sleep for about a year. Call me if you need anything."

"I will, sweetie. Have a good nap."

I knocked off the last few clumps of melting ice that clung to the wires of the shelves, swept out the remaining watery slop until the freezer was clean and replaced the half-thawed food. As I placed the last box of green beans in its place, I stood back and admired how it looked.

All ready to go again.

If only it were so easy with Theresa.

CHAPTER 9

Who, Me, A Homemaker?

Questions for Discussion

§

1) I once read an autobiographical blurb written by a highly professional woman who said that in addition to all her other accomplishments she raised two children "in her spare time". What does that remark convey to you about how she regarded the job of child-rearing?

2) Not every stay-at-home mother is a good mother and not every mother with a career outside the home does her family a disservice. How much was your mother around when you were little? Do you wish she'd been around more, or was it enough?

3) Based on how you were raised and what you felt you received or didn't receive from your mother, how important do you think a mother's role—and a mother's time—is in the life of her family? Do you think it's important for her to stay home with her children? If or when you have children, do you plan to stay home with them or pursue a full or part time career outside the home? (Understanding that for many women, finances dictate that decision.)

4) If you are a stay-at-home mother, how do you balance your needs against your family's needs? Families are often unaware of all the things a stay-at-home mother does to take care of her home and family and they often take her and her work for granted. How can a stay-at-home mother keep herself encouraged in a situation like that?

5) Katie quoted Jesus as saying that unless a grain of wheat falls into the ground and dies *(John 12:24)*, it will not bear much fruit. What do you think this means?

6) For some women, staying home with children all day is more stressful than working outside the home. For other women, it is leaving the family each day that causes them the most stress. If you have children, where do you fall on that spectrum? Are there other options?

7) Discuss stress on a family. What are its effects on you as mother, wife and woman; on your husband, and on your children? Can it be damaging or have long-term effects?

CHAPTER 10

Letting Anger Go

§

A couple of days later I was bustling around the kitchen getting an early start on supper. Craig and I had a church meeting at seven that evening and I wanted plenty of time for a family supper before we left. Eating dinner together was our only chance to catch up with each other during the day and it also gave Craig and me an opportunity to gauge how each of our brood was doing. Without this time to touch base it was too easy for us to fly off in our own directions, each of us absorbed in our own lives. I had learned, during a brief full-time job outside the home years ago, how easy it was to emotionally lose track of a child even while living in the same house. From then on, Craig and I insisted that everybody make it to dinner each night if at all possible.

Theresa wandered into the kitchen. She hadn't said much since our time down by the freezer, and I hadn't wanted to pry. She sat down at the breakfast bar and looked at me.

"So, Katie, can we talk? I can peel carrots or something."

"Fine by me. Here's the scraper. Don't take too much of the peel off; that's where the vitamins are stored."

She peeled slowly and deliberately. I usually peel a mile a minute so I glanced her way.

"Got something on your mind?"

"I kind of feel like this carrot here, with the first layer of my skin being scraped off. I feel all raw inside."

"After the other day, you mean?"

"Yeah. Somehow you got down to where it hurts and I'm not sure I like that. It's easier to keep your skin on."

"Be tough, you mean? Not let anybody into your heart?"

"Well, yeah! It's easier that way. Nobody can get in to hurt you and you don't have to face how much you hurt down there."

"Do you really want to keep carrying this hurt and anger around with you for the rest of your life, Theresa?"

"It's not that I exactly like it, but what choice do I have? The damage is done and I'm kind of ruined. Not much anybody can do about it."

"What if I told you there was something you could do about all this hurt? Would you want to get rid of it?"

Theresa stopped peeling. "Would I want to get rid of it? I don't know, to be perfectly honest. It's been with me so long I'm not sure what I'd be like without it. I mean, wouldn't there just be a huge hole left in my heart? I don't know what kind of a person I'd be without all that anger and bitterness."

"You willing to give it a try? I have a feeling there'd be a lot more room for you to be the Theresa God made once you got rid of all this anger and bitterness."

"Heck, what've I got to lose? So what's your solution?" She turned and looked glumly at me.

"You need to forgive your mother. And your father too, although you don't speak of him as much."

"Yeah, right! Why in the world would I want to do that? *They're* the ones who screwed me up. *They* should be the ones who come groveling to me and ask my forgiveness. They should pay for what they did to me. I'm not gonna just blow it all away as if it never happened and forgive them! Good grief, Katie! Get a life!" She slammed the peeler down on the counter and stared at me.

"Theresa, you've peeled half that carrot away. Here, try another. And remember, the carrot isn't your mom." I said mildly, handing her another carrot.

"Yeah, but this is what I'd like to do to her." Picking up the peeler, she furiously peeled all the skin off the carrot. Sighing, I took it from her and gave her another one.

"You want to make her pay. Is that right?"

"Of course I do. Wouldn't you want to make someone pay if they'd completely screwed up your life? I bet you would. Even you."

"And what could she possibly do to 'pay' for all the hurt you've received at her hand? How could she pay you back?"

"Oh, maybe just come to me and admit to me what a lousy mother she was and beg me to forgive her. I'd just tell her that I'd think about it and that I'd get back to her when I had the time. And then I'd show her the door. I wouldn't get back to her for a year or two or three, no matter how many times she came groveling. If she called, I'd just tell her I was too busy to think about her needs right now and that I had my own stuff to tend to."

"Sounds like what you heard her say to you when you were little?"

"You'd better believe it! And I'd shove it all right back in her face and let her feel what it's like to be little and ignored and helpless. Then maybe she'd feel sorry for all the lousy things she did to me."

"And then where would you be? You'd both be miserable, but the anger and hatred would still be there."

"So? Maybe I like the hatred and anger. It keeps me going."

Slash and peel, slash and peel. Carrot skin flew all over the counter.

"It'll keep you going right into an early grave, Theresa. By the way, did you know that the Bible has some very specific things to say on this subject?"

"Who would have guessed? And I bet I'm about to hear them whether I want to or not."

I took the skinny little stick of a carrot she was about to peel into oblivion and gave her another.

Lord, I need Your love and patience here. Quick.

You know it's always available—as much as you need.

I need Your wisdom too.

You've got it. As much as you need.

"If you don't want to hear them, girl, that's fine. We'll just talk about something else. But one thing I will tell you: you're going to be miserable until you get all this stuff worked out."

"Okay, okay. So tell me what I have to do. I'm not saying I'll do it, but at least you can tell me."

"Well, the Bible tells us to honor our father and mother so that—now catch this—so that life will go *well with us*. That means if we honor our mother and father, our lives here on earth won't be tangled, hurting and angry. If we don't honor our parents, things will not go well with us *(Eph 6:2)*."

"Well, I'm a living testimony of that!" She tossed the scraper on the counter. I looked at the huge pile of peelings and the scrawny little carrot sticks that were left and laughed.

"Oh, girl, I love you."

I chopped up what was left of the carrots and dropped them into the stew pot. Wiping my hands on my apron, I turned to Theresa.

"You have the choice of forgiving your parents and being free of all this hate," I gestured to the large pile of peelings, "or continuing to carry all this bitterness and probably spread it to your baby one day."

"But if I forgive them, isn't that like saying they never did anything wrong? That's the lump I can't get past."

"Oh honey, no. It's not saying they never did bad things to you. They did, and that was hurtful and wrong. Every child needs and deserves a loving mom and dad. You did suffer; you were hurt. It is a fact, and it is awful. You have a right to be mad about it. Unfortunately, being mad about it isn't going to bring you any peace."

"So what's gonna bring me peace, if that's even possible? Huh?" She glared sullenly at me, her eyes veiled and angry.

"Forgiving them. Letting God take care of paying them back, as you say. Rolling the whole mess onto His shoulders and let Him take care of it. I once heard a good definition of forgiveness as 'Giving up my right to hurt someone who's hurt me.'"

"That would definitely be me. I sure have the right to hurt them after all they've done to me. And I'm not sure I want to give up that right just yet."

"Well," I said, turning back to my cooking, "let me know when you are ready. Until then: enjoy."

"Hmmm. 'Giving up my right to hurt someone who's hurt me'." She slumped over onto the counter with her face hidden in her arms and stayed that way for at least five or six minutes. I could see her shoulder shaking but I figured this was between her and God so I went on with dinner preparations.

Finally, she lifted her head and looked at me with a wet face. "You know what? I changed my mind. I'm so tired of all this, I just want it over with. I don't even want to hurt them. I just want to get away from all the pain."

"So forgive them. Just let it all go. Tell God you forgive them and you don't want to carry this burden anymore and so you're cancelling the debt they owe you. Can you do that?"

"If it'll make *you* feel better. . .Mrs. Holy Christian. . ." she mumbled, looking anywhere but at me.

I began to hum, stirring the stew.

Ama-zi-ing grace. . .how sweet the sound. . .

"No, I guess what I really mean is if it will make *me* feel better. Yes. I want to do it, but I'm not sure I can. Will you help me? Can you lead me in a prayer or something?"

She leaned both elbows on the counter, holding her head, her hair dripping over her face like tears.

"At this moment, nothing would make me happier. Ready?"

"Yup."

I took both her hands in mine and bowed my head.

"Follow after me if you want.

"Father, I come before you now to get rid of this burden–"

"Father, I just want to get rid of this burden. I'm sick and tired of carrying it, so God, I don't exactly know how this works, but here goes. I forgive you, Mom and Dad. I forgive you for being lousy parents. I forgive you, Dad, for walking out on us and never looking back. That was a lousy, selfish thing to do and it's screwed me up for the rest of my life. But I'm choosing to let it go, Dad, because I don't want to carry this anger around any more. And Mom, I forgive you for never having enough time for me, for being hateful to me when all I wanted was your love." Her voice quavered, but pressing her fist to her mouth she pushed on.

"I forgive you for screwing up my life by not loving me. Even though I *hated* you for what you did to me," she moaned with the effort of saying it, "I forgive you both. Right now, *I'm* choosing to let all this anger and hatred go," she opened her clenched fists and spread her fingers wide, "because it's tearing me up just as much as anything you ever did to me. From now on, I won't make you pay for what you did, in my mind or anywhere else. You can never take back what you've done, so we're just going to draw a line and forget it, here and now. Your stupid mistakes and selfish actions aren't going to control my life any more.

"Maybe next time I see you I'll tell you all about this but in the meantime, go on with your life. Maybe someday you'll know your bratty, screwed-up daughter doesn't hold bitterness against you any more. It's over; it's done with. You're free to go on with your life. And so am I." She looked up at me, tears soaking her face.

"You sure didn't need me to lead you in that prayer!" I put my arm around her a gave a squeeze.

"No, I didn't, did I? It just sort of poured out of me. I'm glad it's done, though. You know, I think I feel some better. A little lighter somehow. Not so angry. Wow, I kinda like this feeling. I did it, Katie! I actually did it. I forgave them. I dropped all this heavy anger and resentment. They're free to go on with their lives, and you know what? So am I."

"Right. So are you. That's the best part; you are free, girl."

She kissed me on the cheek and wandered out of the room in a daze.

Thank You, Father. Thank You so much!

*   *   *   *   *

Theresa came up to me after supper, just before we left for our meeting.

"Do you think Craig would mind if I rode with you guys as far as the pharmacy? I want to buy a notebook to start writing some of this stuff down. I can walk back."

"Not a problem at all."

*   *   *   *   *

The next morning Therese caught me just as I arrived back from taking the kids to school. She was actually cleaning up the kitchen and humming, a smile tweaking the corner of her mouth.

I tried not to be too obvious about staring.

"Hey, Katie, guess what?"

"What?" I mumbled, as I stuffed my purse back on the shelf, mentally going over the things I needed to do today.

"Turn around and look at me, Katie. I'm talking to you. Guess what?"

I blinked and turned around. "Okay, what?"

"I've got a job! When I went to the pharmacy last night I noticed they had a 'Help Wanted' sign out front, so I asked them about it and they hired me on the spot! It's just part-time, and of course there's some paperwork to do still, but they said I could have the job if I wanted it! How cool is that? I can start making my own money now and not have to depend on you guys for everything anymore. Not that I'm ungrateful for what you've done; I just mean I'll be able to start paying my own way now." She turned a beaming face to me. I'd never noticed before just how pretty she was when she smiled.

CHAPTER 10

Letting Anger Go

Questions for Discussion

§

1) Have you ever struggled with bitterness against someone and do you find that it is keeping you angry and unhappy? After this chapter, do you have an idea how to fix the situation?

2) In the Lord's Prayer, Jesus teaches us to ask God to *"Forgive us our debts as we forgive our debtors"* (**Matt. 6:12**). Given that admonition from Jesus Himself, what happens to us if we don't forgive others' sins, especially those that are directly against us?

3) What does anger and a lack of forgiveness do to us when it stays with us, sometimes for years? Can it affect us physically, mentally, emotionally, and spiritually?

4) Does forgiving someone who has hurt you mean that you're denying that there was ever any hurt done?

5) Is there a difference between forgiving someone—*letting go of your right to hurt someone who has hurt you*—and asking him or her to make restitution, such as paying for a broken window, or a damaged car? Are there times when no restitution can be made and we just have to let go of the anger and hurt?

6) The Amish are a people who always forgive, by religious conviction and by choice, no matter what the sin against them might be. They forgave the driver who killed several of their little girls some years ago. If you had been one of the parents, do you think you could have forgiven the driver? Why or why not?

7) What might happen to you in the next several years if you chose *not* to forgive, even in a situation like that? (*Not* forgiving is always a choice, just as forgiving is a choice.)

8) Discuss the saying of Jesus when He said that *"the measure you give will be the measure you get, and still more will be given you"* **(Mark 4:24 RSV).**

CHAPTER 11

Plunging into a New Life

§

The school year rolled on by. Theresa had been with us for two and a half months now and we all felt like she was part of the family. She worked her pharmacy job in the evenings so I had plenty of time to see her during the days. Her whole demeanor had changed; she fixed herself up to look nice at work and a certain self-confidence seemed to be creeping in. I rejoiced.

She was well into her third trimester and I made a mental note to find out about childbirth classes and encourage her to take them but as so often happened in our household, it slithered down to the bottom of my to-do list.

Then one day, just before the end of the school year, it happened, catching us all off guard.

I was flying around the kitchen, late as usual, throwing supper together so we could all eat before Craig left for a 7:00 meeting. I was on a roll—not needing any distractions—when I heard Theresa come upstairs, breathing hard. I called out "Hey there, girl!" from the depths of the fridge where I was rummaging around for lettuce and green peppers.

She was silent, except for the heavy breathing. I straightened up and turned around. "What's wro. . .oh glory, is it the baby?" I asked as she gripped her belly in sudden pain and hunched over a barstool. Her white face and ragged breathing told me all I needed to know. I ran to the stairs, yelling, "Molly, Lizzie, come here quick! I need your help, *now!*" Something in my voice must have let them know I was serious; they both came leaping down the stairs within seconds.

"Girls, Theresa's in labor, and she's way premature. We've gotta go to the hospital, right now!" Trying to think clearly, I handed out instructions as I whipped off my apron and washed my hands. "Would you two please finish making dinner—tuna salad and raw veggies—and set the table? Dad'll be home soon; I'll call him on my cell as I drive. He's got a school board meeting tonight and I don't think he can get out of it. Rob and Jeff should be home soon and Jason and Jossie are upstairs. You can help the twins with their homework if they need it, okay? Thanks, girls; you're sure precious to me." I hugged each one hard and kissed them on their foreheads. They hung back wide-eyed, watching Theresa moaning and holding her belly, turning whiter by the minute.

"Think you can walk, honey?"

"I don't know—oooh! Here comes another pain! I'll try." She breathed hoarsely, looking at me with panic in her eyes. I reached out to steady her. The girls shrank back against the counter to let us by. I kissed my fingers to them as we walked past, mouthing to them, "You'll be fine," before turning back to Theresa. I put my arm around her to steady her.

"Don't walk just yet. Breathe deeply and steadily. In, out. In, out. The pain will pass. That's right. In, out. In, out. Easy does it. Just twenty more seconds and it'll be over. There we go. Good girl."

Oh, why didn't I take her to childbirth classes before this?

"That's right, in and out, slow and deep. Good girl. Okay, now one more deep breath when it's over. There. Is it over now? When did you have the last contraction?"

"About six or seven minutes ago. Just before I came upstairs. That's why I came to get you. Oh, Katie, I'm wetting all over your floor! I'm so sorry! What a mess. . ." she began to cry.

"Honey, it's nothing to worry about. Your water's breaking, that's all. No problem. Lizzie, run and get some towels from the laundry room shelves, will you, honey? Thanks. Get a bunch; Theresa'll need a couple on the way to the hospital, too. Can you walk now, girl?"

"I think so."

"Here, take my arm. Lean as hard as you want. We need to get you to the hospital, so we're going to have to get you in the car even if you are in labor. Okay? Let's go." Leaning heavily on my arm and holding a towel between her legs, she waddled with me to the garage. Her bony shoulders trembled beneath my arm.

The thirty minute ride was tense, to say the least. I happened to glance at the gas gauge; it was right on the *E* and we were in the middle of rush hour traffic.

Oh God, please help us get there in time without running out of gas. I don't know how to deliver a baby in a car on the side of the road. God! Please!

I'm watching over the whole situation. Don't worry.

It seemed like every two minutes that Theresa let out a moan and began to breathe heavily. I coached as well as I could while still keeping an eye on the road. Traffic had never seemed to move so slow.

"Breathe, girl. Slow and deep. Don't let yourself panic. You can breathe your way through these pains. Don't fight it; go with the flow. Gently now." Theresa's eyes were shut, her nostrils flared and her knuckles white where she gripped the armrest.

"Katie, I can't do this! I'm sitting on her head! She's about to come out!"

Dear God, help!

"Okay, we're turning into the emergency entrance now. Don't hold your breath! Open your mouth and pant like a dog. Hold on just a little more, girl, you're doing great! Keep panting!" I hoped she felt more confident than I did. Putting the car in park, I left it running and dashed around to her side. Flinging open the door, I practically caught her in my arms as she tumbled out.

"Okay, easy now, breathe deeply," I coached, helping her walk toward the entrance.

"Can somebody please help us? We've got a mother in hard labor here!" I yelled.

Thank God, two nurses came running.

I babbled as we half carried her to the entrance. "Her contractions are coming every three or four minutes, and her water broke about twenty minutes ago. She's only about seven and a half months along and I don't know if she has any insurance. This is her first baby. I'm not her mother, just a good friend."

* * * * *

Not more than ninety minutes later, the doctor poked her head into the waiting room where I sat, pretending to read old parenting magazines.

"You can go in and see her now. She did great and she's got a cute little girl."

Thank You, God, thank You, for the safe delivery of this baby!

But, oh Lord, I'm not sure any of us were quite ready for this yet. We all need Your help here!

I pushed the door open quietly and walked in. Theresa lay on the bed with her eyes closed, her sweaty wet hair slicked back from her face and a look of utter exhaustion and contentment on her face. I stood by her bed for a moment, just enjoying looking down at her.

"What'cha lookin' at?" she asked, lazily opening her eyes and grinning at me. "I did it, Katie. I did it. All by myself. I had a baby, and I didn't even scream once. Aren't you proud of me?"

I pulled a chair close and sat down, stroking her hair.

"I sure am, sweetie. Where is this little bundle of joy?"

"They cleaned her up and took her away to the nursery. I got a chance to look at her first though, and cuddle her for a minute. They say I'll get to see her more a little later on, but they have to get her stabilized first. Her lungs are kind of small still. But she'll be fine, won't she, Katie?"

"I'm sure she will. Have you thought of a name for her?"

"Her name's AdaLayne," she said dreamily, her eyes closing again. "Ada is spelled *A-d-a* and sounds like "atta" except with a *D*. You know, like in, ''atta girl, way to go!' That's after my grandmother Ada. Everybody called her Addie, but her real name was Ada and I think that's prettier than Addie. Layne is spelled *L-a-y-n-e* and is for my grandfather who spelled his name L-a-n-e, no *y*. I added a *y* in there to make it look special. Do you like it? I loved my grandparents so much, Katie; I've always wanted to name my first baby after them. If it had been a boy, he would have been Lane Adair."

"I had no idea you'd been thinking about this all this time." I took her hand and began stroking it.

"Yup. I've had these names in my mind ever since I was a little girl." She opened her eyes and looked at me. "Do you like her name? I did good, didn't I, Katie? I did it all by myself."

"You did great, girl. I just wish I'd thought to take you to childbirth classes before this. And yes, I do like her name, very much."

"I told you, didn't I, that I used to spend summers with my grandparents?" she asked dreamily. "My mom would drop me off there and not come back for weeks. I loved it there. They were so kind to me. That's where I learned to love flowers and climb trees. And, like I told you before, they took me to Sunday school every week, where I learned everything I know about Jesus. Except for what you've taught me, of course." Her eyes drifted closed again.

"You sleep, Theresa. I'll check on you later."

"Stay here just a little longer, Katie, please," she murmured, almost asleep, reaching for my hand. I sat down again and took her hand in mine, rubbing it gently.

A little longer can't hurt. I'm sure all is well on the home front.

*   *   *   *   *

At six weeks premature and less than three pounds, AdaLayne had to stay in the hospital for a few weeks in an incubator. Theresa was discharged after a day or so but she refused to leave her baby. I finally had to force her away and take her home, weeping. Both of us were crying by the time the car pulled into the driveway but I couldn't tell if I sympathized with her anguish or if I was exasperated at her for making such a fuss.

She showed up in the kitchen at 7:15 the next morning, washed and dressed, with her huge, fake leather purse slung over her shoulder.

"Hi, honey. How're you feeling today?"

"Great, and I'm ready to go to the hospital to see my baby."

"Theresa, it's only 7:15. I can take you a little later; just not yet."

"Anything I can do to help you get ready?"

"Um. . .take a shower for me? Comb my hair? Make my bed? Straighten up the kitchen?" I was a little shorter with her than I meant to be.

Good grief, Katie, lighten up! The girl's just had a baby and wants to go see her. Give her a break!

"I'll clean up the kitchen for you. Can we go after that?"

"I'll do my best, honey." With that, I escaped up the stairs.

An hour later, I stood with Theresa, looking down at her tiny daughter. Baby AdaLayne's eyes were shut tightly, a tube in her nose brought oxygen to her lungs and her translucent skin showed every vein. Her little belly rose up and down in the warmth of the incubator. Theresa slipped her hands through the rubber-lined holes in the side of the plastic womb her daughter lay in and gently stroked the fragile skin. The baby startled, flinging her pinky-sized arms straight out.

After half an hour, I turned to Theresa. "Honey, I need to go. Want to come with me or shall I pick you up later?"

"Oh, I'm staying until ten tonight. You can pick me up then." She turned back to her baby, focused on her and nothing else.

"I'll see what I can do. Have a good day, and enjoy your little one." I kissed her on the cheek and left.

This pattern was repeated daily for the next three weeks. Some days Theresa stood by the back door, tapping her fingers and looking at her watch even before Craig and the kids left for school.

Finally, I'd had enough. My schedule was thoroughly disrupted by the hour's round trip driving Theresa to the hospital in the mornings and picking her up in the early afternoons so she could go to work for a few hours at the pharmacy, often taking her back again for a few hours in the evening and arriving home after eleven each night.

Theresa herself was becoming wan and pale. Each evening when I arrived at the hospital to bring her home she went through the same routine: asking the nurses what they would do if little AdaLayne cried, how often they were going to feed her, how many times they were planning to hold and snuggle her throughout the night, what they would do if she stopped breathing. She seemed to feel that unless she was there all care for her little girl would come to a halt. I could sense the nurses' growing irritation about the whole thing.

"Theresa," I said as we drove home at the end of the third week, "tell me how you're doing. You look exhausted to me. What's going on inside?"

"Katie," she started, then her mouth crumpled and she hid her face in her hands, weeping. "I don't know if I can do this! All the responsibility. How do I know that the nurses will take good care of her? I feel like I have to be there every waking minute of the day to see that she gets enough care. I'm overwhelmed and scared. What if something happens to her? It'll be all my fault!"

Exhausted sobs rose from her very gut and she hunched over in her seat, her head down in her hands, her hair falling forward.

"Honey, honey." I reached over and stroked her hair as I drove. "Sounds like we need to talk. You're taking on way too much responsibility for this little daughter of yours."

"Yeah, but isn't that what parents are supposed to do?" she wailed. "Nobody else could possibly love her the way I do, so obviously nobody can take as good care of her as I can. But it's just too hard! I can't do it all on my own. I feel like I'm gonna break if I have to keep this up for the rest of her life. I *knew* I'd be a bad mother!"

"Listen to me; can you hear me in there? Tomorrow I'm taking you out to lunch. We're going to buy you some clothes that will fit your new shape, and we'll talk. Sound good?"

"But what about AdaLayne? Won't she miss me?" Theresa's voice was so weak I could hardly hear it.

"I'll call the hospital and let them know that you'll be there in the evening tomorrow. I'm sure the nurses can take care of her for the morning."

CHAPTER 11

Plunging into a New Life

Questions for Discussion

§

1) Have you ever felt like you were plunging into a new life with some new responsibility suddenly thrust on you? How did you handle it?

2) We all have a first reaction when faced with something scary, difficult, or unknown. What is your typical response? Where do you go for help?

3) Many people depend solely on themselves in a time of challenge; they're survivors and they trust no one but themselves. Others are trusting and able to depend on others in a crisis. Where do you fall on this scale? Are there downsides to either of these mind-sets?

4) When we first get to know God, we often don't trust Him fully, if at all. As we grow in our knowledge of Him, we (hopefully!) learn to trust Him more fully. Where are you on the spectrum of trusting God, if one is little or no trust and ten is full trust?

5) Part of the process of learning to trust God comes by experiencing His faithfulness through different experiences. Years ago, I prayed with my thirteen year old daughter for the funds to come in for a mission trip she wanted to go on and watched with amazement as God brought in the funds, little by little, until she had enough. That experience strengthened both her faith and mine in God's ability to provide. Have you had a similar experience of any kind?

6) Discuss how early experiences in our lives make us more—or less—able to trust that God loves us and always has our best interests at the center of His heart.

CHAPTER 12

Can Anything Come before God?

§

The next day after shopping for some new clothes for Theresa we sat at a corner table for two at my favorite lunch place. I ordered a chicken Caesar salad and Theresa ordered a double cheeseburger with everything on it, super sized fries, and a milkshake. Needing some time to collect my thoughts, I let her eat a minute before I launched in.

"So, girl, you've been plopped into motherhood without much preparation. We've been talking about how to be a follower of Christ, but we haven't gotten to motherhood yet. I'm sorry, I should have prepared you better."

"I know I'm not ready. I'm really gonna need your help, Katie. I'm not sure I can do this mothering thing," she said around a mouthful of fries.

"I'm glad to hear you say that, because so far it hasn't looked like you've wanted anyone's help in taking care of AdaLayne. One of the first things you're going to have to learn is that you can't do it all on your own, and you can't make an idol of your baby."

"What do you mean—make an idol of her? She asked testily, laying down her burger and looking me straight in the eye. "Don't give me all kinds of religious talk, Katie. I'm way too tired to try to understand all that right now."

"I'm sorry, girl. I'm not trying to overwhelm you. I just want you to get started on the right foot as a parent. None of us can do it all on our own. We all need God's help."

"Right, but what do you mean about idols?"

"An idol is anything that gets first place in our hearts before God. It's easy to make an idol of someone as small and vulnerable as a newborn baby, since babies need so much care, and we start thinking we alone are responsible for raising this baby. We get so focused on trying to do everything right that we forget God's in charge and it's His strength we need.

"God's gotta have first place in our hearts, honey. Otherwise everything gets out of whack. If we go to Him for the strength and wisdom we need to raise our children, we don't get so weary and over-whelmed. But if we let our children become the primary focus of our love, they crowd out our need for God."

I stopped for a bite and to see if she was taking any of this in. She took a huge bite of cheeseburger, looking at me, frowning but nodding slightly. I took that as a sign of interest and continued.

"If we struggle to be perfect parents, trying to do it all ourselves without God's help, we're putting our kids before God in our hearts. We're saying, 'Lord, I'm afraid You won't do a good enough job taking care of my children, so I have to do it all. I trust myself to take care of them more than I trust You.'

"Do you see how that puts your children and your need to be responsible for them above God? Anything that you esteem higher than God becomes an idol, since you love it more than you love God. We can't put our children before God, Theresa, no matter how much we love them."

"I think I'm beginning to see. . .maybe." Head down, she played with her fries, swirling each one in catsup before taking a nibble of it.

"Basically, honey, it boils down to turning your children over to God. One of His highest priorities is helping us to raise the children He's given us and He's the one guiding us, giving us the strength and wisdom we need.

"You can go to God and say, 'God, she's Yours. I'm her mother, but You're the Father of us both. Please help me take care of this baby You've entrusted to me."

"So I don't have be on guard 24/7 watching out for her?" Brushing aside her hair—once again limp and flat—she looked at me warily. Dark bags hung under her eyes and her thin cheeks were pale.

"You need to be a diligent mother, but no, not even God expects you to be on duty twenty-four hours a day, seven days a week. He's the God who never sleeps; He's always awake, always watchful, but He doesn't expect you to be. In fact, He says that you don't need to anxiously rise up early and stay awake till all hours of the night, for He gives sleep to those He loves *(Psalm 127:2)*. He loves us, and He's telling us that we don't need to be so anxious and worried; we can lay our concerns in His hands and get some rest. He'll watch over our little ones for us."

"Oh my gosh, Katie, I can't tell you how relieved that makes me feel. I thought it was all on my shoulders. I thought if I didn't do everything perfectly, I'd be a lousy mother."

Licking catsup off her fingers, she sniffed, running the back of her hand under her nose and down the new jeans I'd bought for her a few hours earlier. I pretended not to notice.

"I understand. Most of us are worried the first time through. But eventually we find out that none of us can do it all by ourselves; we all need God's help to raise happy, healthy, godly children."

I reached across the table and tucked a strand of hair behind her ear. She raised her head just a little, and looked at me.

"I'm gonna have to practice this trusting business. I'm not very good at it." One corner of her mouth lifted in a half-hearted smile but sank again just as quickly.

"Nothing like raising kids to teach you about trusting God!" I laughed. "But you know, there's something else I want you to remember about this talk."

"And what's that?" she asked, slurping the last of her milkshake through her straw.

"This whole idea about idols. You might as well get this straight right here in the beginning of your life with God, especially as a parent. In the Bible, God is absolutely passionate that we worship nothing and no one but Him, and that's because He knows He is the only one in the whole universe who will never fail us, will always love us, and will always have our best interests at the center of His heart. No one else can fit that bill, not even the most loving parent, spouse, or child."

"Well, isn't that kind of obvious? I've sure never had any person love me with that kind of love."

"You'd think it would be, but we frequently get off track anyway. As humans, we're created to worship someone or something, and if it's not God, it will be something else— guaranteed. It may be our children, a spouse, or a job. Perhaps it's the desire for a bigger home. Maybe it's a desire to be married or well educated or well thought of. Maybe we crave praise or honor. Maybe it's our own intellect we revere above all else."

"So are all those things bad, then?"

"No, they're not bad. What's bad is when those things get between us and God and we become more absorbed chasing after them than in loving God and trusting that His plan for our life will include all the good things we need."

I stabbed at a cherry tomato as I spoke but it popped out from under my fork and flew right into Theresa's milkshake glass. She giggled and then laughed out loud. Stifling a grin and trying to preserve my dignity, I pretended nothing had happened. In a few seconds, though, I gave in and laughed right along with her. It was so good to hear her laugh out loud like that.

"God's plan is *always* better than our own, even if we don't understand it, and He wants us to believe that and to trust Him with all aspects of our life," I continued, settling back into our talk.

She fished the tomato out of her glass with her long spoon and popped it into her mouth.

"So what do I do here and now? What does it take to put all this into practice?" she asked, chewing the tomato and leaning forward with her 'let's get this show on the road' look.

"Oh, Theresa, that's one of the things I love so much about you!" I reached across and squeezed her arm. "You're so practical. You don't just want to *talk about* following Christ, but you actually want to know how to *do it*! Once you see the reason to do something, nothing stops you from wanting to put it into practice. I love that. I wish we were all so gung-ho!"

"I've spent enough time screwing things up. I want to start living right for a change," she muttered, using her last french fry as a mop to wipe up the blob of catsup on her plate.

"So, on a practical level, you could start by giving AdaLayne to God."

"I thought He just gave her to me. What's the deal?" She eyed me suspiciously.

"He did, but He gave her to you to raise, and you're going to need His help in raising her, so you might as well give her back to Him. It's kind of like the story of Moses in the Bible."

"Refresh my memory." Pushing her plate away, she sat back, ready for a story.

"The Hebrew people were slaves in Egypt at this point in their history, and because their women were healthy and fertile their nation was increasing rapidly. Pharaoh did not like this and he made a law that all Hebrew baby boys born from that time forth would be killed. Moses' mother knew this law so when she had a baby boy she put him in the Nile in a little woven basket. That's like giving him back to God. Then God arranged for the daughter of the Pharaoh to come along and find the baby boy in the basket. She wanted to raise him as her own but she needed a wet-nurse to feed him. Moses' sister was hiding in the bushes, keeping an eye on her baby brother, so she stepped out and volunteered her mother to raise the child until he was weaned *(Ex. 1:9-2:9)*. In that way, God provided Moses' mother with the protection she needed to raise her son. In the same way, He gives us children, and as we commit them back to Him, He'll provide the means—the wisdom, the finances, the strength—for us to raise them."

"Well, if He could do it for the mother of Moses, I guess He can do it for me. I sure don't want to do this child-raising thing all on my own if I don't have to! Here and now okay to pray?"

"Anywhere's fine."

She leaned her elbows on the table, resting her head in her hands.

"God, I give AdaLayne to You. You've given her to me, but really, she's Yours; You made her. God, I don't know the first thing about how to be a good mother. You know what kind of an example I had. But since You've made me her mother, please help me be a good one. Please help me raise her, and please help me teach her about You, the way Katie's doing with me. And please help me learn to trust You more. Thank You, God. I pray this in Jesus' name. Amen.

"Whew, I do feel like a load's been lifted off my shoulders! How cool is that, to know that God really will help me out with being a mom, even though I don't have a clue."

"Way to go, girl! We need to celebrate! How about the biggest, gooiest chocolate sundae with extra nuts and whipped cream they have on the menu?"

"Sounds good to me." She grinned at me, then suddenly sobered. "And Katie?" she ducked her head, her hair across her face again.

"What?"

"Thanks for your help. I love you," she murmured.

I looked away and bit my lip before rising and planting a kiss on the top of her head on my way to the counter to order our sundaes.

*   *   *   *   *

A week later, the whole Tucker family accompanied Theresa to the hospital to bring little AdaLayne home. I was surprised the older boys were interested but they both said they wanted to come along so off we all went in a caravan.

Much to my relief, AdaLayne turned out to be a peaceful baby and Theresa a loving and increasingly confident mother. She'd bring the baby upstairs in the evenings and let Jossie, Molly and Liz hold her and give her a bottle. The nurses at the hospital had shown her how to pump her milk which she was feeding to AdaLayne in the tiniest bottles I'd ever seen. It took a while to feed her so she was grateful for the help and our girls loved it. Molly was full of advice from her parenting class at school, to which Theresa listened patiently. Jossie began to develop a full-blown case of premature motherhood, cooing "And how's my baby doing today?" as she cuddled little AdaLayne, unconsciously doing the motherhood sway. I began to fear for her ability to disengage when the time came for Theresa to leave. For it was becoming increasingly clear that the time was fast approaching.

One afternoon when AdaLayne was about six weeks old, Theresa approached me with two cups of tea.

"AdaLayne's asleep; can we talk for a few minutes?"

I laid down my dusting rag, and we headed through the kitchen for the back porch; although it was the last week in June the day was unusually mild with a soft breeze. It had been a while since we'd talked and I wondered how she was doing. We went to the other end of the porch this time, away from the sun, where two chairs sat in a corner with a small table between them. She set the cups on the table and pulled her chair out so it faced mine. I sat down and asked her, reaching for my tea, "So what's on your mind these days, besides getting enough sleep?"

"Do you *ever* catch up?"

"Yeah, I'm beginning to about now," I answered, grinning at her.

"Oh, great! You're a lot of help. So I have approximately twelve years to go?"

"You get used to it. You learn to sleep standing up; it's not too bad."

"Terrific!

"Well, on that encouraging note: I need help with my next step. I can't live here forever. I've imposed on you guys long enough; I think it's time I found my own place to live. I'll need a more full-time job than what I have at the pharmacy, and someone to watch AdaLayne. . .it seems overwhelming, to be honest."

"We'll take it one step at a time. I'm sure one of us will be available to watch the baby while you look for a job. Don't worry; we're not going to kick you out 'til you have a good place to stay and someone to watch AdaLayne."

"I can't tell you how much I appreciate that. You've been so good to me, Katie. Kind of like the mother I never had. Even if I move away, can we still meet once in a while on kind of a regular basis, just to keep tabs on each other? You know, to talk and stuff."

She ducked her head and looked away, pulling a strand of hair out of her ponytail and playing with it.

"You'd better keep tabs on me, girl. I'm pretty wild. You never know what I might do; I need someone to keep me in line."

Theresa just kicked me.

"No, seriously, I'd love to. I could write a book about the things I've learned about mothering; I might as well pour it all out on you."

"I'm just a little baby bird with its mouth wide open. Pour it in, mama," she said, grinning.

I laughed, shaking my head and looking at her. "You're something else; you know that?"

CHAPTER 12

Can Anything Come before God?

Questions for Discussion

§

1) Can you relate to Theresa when she says, "I'm gonna have to practice this trusting business; I'm not very good at it"? How and why do you relate to that?

2) All we can see in the face of any challenge is a huge obstacle. We're like ants looking up at a ten-foot high wall; it seems utterly insurmountable. But God can see the other side as well as we can see the other side of a brick; it's no problem to Him. Do you know this deep down in your gut or do you try to figure out all your challenges with the limited, human knowledge that we all have?

3) What does Katie mean when she says that we are all created to worship something? What does it mean to worship?

4) If you were to be honest with yourself, what would you say you worship? Most of us have things we think we couldn't do without: security, running water, a safe house to live in, heating and air conditioning, money, an education, or even a TV for some people. If God took all those things away, could you trust Him to meet your needs? (For most of us who live in the U.S., this is still a rhetorical question, but there are plenty of people on earth who live without those things.)

5) Have you ever committed the important people—or even things—in your life to God?

6) Our very lives are a gift from God. Have you ever given your life back to Him and told him that you want to live your life doing

what He wants you to do? When you think about it, our lives are all we have to give.

7) Discuss the things in your life that might come between you and God.

CHAPTER 13

Who Do I listen to for Advice?

§

A month later I got a call from Theresa. "Hey, Katie, I could use some 'Mom time'. You have any time to get together in the next week or so? I'm free in the mornings these days. Would that work for you?" She sounded a bit blue.

"Hey, girl, it's good to hear your voice! Sure, I'd love to see you; I've been missing you. How does Thursday look to you?"

"Sounds okay. Can you come to my place? I want you to see it."

"Just give me the directions and I'll be there. 9:30 okay?"

* * * * *

Later that week as I climbed the metal steps to Theresa's apartment rust brushed off the rickety iron railing onto my slacks. Traffic sounds roared up from the highway below and garbage cans lined the side of her building like battered metal sentinels.

She opened the door at my knock and unsmilingly stepped back so I could squeeze past the fridge into her kitchen. A kettle whistled on the stove and two cups sat on the worn linoleum counter. I sat in one of her unmatched wooden kitchen chairs—tucking my legs out of her way so she had room to walk—and watched her as she fixed the tea. Her movements were tired and slow and her face bleak. Her hair hung flat and greasy and dark circles sagged below her eyes. She wore the same old skuzzy tank top and sweat shorts she'd worn when she first came to our house. A fly buzzed at the torn screen in the window.

Holding both cups, she motioned with her head for me to follow her into the living room two paces away. She'd tried to make the room pretty by tucking worn red plaid bedspreads around an old couch and overstuffed chair and by placing a blue pillow in each corner of the couch. She'd folded a piece of red and blue fabric over a large box in front of the couch, forming a makeshift coffee table. A catsup jar holding a limp silk rose stood on top. A mild breeze—unusual for late July—stirred the too-short grayish sheers at the partially open window. I could hear the traffic below.

I sank into the well-worn springs of the overstuffed chair, and she plopped down at the end of the couch, drawing her legs up so they wouldn't tangle with mine.

"So, girl, how are you doing out on your own? Catch me up on what's going on in your life." I asked, concerned about her haggard looks.

"I will, but first I have some questions for you and I want to make sure we get to them while AdaLayne's still asleep since I have to go to work in an hour, so can we start with them?" Curling her legs up under her, she hugged the blue pillow to her bony chest. She looked thinner than I'd ever seen her.

"Fire away, girl. You know I love questions."

"Well, this whole parenting thing: it's overwhelming, Katie. I've been pretty down lately. I mean, I've had some bumps in the road before—you know that—but this is different. I can't shake it. I love AdaLayne, but. . ." putting her tea down, she sagged forward and let her head fall onto her knees, hidden behind her hair. Her shoulders shook.

I leaned over and kissed her head. "It's not surprising, honey. You're coping with a constant lack of sleep, there's the insecurity of being a first-time mom, and your baby is still getting her nights and days straightened out. Plus, you have no other adult to talk to most of the time. No wonder you're worn out!"

"I get so tired and discouraged; I just want to cry sometimes," she moaned.

"Well, go ahead and have a good cry; it'll do you good."

"I don't know if I can just now. I think I've cried all my tears away. I just feel so alone. Is God really there? Does He even care?"

"Yes, He does. We don't always feel His presence, though, especially when we're feeling down and blue. When I was worn out and exhausted like you are now, I hung onto this scripture: *"He will feed His flock like a shepherd; He will gather the lambs with His arm, And carry them in His bosom, And gently lead those who are with young" (Is. 40:11)."*

I stroked her hair as she remained with her head flopped down onto her knees and her arms clasped around her legs.

"I used to love to think of Jesus gently leading me and my young ones. Jesus will gather you in His arms, Theresa, and He'll carry you when you're too tired to take care of yourself or your baby. Like a shepherd who makes sure that his flock has plenty to eat and who finds the best eating and watering spots for his sheep, He will provide food for you. He will protect you and AdaLayne from harm. He will gently and patiently lead you along the path. Can you imagine Jesus doing that for you?"

"I sure feel like I'm the one who has to do all the caring and feeding around here," she muttered.

"I know how you feel. But if you think about it, He is taking care of you, isn't He? You have a roof over your head, food in your cupboard and clothes on your back. This may not be the Ritz, but it's your home and it's snug and pretty. You've done a great job, by the way, of making this apartment into a cozy and inviting home. Sometimes we have to look for how God is blessing us when things seem bad. Usually if we look, we'll find His blessings, because our Father loves us with all of His incredible heart."

Theresa lifted her head from her knees and propping her chin on her elbows she faced me. "Yeah, I guess. Even though this apartment is small, it's enough for AdaLayne and me. And besides, there's less to clean." She gave me a wan smile.

I smiled back, loving her.

"You know, the post-partum blues are a real problem for many women after a baby is born. It can be a horrendous time of hormone imbalance and mood swings. For some, like me, it was just one bad day shortly after the birth of each baby. Nobody could do anything right on that day. I cried most of the day. I was fearful, angry, depressed, and I hated the world, including my husband and baby. Fortunately for me, it passed quickly, but for some women it lasts a long time and can make the first several months even harder than they already are."

She nodded bleakly. "Tell me about it."

""Every woman needs to know that post-partum blues can hit anybody and it has nothing to do with whether or not she's a good mother or whether or not she loves her baby. If the blues are severe, women need to know that they can't beat them by putting on a happy face or just trying harder to feel cheerful. These blues are caused by a hormonal imbalance and they can send our emotions into a tailspin. Sometimes we can't get out of it without help from medication or some counseling to get us over the hump. Feeling blue like this is nothing to be ashamed of," I said, leaning down and looking into her eyes behind that curtain of hair.

"The worst thing you can do, girl, when you're feeling like that is to hide it and try to handle it all on your own. Sometimes a good cry and a cup of tea with a friend helps immensely."

"Wow. I wish I'd known that earlier. I thought I was a failure of a mother as I cried myself to sleep night after night." She scrubbed the back of her hand over her eyes, trying to keep the tears from overflowing.

"Oh, honey, I wish you'd called me!" I moved over to the couch and put my arm around her.

"I couldn't. I was too down, I guess. I just sort of muddled through. I'm better now, but it was kind of scary."

"I know. And the scariest part is feeling like you're the only one in the whole world who feels this way. That's why the best thing you can do is tell someone how you're feeling and what you're going through."

"And another thing," Theresa continued, sniffling, "how do I know whose advice to take? Everybody has their own advice about how to be a parent these days. I can't go anywhere without somebody saying to me," she pitched her voice higher, "'When I had my babies we didn't spoil them like you girls do today. Honey, you gotta let'em cry it out. Your baby will be spoiled rotten if you don't.' And then the next person tells me to hold my baby all the time or she'll grow up insecure. And some other person says to start feeding her solids by three months or she's sure to grow up sickly and puny, and then someone else tells me to wait for six to nine months before I give her anything solid. I don't know *who* to believe. It makes me feel like I can't do *anything* right!" She flopped her head down again.

"Okay, honey, let's see if we can't straighten this mess out. First of all, you have way too many voices telling you what to do. You need to listen to what God says about raising your baby and disregard the rest since every woman who's ever given birth has an opinion about how to raise children."

"But I don't see anything in the Bible about how much to let your baby cry or whether or not cuddling her will spoil her or when to start her on solid food!" Theresa wailed. "I need specifics! And most of all, I just need to know if I'm doing things right so she'll turn out okay. I'm so afraid that I'm going to mess her up forever, like my mother messed me up."

"I understand." I put my arm around her shoulder and gave it a squeeze. "You know what I do when I can't find anything specific in the Bible about something I need help with?"

"No. What?" Theresa moaned.

God, please give me wisdom here.

"I look at God's character. Like that little saying 'What Would Jesus Do?' You've heard that, haven't you?" I asked, pushing her hair behind her ear so I could see her face.

"Yeah. Go on." She mumbled through her fingers.

"If I can figure out what God might do in my situation, it helps."

"So what does God say about how long I should let AdaLayne cry at night before I go in to pick her up?"

"The more we know God, like we might know a friend, the more we can guess what He might do. You know me well enough to have a good idea of what I might do in a particular situation. It's the same with God; the better we know Him, the more we can guess what He might do."

"Go on. I'm listening." She propped her cheek on her fist again, and looked over at me glumly.

"One thing is sure about God: He *is* love. It's not just that He *loves*; He *is* love. So *everything* He does is motivated by His love for us."

"OK. . . but I'm still not getting the connection."

"Stay with me. We should be following God's example, right? So if everything God does is motivated by love, it should be the same with us. Everything we do should be motivated by love as well. We can make all our decisions by that yardstick: is it loving?"

"But how do *I* know what the most loving thing is for AdaLayne? Some say the most loving thing is to let her cry herself to sleep at night; others disagree. How am *I* supposed to know?" She let her head fall forward and held it there by gripping a handful of greasy hair on each side of her head.

"You know what, Theresa? God gave you mother instincts. Follow them. What does your heart say when you hear her crying at night?"

"I just want to go get her and hold her and make it all better for her."

"Then do that. Trust your instincts; God gave them to you for a reason."

I rubbed her back gently.

"So if I think it it's best to rock her at night when she's fussy, I should do that and not worry about whether or not I'm spoiling her? Not care what people say?" she asked, flattening her back against her knees so I'd continue to rub it.

"Absolutely. Remember the scripture we just talked about? What does Jesus do for us? He holds us in His arms and gently leads us like a shepherd. Do you think a good human shepherd would let his little lambs cry and cry without going to help them?"

"No, I guess not."

"Neither would Jesus."

"So you mean I really can trust my instincts and do what *I* think is right for my baby?" Pulling up the cloth covering the packing box table in front of us, she took a Kleenex box out from the storage space under it. Pulling a tissue out, she blew her nose loudly.

"Nobody's better equipped than you. Nobody loves her more than you do. Nobody wants the best for her more than you do. Why is it so hard to believe that God would give you the wisdom you need to take care of her?"

"This is just such a new idea. . .that I actually might be an expert on my own baby. Wow. That's kind of cool!" She sat up and brushed the hair out of her face, tucking it behind her ear, and rubbed her fists under her eyes to wipe away any stray tears. Her birthmark stood out in bright red contrast to her pale skin. Balling up the Kleenex, she tossed it across the room, missing the wastebasket by a few feet.

"It *is* cool. Absolutely. And each mother may have a slightly different way of taking care of her own baby. The important thing is that she feels confident in her own abilities as a mother, the expert on her own baby."

"But what about the real experts, you know, the ones on TV? The ones that've written all those books I'll never in a million years read? Shouldn't I listen to them?"

"Are they experts on AdaLayne? Do they know her like you do? Are they following the pattern God set down for us?"

"Hmmm, maybe not." She crossed her legs and began to waggle her top foot up and down.

"You know, Theresa, 'experts' are a dime a dozen and their advice changes every few years. First it's, 'Don't hold your baby too much; you might spoil her.' But soon, it's 'Wear your baby next to your skin so she'll be secure.' Then, 'Lay your baby on her tummy to sleep.' And then, 'Lay her on her back.'"

"Don't I know it! That's exactly the kind of confusing advice I get from ladies in the check-out line, or at work, or at the beauty salon."

"Honey, each one of them is just parroting the current thinking of her day. That's why going by what the Bible says makes so much sense; it doesn't change from day to day or even year to year. It's God's wisdom and it's always the same. It always works and it's always available.

I took a sip of tea, watching her. The light was returning to her eyes, like a slow dawn on a cloudy morning.

"That's kind of comforting, when you think about it." She said, chewing a nail thoughtfully, leaning back against the couch, holding the blue pillow in her lap.

"You know the best place to get practical wisdom from the Bible? The book of Proverbs, which is full of God's wisdom. If we read it and follow it we can't go wrong. I love the proverb that says, *"Train up a child in the way he should go, And when he is old, he will not depart from it"* (Pr. 22:6). Believe me, I've held onto that scripture over the years!"

"Wow, you can just spit these scriptures out like an expert!" She turned around on the couch to face me, bringing her knees up again and wrapping her arms around them. Resting her chin on them, she looked over at me expectantly.

"When you reach for a tool often enough, eventually you learn where it is without having to hunt for it each time."

"What else does Proverbs say about raising children?"

"Tell you what. You read it through, and the next time we get together, we'll talk about it. Fair enough?"'

"Sounds good. Oh my gosh, look at the time. And I've got to get AdaLayne to the babysitter and everything! I've gotta fly, Katie."

"Can I help you with anything?"

"Check my diaper bag? Make sure I've got all she'll need for the next eight hours?"

CHAPTER 13

Who Do I Listen to for Advice?

Questions for Discussion

§

1) If you've had a baby, did you suffer from post-partum blues either mildly, like Katie, or severely, like Theresa? If so, what did you do about it?

2) Did you ever experience feelings of helplessness, inadequacy, hopelessness, or depression at any time after the birth of a baby? (Sometimes, with a colicky or difficult baby, these feelings can be due to simple exhaustion, and are not a full-blown case of the blues.)

3) Did you have someone like Katie to whom you could turn for help? Even though I had five babies, I still had to call for support and encouragement from an older friend at least once after the birth of each baby.

4) Have you ever felt the same bewilderment that Theresa describes over all the conflicting advice that a new mother receives?

5) If you've had more than one child, did you find that after a while you found your own way of doing things, and stuck with that— even if it didn't line up with the "experts"?

6) Some women start motherhood having had years of experience with babies and small children like one of my daughters-in-law who—as the oldest of nine homeschooled siblings—had been mothering for years before she got married. Others approach it with no previous experience whatsoever. Where do you fall on that scale, and how confident were you the first time around?

7) Discuss the idea of mothers being the experts on their own babies. What do you think of that idea?

CHAPTER 14

Bonding with Your Baby

§

Theresa called me again some weeks later. Her voice sounded more upbeat this time.

"Okay, Katie. I'm ready for the next installment. Can you come over again? I have next Thursday off; is that a good day for you? We could take AdaLayne out for a walk while we talk."

"It's a deal, girl. I just have to be back by 4:30 to pick the twins up from ball practice."

"How about 9:00, while it's still cool?"

"Sounds good to me. I'll meet you at the park."

*   *   *   *   *   *

"So," Theresa asked as she started pushing AdaLayne in the stroller on the trail around the park in the August morning sunshine, "start at the beginning about being a parent. If you remember, I haven't had the best training in this area. Got any overall plan for parenthood I could follow? You know, like ten tips for being the perfect mom?"

"If I knew those ten tips," I laughed, "I'd have patented them by now and become a millionaire!"

*Wow, if only. . .*I shook my head. Foolishness. I continued, "But there is something I want to talk about today. I've been thinking about it since our talk last time."

"And what's that?"

"Bonding between mother and child. You asked me how much to hold and cuddle AdaLayne, how much to pick her up when she fusses, and how long to let her cry it out at night."

"Yeah. I'm gaining confidence in that area. I've been reading in Proverbs like you suggested. But go on."

She strode on confidently, assuming I'd catch up.

"Did you know that the loving and cuddling you're doing with AdaLayne in these early months of her life are about as crucial to her development as her growth in the womb? Actually, the development started in the womb doesn't complete until she gets the kind of cuddling and holding that you're doing?"

"Wow, I didn't know it was all *that* important! What do you mean?"

"What you're doing now, teaching her that you are warm, loving, and can be trusted to come when she cries, is teaching her what she can expect from other human beings. Your responses to her are establishing patterns in her brain that will last for the rest of her life."

"I'm not sure I understand. Explain."

"I can't give you a scientific explanation but here's a word picture." I hustled and drew up next to her on the sidewalk. "Imagine a freshly plowed field. The soil is soft and plowed into furrows. Then it rains and water pours over the field, digging into the soil, sometimes running down the furrows and sometimes cutting new paths. The more water there is, the more the soil is moved and the more the paths are deepened. When the soil dries out and becomes harder, the grooves are left."

"Yeah. . .and?"

"So, the soil is like AdaLayne's brain—soft and malleable, fresh from the womb. Like the field of soft soil, it hasn't been fully shaped yet. The flood of information that washes over her brain in these first months of life will shape her brain to a large extent."

"What kind of information?" she asked, looking over at me.

"Information like what your arms feel like. Are they safe and warm, giving her a sense of security? Or is there fear, impatience, or indifference flowing through them to her? Information like what your voice sounds like. Is it reassuring and gentle? Information like how consistently you come when she cries. Can she count on you, or are you erratic and unpredictable? All this information begins to shape how she sees the world, forming deep, underlying perceptions that can affect her all her life.' "

"So you're saying what I'm doing now with AdaLayne matters for the rest of her life?"

"Exactly. God, in His wisdom, arranged it so that human babies are not complete without interaction with their parents—primarily their mothers—in their early months. Babies left without human inter-action will literally die. It's called the 'failure to thrive syndrome'."

"I never knew that!"

"You're not the only one. I think if more people were aware of this, there might be fewer babies in daycare. Because it's not just any old human interaction that helps a baby thrive. Yes, anybody can feed and change a baby, but there's something about that initial mother-child bond that's irreplaceable. And it's that love, that sacrificial, constant, patient love that says, 'I would die for you,' that creates the patterns of trust and security in the baby's brain that I'm talking about."

We walked single file for a moment as we skirted a large puddle from a recent downpour. Catching up to her, I continued.

"What your baby learns about the world around her in the begin-ning of her life shapes how she sees the world from then on. And how she attaches to the most important person in her life—who, at this point, is you—affects her ability to attach to people for the rest of her life. It's as if the tools for forming relationships are created by her first experiences with the world, which is what you provide."

"Wow. All these thoughts make motherhood look pretty important all of a sudden," she commented, looking over at me with lips pursed thoughtfully.

"It does; you're right. And it's because attachment is probably the most basic emotional human need there is. People who aren't attached to other human beings, who don't know that they are loved and cared for, are the saddest and most dangerous people in the world."

"Dangerous? What do you mean?" I could feel the protective mother vibes bristling.

"Yeah, dangerous, because those who can't form healthy rela-tionships with others often simply use people for their own pleasure, sometimes with horrendous results. Someone who has never bonded with a parent or whose original mother-child bond was broken and never replaced often has a hard time creating healthy relationships. He doesn't know what a loving, reciprocal relationship is since he's never experienced one.

"Think of all the times you play with AdaLayne. You look into her eyes; she looks into yours. You connect. You smile; she smiles. You make a face; she laughs. You hug her; she wriggles with pleasure. In all this mother-child play, you're teaching her the importance of reci- procity—the back and forthness between two people who love each other.

"Without this, she could grow up not knowing that other people have feelings and needs just like she does and that relationships go two ways, which is how empathy and love for others is developed."

"I had no idea I'd have that much affect on AdaLayne." She gazed down at her sleeping baby in her stroller.

"I know. It's amazing to me how important the mother is in all this. Studies have shown that babies respond best to their own mothers— before all other child-care workers, including grandparents."

"What about adoption?"

"Good question. Did you know that at one time Craig and I wanted to adopt?"

"Why didn't you?"

"I guess we figured six children were enough for us. We weren't exactly expecting twins, or even a fifth pregnancy for that matter!

"But still, I think adoption is about as close to God's heart as you can get. After all, He adopted all of into His family, and I think it gives Him great pleasure when we adopt children whose parents can't take care of them into our families."

Theresa pulled AdaLayne over to the edge of the sidewalk to let a kid on a bike speed by. Earbuds in, hat on backward, he seemed not even to notice us as he rode by, brushing roughly past AdaLayne's stroller. Theresa glared after him, muttering, "Bratty kid!" under her breath before turning back to me.

"You were saying?"

"But wonderful as it is, at the beginning of every adoption is the breaking of that original, biological, mother-child bond. For some babies—often those adopted at birth—who establish a bond with their adoptive mother in the first months of their life, this rupture of the original bond isn't a major issue. But for some, those separated from their mothers as toddlers, for example, and raised in an orphanage or foster care for several years before being adopted, establishing a bond with new parents can be difficult or impossible. The breaking of the old bond often needs to be acknowledged and grieved over.

"A friend who works with adoptions once told me that the babies who are heartbroken and wailing when they're taken away from their caretakers were the ones best able to form a new bond with their adoptive mothers. The ones who sat passively and showed no emotion about being taken away from the only home they'd ever known often bonded poorly with their new mothers, if at all. It was almost as if their little hearts were already sealed over against becoming attached to anybody. It was the latter group that really broke her heart, she said."

"I don't know if the bond between my mother and me was so wonderful," she muttered, striding on ahead again. I had to jog a few steps to catch up to her.

"It may not have been wonderful, but it's still important to you. You wouldn't be mentioning your mother so much if it weren't. That bond can be just as broken in a biological relationship as in an adoptive one if the mother isn't able to be there for her child, as I gather yours wasn't."

"Yeah, I guess. I just wish. . ." Pushing the stroller with one hand, Theresa twirled a strand of hair behind her ear and looked away from me as we walked.

"Wish what?"

"I don't know. That she could have held me more often, I guess."

"Oh, honey, I wish so too! God created mothers to want to hold and care for their babies and to respond to their cries and He created babies to need their mothers. It's just that sometimes that pattern gets twisted around in this messed-up world of ours, and mothers can't do the mothering they were created to do."

"Don't I know it!" she jerked the stroller up over an uneven crack in the path. AdaLayne's little head bobbed back and forth, but she didn't wake up.

"And did you know that when a mother consistently picks up and tends to her baby's needs when he or she cries it teaches the baby about cause and effect? Baby cries, mother responds. The baby learns the rhythm of need and satisfaction of that need. I call this the mother-baby dance. Because of this, babies learn they can affect the people around them."

Theresa looked at me, chewing on the inside of her lip. I could tell this brought up sad memories for her.

"But babies whose moms don't respond to their cries or who only respond erratically— sometimes there, sometimes not; sometimes comforting, sometimes angry—often have a hard time learning that their actions affect the world around them. So, they have difficulty connecting the cause and effect of their actions as they get older. They never seem to learn that early rhythm between baby and mother of cry and response, cause and effect. They go through life without realizing that their actions affect people and have consequences.

"It's almost as if a baby's development is like building blocks placed one on top of the other," walking beside her, I stacked my fists one on top of the other, "and the concept of cause and effect is put into place at a certain time in a baby's early development. If it doesn't develop then, it's as if that building block is missing from their early mental and emotional structure and it can only be inserted later with a good deal of effort, if at all."

"So that's why some of us make the dumb decisions we do!"

"Could be."

"So is there any hope for those of us who've had a lousy early childhood?" she asked, not looking at me but staring straight ahead as she walked along.

"Of course there's hope, Theresa. With Jesus there's always hope. He can restore us and help us heal, no matter what kind of upbringing we've had, but it can take a lot of work on our part. How yielded we are to Him, and what we're willing to let Him do with us makes a big difference in how our lives turn out."

"You mentioned trust earlier. I have a real problem with that. Explain that to me," she demanded.

"If the adults in a baby's life don't meet her needs on a consistent basis, it becomes difficult for her to trust them and she learns that if her needs are going to be met, she will have to meet them herself. Instead of blossoming outward and allowing herself to be vulnerable and trust others—really believing that they will love her and take care of her—she turns inward, learning to depend on herself alone to get her needs met. Often babies like this will learn to practice self-gratifying behavior, like rocking themselves or banging their heads—anything to make themselves feel loved and cared for. You see a lot of this kind of behavior in orphanages or substandard foster homes."

All I could see was the side of Theresa's face but her tight jaw and compressed lips told me all I needed to know.

"Makes me think of when I was a kid," she muttered angrily. "I can't count the number of times I went to bed scared and hungry and lonely. Maybe my mom had just yelled at me and sent me to bed without any dinner, or maybe she just forgot to fix dinner and we kids had to scrounge for ourselves. All I wanted was for her to put her arms around me and hold me. She rarely did. So I sucked my thumb and rocked myself to sleep night after night."

"That's so sad, Theresa. Makes me wish I could have been back there with you. I would have loved you."

I put my hand on her back. She shook it off.

"Probably not. I was a bratty kid. Pretty unlovable."

"Kids get that way when they don't get the love they need. They don't learn how to love because they've never been loved right."

"What do you mean, loved right? How many ways are there to love a kid? It can't be that hard, can it? Jeesh, just hug the kid once in a while!" She ducked under an evergreen hanging over the sidewalk, impatiently brushing the branches away from AdaLayne's face.

Ducking my head as I followed her, I continued, "It seems easy from this angle but haven't you ever felt like AdaLayne needed more from you than you could give her? Maybe at night, when you'd already been up three times and you knew you had to go to work the next day? You're exhausted, she's crying, and you just don't feel like you have anything left to give?"

"Well, yeah, but—"

"So imagine a mother who is depressed or on drugs or addicted to alcohol or in an abusive relationship. Now, imagine that she loves her child, but every time her baby cries, she doesn't know how to make her stop, or she's too tired or has been so neglected herself that she has nothing to give. So she doesn't hold and soothe her baby; instead she yells at it or shakes it or worse, she leaves it all by itself to cry its little heart out night after night."

"I don't even have to imagine." She bit off the words, staring straight ahead as she stalked along, jerkily thrusting AdaLayne ahead of her. The baby began to whimper.

"So after a while, the baby starts to turn inward to comfort herself, and begins to recoil from her mother's touch. How do you think the mother reacts then?"

"Finds the baby hard to love. Stops trying to love it. Leaves it alone."

"And so the cycle continues. I hate it that you seem to know all this stuff from personal experience."

"I do too. But I'm determined to do better with AdaLayne. Speaking of which, she's waking up. Think we could stop for a few minutes so I can hold her? All this talk of unloved babies makes me just want to sit and cuddle her. That okay?"

"It's your most important job. Go for it. I don't mind a rest."

*   *   *   *   *

Leaning my head on the back of the bench where there was a bit of shade, I stretched my legs out to catch a few rays. The sun on my skin felt good, like the warmth of a loving mother's touch, I thought lazily. I watched out of the corner of my eye as Theresa unbuckled AdaLayne from her stroller and held her on her lap, bouncing her up and down.

"Look at those legs, baby. Such a strong girl you are. Mama's big girl, that's what you are. And mama loves you, too." She leaned in and kissed her baby's hair. AdaLayne responded with a wet and toothless grin, her whole body wriggling with delight.

"Mmm, she smells so good, Katie. I just love her so much. Especially at times like this, when I can meet her needs and she seems happy and content. Times like this I feel like maybe I'm doing a halfway decent job as a mother."

"Honey, you're doing a great job as a mother. You're giving your baby plenty of cuddling and affection and at this stage that's what she needs most of all."

"Yeah, but there are times when she just cries and cries and I have no idea what to do for her and then I really begin to feel like a bad mother. Like I just can't meet her needs."

I rolled my head on the back of the bench to my right to see her better.

"Did you know that different babies have different needs for being closely attached to mom, for being held and cuddled by her? Some babies are laid-back and easy-going and can go with the flow, while others are high-strung and need a good deal of holding and attention. They cry to express their needs. If AdaLayne could talk when she cries, maybe she'd say, 'Mom, I need you. I want to feel your warm arms and skin. I need to be close to you.'"

"Wow. I never thought of babies trying to express actual needs. I just thought she was having a fussy spell."

"That's because most of the time we don't take the time to figure out what they might be trying to say. Babies are people, just like grown-ups, and they have their needs, likes and dislikes. That's why I say you're the best expert on AdaLayne, because you're the one who knows her the best; you know her cries and her moods. You can tell when she's happy and secure or tired and frightened. Most importantly, you're her mom. No one else can fill that role like you can. You're the person she needs most in the whole world right now."

"You're right. I *am* learning those things about her. I like knowing her that well."

She made googley eyes at her baby, leaning in and nuzzling her soft neck crease.

"Don't ever hesitate to give her the cuddling and affection she needs, even if it means your dirty dishes have to sit in the sink another day, or the apartment isn't as clean as you'd like. I ran across a poem by Ruth Hulbert Hamilton back in the days when I was struggling with things like this. I don't remember how the rest of it goes, but here's the part that helped me so much:

'So quiet down, cobwebs.
Dust, go to sleep.
I'm rocking my baby,
And babies don't keep.'

"That's about the truest thing I've ever heard about child raising: babies don't keep. They need you now, not later when it's convenient for you. This moment, this day, will never be repeated in her life. You'll never get another chance at it, so be with her while you can."

"So enjoy them while they're little; is that what you mean?" she asked, holding AdaLayne close to her and looking at me.

"What I mean is to enjoy them at each stage, and that includes when they're little. You'll never have another time like this with AdaLayne, when you're the sum of her universe and she looks to you for all her needs. You'll never again be able to satisfy her so completely by just being you, her mother. There will probably never be another time when she adores you quite so much, either! So enjoy."

"Hmmm. Enjoy. I like that word. I never thought much about *enjoying* my baby. I mean, all the care involved, all the time, all the responsibility; it always seemed like such a heavy load. You mean I can just *enjoy* her? For the fun of it? Like just *enjoying* her and playing with her?"

"That's exactly what I mean. When I was a new, first-time mother, I asked my pediatrician for advice in raising healthy, happy children. 'Enjoy your baby,' he said. I was dumbfounded. 'That's it?' I asked. 'Yep, just enjoy him,' he repeated. So, even from a pediatrician, that's the best thing you can do for AdaLayne. Go ahead and be a conscientious mother and play with your baby. Take delight in her. Show her the pleasure she brings you. You're already doing a great job of it, by the way."

"Yeah, well, all I know is I don't want to do it like my mom did. So I try to do the opposite. But I never really thought about just enjoying her for her sake. That's so cool! It gives me a whole different perspective on being a mother."

She focused on AdaLayne's face, waiting until they'd made eye contact. Bringing her forehead down to her baby's, she gently bumped it, murmuring, 'Ahhhh, boo!' each time they made contact. AdaLayne hiccupped with laughter and Theresa did it again and again.

"Did you know that the more you play with her and enjoy her, the more you're giving her a sense of self? A sense that she matters in this world?"

"How's that?" She looked over at me in the middle of a boo cycle.

"If you're taking the time to play with and enjoy her, that tells her that she is worth your time. For children, love is spelled *t-i-m-e*. As we spend time with them, we give them the message that they must be special and worth spending time on. The saddest thing is to see a child who doesn't think he or she is worth anything because no one has invested their time or love into him or her."

"Don't I know it. You're preaching to the choir, you know."

AdaLayne kicked her feet in delight as her mother made bubbling sounds through her lips at her.

"Theresa, if it makes any difference to you, I love you. I don't think your mother was able to love you the way even she probably wanted to; she was overwhelmed, I'm sure. But that doesn't mean you're unlovable. I find you very lovable."

"Thanks. I'm getting kind of excited about being a mom. Instead of it being an incredible burden of work and responsibilities always demanding more than I can give, I think it might be kind of fun. I always thought I'd never measure up, especially being a single mom. But enjoying her. . .now that's something I can do. Especially knowing that Jesus is gently leading me since I'm with young. I like that. Gently leading me. . .Wow."

Wrapping her arms around her baby, Theresa rested her cheek against AdaLayne's head and stared off into the distance. I noticed her eyes were brimming. I sat back in silence.

Thank you, God.

CHAPTER 14

Bonding with Your Baby

Questions for Discussion

§

1) Have you ever considered the concept of bonding and attachment, either in your own life or that of your baby?

2) The early attachment between mother and child can be broken—or never formed—due to many circumstances: a mother leaving her child for an extended period of time shortly after birth; the mother's mental illness or emotional instability; prematurity or illness on the part of the baby requiring hospitalization, etc. Were any of these present in your early infancy?

3) Have you ever thought about the idea of babies having different personalities and needing different amounts of attention from their mothers?

4) What do you think of the concept of being the expert on your own baby?

5) If you harbor anger against your mother for not being there for you when you needed her as an infant and small child, have you ever thought about that same situation from her point of view? What was going on in her life at the time?

6) Have you ever felt like your baby demands more of you than you can give? What do you do when you feel that way? Do you have someone you can turn to at times like that?

7) Discuss ways in which you can enjoy your baby. What do you think of this concept?

CHAPTER 15

Training Your Child

§

"Katie, hi there! Hey, Jeannyne's actually playing with AdaLayne for a few hours to give me a break, can you *buh*-lieve it?"

I smiled as she mimicked her sister perfectly.

"Do you have time to get together? I'd love to pick your brain some more. Can we meet for coffee or lunch somewhere?"

I couldn't resist, even though I had a full day's worth of activities ahead of me.

"Sure, I'll meet you for lunch at The Soup and Sandwich."

"Wonderful!"

Oh, well, raking leaves and clearing out the gardens can wait for another day.

*   *   *   *   *

The weather was unusually balmy for early November. At the restaurant, I found a table outside in the mild sunshine and smiled as I watched Theresa came swinging up, wearing a short, flippy white skirt, high-heeled sandals, and a knit navy and white top. Her hair bounced in a high ponytail and make-up covered her birthmark.

"Hey, girl, you look great! Looks like life is agreeing with you."

"I can finally say that it is, for once. AdaLayne's smoothing out some, and I feel like I'm handling things well for once in my life."

"There's something else; I can tell. Or is it some*one* else?"

"Boy, are you ever nosy! Almost as bad as my sister. What, do I have a sign across my forehead saying, 'I've met a man who might be halfway decent'?"

"You might as well; it shows all over you. You're actually smiling and for no particular reason. Not to mention the outfit. It's gotta be love."

"Okay, okay, I met a man who is actually a decent guy. He's hardworking, kind, and considerate, and he hasn't even *hinted* at sex yet! He's gentle and funny. Oh, and he has some money, too."

"Wow, what can I say? If he's kind, funny *and* has money, what more could a girl ask?"

"Don't tease me, Katie. This is the first male I've ever met who didn't either abuse or ignore me. He actually seems to like me!"

She pulled out the little wrought-iron chair and sat down, crossing her legs and jiggling one sandaled foot up and down, looking up at me expectantly.

"Well?"

"Does he love God? Is he a Christian? In my mind, that's gotta be the first thing to look for in a possible husband."

"Yikes, don't use the H-word, please! I think he's a Christian; he goes to church sometimes. I haven't gone with him yet; I don't know why. Just not ready, I guess."

"Well, there's no need to rush things. If this is the real deal, it will last."

"Good old Katie. Always giving me solid advice."

"So you want advice on courtship and marriage?"

"Good grief, no! Not that I don't want your advice, but I'm not ready for courtship or dating just yet. I'm barely sticking my toe in the water again. Hear that? *Barely.*"

She pointedly directed her gaze–and mine–to her pink-nailed big toe, peeking out at me from her sandal. "See? Just *one* toe, Katie. No more."

"Well, if he's a good guy, he'll go your pace. So, what do you want to pick my brain about if it isn't romantic stuff?"

We gave our orders to the hovering waiter: hers a Reuben with fries and a coke, and mine a Caesar salad and water with lemon–no ice, please.

"I'm not sure about the next step for AdaLayne. When does a baby start yelling for what she *wants* instead of what she *needs*? I swear she yells out of pure willfulness sometimes. Do I spank her bottom? Do I speak sternly to her? Do I ignore her? How can you tell when a kid is old enough to know the difference between right and wrong? Sometimes I'll tell her 'no' about something that could be dangerous–like playing with the light sockets–and she'll look right at me and crawl over there and try to stick her finger in them. What am I supposed to do?"

"Ah, the perennial question about discipline. I've been thinking about it lately, wondering when you'd ask. Not that you ever really stop thinking about it once you start raising children…they give you plenty of occasion to think about it. So first, let's look at the big picture: what's the point of disciplining your child? What are you trying to accomplish?

"Ummm, to get her to behave? To mind me? I don't know; you tell me."

"Let's look at what the Bible says about this in order to put it all on the right foundation. I just happened to have brought mine."

"How'd I guess?" Theresa muttered. She rolled her eyes at me, but I could see a tiny grin behind the scornful look.

Ignoring her, I leaned down and pulling my Bible out of my purse, flipped it open to Ephesians.

"Well, if you want wisdom, girl, this is where to get it. Here, in Ephesians 6:1 it says, *'Children, obey your parents, for this is right.'* That's step number one; we'll get back to that in a minute.

"Now let's see what Solomon has to say about raising children. He's referred to in the Bible as the wisest man who ever lived. Listen to the words he uses to open the first five chapters of Proverbs: *'My son. . .receive my words. . .treasure my commands. . .keep my commands. . .hear, my children, the instruction of a father. . .give attention. . .pay attention to my wisdom.'* What's all that saying to you?"

"Sounds like he's trying to get his son to listen: 'Pay attention, bud, listen up!'"

"Exactly. Seems to me that should be the first goal of training our children: to get them to pay attention to us; to listen to our voices and not just tune us out."

"Right. Like I used to do with my mom. She'd yell at me so much that I just tuned her out. She never meant half of what she said, anyway, so we kids just ignored her. Then she'd chase us and smack us with a flyswatter or a yardstick across our legs. We just laughed at her and ran out of her reach."

"And what did that accomplish?"

"Oh, she'd get as mad as all get out and yell all the more."

"I'm sure she did. So the first goal of training our children is to get them to pay attention to us: to stop and listen to what we're saying and to *obey* it. We have to act in such a way that they'll *want* to listen to us and copy our behavior. God has given us the responsibility to teach and train them, and them the job of learning to obey us. We have the wisdom, the authority and the experience they need to become healthy and loving adults. That's the way God set it up.

"So you mean I can have the confidence that what I say will be right for AdaLayne? I really am the boss?"

"You're the boss, girl, and she is *not*. We're all born wanting our own way and the sooner we learn to submit to those in authority over us, first to our parents and then to God, the better off we'll be. Adults who haven't learned this lesson yet, who still expect the world to revolve around them, are pitiful creatures."

"Tell me about it! That describes every adult figure in my entire life. Except you, of course." She grinned at me with one of her sudden coming-from-behind-the-clouds grins.

"Thanks, girl." I reached across the table and squeezed her arm and went on.

"So, we need to instill good values in our children; values like respect for themselves and others, self-control, obedience, responsibility and compassion. Our goal is to have them adopt these values as their own for life. In order to do that, our training has to be set in the context of love and godly example."

"Let me give you an example of what I mean. I saw a dad and his young son at a funeral recently, standing and talking to people. Every couple of minutes, the dad would lay his hand on his son's head, or draw him close to his side. The message was clear: this is my son and I love him. We belong together. Needless to say, the son's eyes were fixed on his dad, copying and watching him. I don't imagine that dad often had to tell his son to do a thing more than once because his son *wanted* to please him, wanted to be like him."

"Okay, so instilling values is my long-term goal. But what do I do *now* when AdaLayne won't listen to me? Like I said, she loves crawling over to the light sockets and sticking things into them. I'm petrified she's going to electrocute herself. What do I do with her? And how early do I start?"

The server brought us our drinks. Theresa took a long sip of her soda and looked up at me expectantly.

"Start as early as possible, because a child's spirit understands more than his mind does. When Mary, newly pregnant with Jesus, visited her aunt Elizabeth, in the sixth month of her own pregnancy, John the Baptist leaped in Elizabeth's womb upon hearing the voice of the mother of his Lord *(Luke 1:41)*. Even at that pre-born age, he understood who Jesus was. In the same way, very small children can understand our words long before they can verbalize anything.

"So start with training her to be obedient. Remember that training is not punishing. *Training* puts her back on the right path and shows her how to do the right thing, while *punishing* her just makes her feel bad about what she's done."

Theresa sat back, taking a big bite of her sandwich. She slowly chewed it, looking at me expectantly. Speaking through a full mouth, she asked, "Yeah, but how? Give some practical help; some specific tools to use with my eighteen-month old baby."

"Okay, ready to write?"

Putting down her sandwich, she dug in her purse for her notebook and pen.

"The first tool is your voice. Use your voice first to correct and direct. You might say, 'No, baby, Mommy says do *not* play with the plugs. Come play with this instead.' She'll hear the tone of your voice before she can understand the words so make it loving but firm. At her age, you might need to pick her up and move her to another activity."

"She'll crawl right back over there and try sticking something in there again."

"As young as AdaLayne is, it's hard to tell whether she's being deliberately disobedient or simply curious. You don't want to punish curiosity."

"Yeah, but I can't just let her keep sticking metal objects into light sockets," she shot back. "I don't care how curious she is."

"Then start with prevention. Cover all your electrical sockets so she can't stick things into them. That's your first defense with a baby her age. Another effective tool is logical consequences. Sometimes the best way to help her understand why something is off-limits is to let her feel a little pain as the natural result of her choice to disobey you.

"Here's a story to illustrate. When Jossie was just learning to crawl, she headed for the basement stairs the minute I turned my back on her. She couldn't navigate stairs yet, and would start down over the top step head first. I was just waiting for the day when she'd fall all the way down. One day I parked myself about four steps down and waited. Sure enough, here she came, crawling straight for the edge, and this time, with no mommy to pull her back, over she went. Of course I caught her, but not before she'd experienced the feeling of falling, even just those four steps. She cried like she'd fallen all the way down, but after that, until she learned to do stairs, she'd crawl to the edge and peer over, but she never pitched herself over the edge again.

"Hmmm, logical consequences. I'll have to remember that one."

"Obviously you don't want to use anything that would actually injure AdaLayne. As your child gets older, the logical consequence for making a wrong choice is not so much a little physical pain or the fear of it as it is making restitution. If a child breaks a window, he fixes it. Older kids can understand that kind of logic, even if they don't like it.

"We had a rather dramatic example of that once. One of our sons had a BB gun at about age 12 and loved to shoot things for target practice: rotten grapefruit, old phone books. . .you get the picture. One day he decided to bend the BB gun barrel around backwards, the better to shoot behind him, I guess.

"He called me out to watch a demonstration of this new invention. Standing in front of our brand-new basement sliding glass door, he aimed at the tree at the end of our back yard and before I could take the whole situation in, he shot that BB gun."

"Uh-oh!"

"Yeah, it was an uh-oh alright! The glass behind him shattered into a million pieces. Did he forget the direction his barrel was pointing? I don't know, but whatever the reason, the window was shattered."

"So what did you do?"

"I asked him to sweep up all the glass and told him he'd have to call the window repair company and pay for a new window. I didn't see the need for any discipline beyond that. He knew he'd done a stupid thing, and he had to pay for it. And sliding glass doors aren't cheap."

"Yeah, I can see that it would work better than just being yelled at. The kid prob'ly felt bad enough already."

"Yeah, he did. He was sorry but mostly embarrassed. He called the glass company—the same one that had installed that door not more than two weeks earlier—and they gave him a special deal on the price since he was a kid. He and Howie installed it that weekend. (I gotta tell you though, Howie was nailing the *very last nail* into the frame, hit it a little off-kilter and the whole window shattered again. That time around there was no discount from the glass company!)"

I shook my head in amusement, remembering that long-ago incident.

"How a child feels about what they did is an important point. If she already feels bad for what she did, and is truly sorry, you as a parent don't need to add any extra punishment. Be aware of the condition of your child's heart as revealed by her attitude. Is she truly sorry, or is she still defiant? Defiance and anger will warrant further discipline.

"But even if she's truly sorry, as our son was, she still needs to take responsibility for her actions. You're not helping her any if she learns that acting sorry will get her off the hook from the consequences of her wrong choices."

"Let's say she's still defiant. Then what do I do?"

"There are four other tools I want to tell you about, in order of severity. The first is a time-out. To me, this isn't an effective way to actually *train* your child, but it is useful for giving everyone time to cool off. Sometimes children back themselves into an emotional corner by being angry or disobedient. Maybe he's frustrated. Maybe his energy and emotions have ratcheted up too high for him to control. At times like that, a short time-out gives him a chance to cool off, think the situation over and change his attitude.

"Once, during our homeschooling days, one of our sons was being a real pain in the neck, so I finally sent him to his bedroom and told him he could come out when he changed his attitude. He stayed there all day. Voluntarily. By the time he came out that evening, he and I were both feeling much more relaxed and pleasant. I'd had a peaceful day and I bet he did too.

"If your child comes back genuinely sorry for what he's done and is ready to change both his attitude and his actions, mission accomplished. Accept his apology and go on. You'll be able to tell quickly enough if he's had a genuine change of heart."

"Do you do that for a big kid too? What do I do if Addie's, say, eight or nine? Do I still give her time-outs? That seems a little ridiculous," she challenged.

"At that age, you can use logical consequences more often. If she abuses your rules about bike riding, she can't ride her bike for a week. If she whines about setting the table, she can set the table every night for a week. Just make sure the consequence you've laid down is significant enough for her to feel, and be consistent about enforcing it."

"Okay, say she's twelve or thirteen. What kinds of tools do I use now?"

"For an older child, grounding or removing privileges works well. Or you might add a few extra chores or temporarily take away a possession: her cell phone or iPod perhaps. Hopefully she's learning that bad choices bring bad consequences. But whatever form of discipline you use, remember, the goal is to help her see what she did wrong, pay the consequence for her bad choice, be forgiven and go on in the right direction with a clear conscience, happy and restored.

"Always distinguish between her as a person and her behavior. Her behavior might be bad, she may make wrong choices, but *she's* not bad. She's always your precious daughter. Never make her feel embarrassed, or stupid, or shamed."

Theresa sucked the last of her soda through her straw with a slurp, wiped her mouth with the back of her hand, and looked at her notes. "Okay, we've covered time-outs, logical consequences and removing privileges or grounding. What else is there?"

"I want to talk about the most controversial one of all: spanking. In our culture today, spanking's gotten a bad reputation, both in the church and out of it. Unfortunately, some who call themselves Christians practice spanking to an extreme extent and it becomes abuse. So let's get it straight what biblical spanking really is."

"You're gonna hafta convince me on this one, Katie. I don't like any form of hitting and I'm not sure I could ever hit Addie. I had enough of that when I was a kid; I want no part of it ever again." She smacked her pen on the table, folded her arms and stared at me, her eyes hard and challenging. This was not going to be easy to explain, I could see that. I sent up a quick prayer for wisdom.

"I know, girl. You're not the only one who has problems with the thought of spanking. It's not for all kids or all situations. You're right, for a child who is already experiencing abuse, it's not a good choice. Nor is it healthy to spank a child who has not thoroughly bonded to you. Some foster and adopted children fall into this category. A child has to be firmly grounded in your love—your consistent, warm love—for a spanking to be tolerable. Nor would you spank a disabled child, or one who was incapable of understanding why he was being spanked. Let's talk about it. Ready?"

"I'll listen, but I'm pretty skeptical, Katie." She slowly picked up her pen, still eyeing me.

"I know. So are a lot of people. But spanking is clearly discussed in the Bible, so we have to at least look at it. It's your choice whether or not you ever spank Addie.

I flipped my bible open to Proverbs and read: ***"My son, do not despise the chastening of the Lord, nor detest His correction; for whom the Lord loves He corrects, just as a father the son in whom he delights (Pr. 3:11-12)."***

Letting that sink in for a moment, I continued.

*"*Our first point is that we are following God's example when we correct our children, even when we have to use a small amount of pain. He corrects us, the children in whom He delights.

"Then over here in Hebrews," I flipped through my Bible, "it tells us that *no chastening seems to be joyful for the present, but painful; nevertheless, afterward it yields the peaceful fruit of righteousness to those who have been trained by it (Heb. 12:11).* The second point is that sometimes discipline is painful, but it brings a child back to peace and righteousness. We all know how unpleasant it is to be around an untrained, willful child, especially as he gets older!

"Then there's the Proverb that reminds us that we are to *train up a child in the way he should go, and when he is old he will not depart from it. (Prov. 22:6).* In other words, if we train them when they are little, we are setting them in a good direction for life. Kind of like the old saying: 'as the twig is bent, so grows the tree'".

"That's all well and good, Katie, but *how* do I spank? The only example I have is of my mom backhanding me across the mouth or pulling my ear. I have no idea how to go about this in a healthy way. If there even is such a thing."

She stared hard at me, a glint of anger still evident in her eyes.

"I just finished reading a book by Chip Ingram called <u>Effective Parenting in a Defective World</u> (Tyndale House, October 2007), so instead of telling you what we did, which was flawed, let me see if I can give you a run-down of what he says." I dug around in my purse for the little notebook that I used for notes on everything from groceries to good books. I knew I had written Chip's points down for just such an occasion as this.

"Okay, here it is." I flipped open the notebook, skimming the page. "He gives us seven steps to keep in mind when we get to the point when we feel we have to spank our children. This is my paraphrase of what he said.

"**Number one:** Be fair. Always give your child a clear warning: if his behavior is bad, tell him so, and tell him there will be consequences if he does that again. Never blindside your child with discipline. Make sure he understands the warning and the consequences of not heeding your voice.

"**Number two:** Require responsibility. Ask her to articulate what she did wrong. It might go something like this:
'Addie, what did you do wrong?'
'I was playing with the ball but I didn't mean to break the window!'
'Have I ever told you not to play ball in the house?'
'Yeah, you did.'

159

'So what did you do wrong?'

'I disobeyed you.'

'What is the consequence for disobeying me?'

'A spanking.'

"We've discussed taking responsibility for our own sins before, remember? In this case, playing ball was not the sin, but disobedience was. It's important for a child to say in his own words what he did wrong so he can own it."

"Yep. I remember." She still looked skeptical, but she was taking notes.

"**Number three:** Show respect. Avoid shaming your child, especially in public. Find a private place to correct her, giving her the same dignity you'd want if it were you being corrected. Training and restoration is your goal, not shame.

"**Number four:** Express sorrow. Sin is wrong and so bad for us that Jesus had to die to rescue us from it. Your child should know that you are sad about the sin she has committed. When any of us sin, it's like letting the enemy score a point against us—"

"That, I can identify with!" Theresa blurted. "I've been letting the enemy score points for years in my life. And look what a mess I've made..." She dropped her eyes.

"A mess you're doing an excellent job of turning around, by the way." I smiled up at her under her glowering eyebrows. She turned her head away.

"**Number five:** Just sting. With your child across your lap, use a small dowel, ruler or a wooden spoon and flick your wrist as you spank her, causing it to just sting the skin, but not bruise it. You're not taking out your frustration on her, or giving her a whalloping; you're just administering a small amount of pain to help her learn not to do that particular behavior again. Proverbs tells us that *Blows that hurt cleanse away evil, as do stripes the inner depths of the heart. (Prov. 20:30)*. A little pain, carefully administered, can be a very effective teacher.

And although Chip Ingram doesn't speak of this specifically I would insert here:

"**Number six:** Control yourself. *Never* spank your child in anger. Ever. Taking out your anger on your child is child abuse. Send her to her room to wait while you cool down if you need to, but *always* control your own emotions."

"**Number seven:** Teach repentance. As soon as she's crying, stop spanking, take her on your lap and hug her. Explain again that you spanked her because of the bad choices she made and help her realize she needs to sincerely apologize to you and God and anyone else she might have hurt by her bad choice. Wait while she does that and reassure her that you both forgive her. If she needs to ask someone else to forgive her wrongdoing, go with her while she does that.

"**Number eight:** Restore peace. Tell her how much you love her and how God loves her even more. Reaffirm what a wonderful kid she is and how glad you are that she's your daughter. Remind her that God has wiped her sin away, He's not mad at her and neither are you. Hug her and let her go back to her play, loved and restored.

"It's absolutely crucial for little kids to return to their play with their equilibrium re-established, completely restored to the family circle. And it's important to you too, so you don't feel any lingering resentment or irritation at them for their actions.

"So, does this sound like the definition of spanking that you had in mind?" I asked, closing my notebook and peering up at her downcast and stormy eyes.

"You know, compared to what my mom used to do, it sounds almost pretty good. Instead of just yelling at me and making me feel bad and stupid, I wish my mom had talked to me when I did something wrong, and even if she did have to spank me, if she'd hugged and kissed me afterward and told me she loved me, wow...I might have grown up a whole lot better." Her voice trailed off wistfully.

I reached over and squeezed her arm.

"Theresa, you keep blasting your mother for the rotten job she did in raising you. But take a look here," I riffled through my Bible to Deuteronomy and read the fourth Commandment: *'Honor your father and your mother, as the LORD your God has commanded you, that your days may be long, and that it may be well with you in the land which the LORD your God is giving you* (**Deut 5:16**).

"In your case, the land that the Lord your God is giving you is your family. But in order for it to go well with you in that land, you must honor your parents. That's an unchangeable law of God, and we break it at our own risk."

"So are you saying that I'm supposed to start loving her all of a sudden? Not in a million years!"

She leaned back and blasted me with a withering glance. Had I *lost my mind?*

"No," I said, gazing back at her levelly, "it says to *honor* your parents; not to manufacture a feeling that isn't there. Love is an emotion; honor is a decision. To honor your mother, start speaking of her positively. Be grateful she gave you life. Maybe she did the best job she could. Maybe she was in over her head and it was all she could do just to get the basics done. Maybe you need to practice thinking up five good things about her every day for a week and see what you come up with."

"You have got to be kidding! Five good things? No way. I'll try one a day, but not *five!* What do you take me for, a *saint* or something?"

She closed her eyes, shaking her head in amazement, unable to comprehend such an outrageous suggestion.

"Start with one then, but the point is to change your attitude about your mother. If you're going to teach AdaLayne about sin, you need to get serious about it in your own life. That way you can be an example to her, identifying with her struggles to be good."

"That shouldn't be too hard!"

"And you know what? The example of your own life will be some of the best teaching you'll be able to give her. Believe me, she'll be watching you."

"Oh, great. Now I have to be the perfect mother again! Just when I thought I was going to be able to handle all this."

She dropped her face into her hands, groaning.

"Nope, you don't have to be perfect. Because you know what you'll get to do when you blow it? Which you will do, by the way, so just get your mind settled on that score."

"Oh, I can hardly wait. Tell me quick," she mumbled up through her fingers.

"You get to model humility, asking her to forgive you when you lose your temper or don't discipline her as you ought or when you speak badly of your mother. You get to show her what it means to be gentle and quick to apologize. Believe me; she'll pick up on your actions fast."

"So I don't have to be perfect? All I have to do is to ask her forgiveness when I blow it? So I can relax, then?" She straightened up, pushing her hair behind her ear.

"Yup. Just relax and be yourself. Love God with all your heart, follow His directives, and love Addie. You'll do just fine, I know you will."

I leaned back and looked at her, just loving her.

"Well, Katie, you've convinced me. Almost. I'll have to think all these things over and reread my notes. This is all pretty new to me. Thanks so much. I've got hope now that I can handle AdaLayne without flying off the handle into a bundle of angry, out-of-control nerves. I was petrified I was going to hurt her."

"I'm so glad, girl. Now, about that other matter…that man in your life?"

"Nope. That's it. I'll call you *if* I ever need advice on that score, which will be never, knowing my track record!"

She stood up, brushing the crumbs off her skirt, her birthmark blazing red even under her make-up.

"Thanks, Katie. I love you. *And* I'll pay the bill."

With that, she kissed the top of my head, laid a twenty-dollar bill on table and whisked away, her high heel sandals clicking briskly as she walked.

Thank You, Lord. I'm glad that *talk's over!*

CHAPTER 15

Training Your Child

Questions for Discussion

§

1) For many of us parents, training and teaching our children to mind us seems to be about the hardest part of parenting. If you are a parent, how do you train your child to mind you? Does it work?

2) How did your parents train you? Was their discipline consistent so that you could count on them punishing you every time you did something bad or was it more haphazard, with your parents sometime punishing you for bad actions and sometimes not? If that was the case, how did it make you feel?

3) Do you think that their method of training you worked? Do you feel like you had a safe, loved and secure upbringing where limits were clear and consistently enforced? Or not? If not, why not?

4) Have you thought about the idea of spanking? What do you think of it? Many people have entirely the wrong view of spanking, thinking it is child abuse. After reading this chapter, what do you think? Why?

5) Does the difference between a careful and deliberate spanking where the pain is real but measured and is followed by cuddling and repentance, and a quick, angry swat to the head or backside make sense to you? Which would you prefer to have if you were the child?

6) Why do you think many people are so averse to causing their child a small amount of pain now, (as in a spanking) if that will help them avoid more serious kinds of pain later on in life? What is

it about pain that we are so averse to? Think about the tee-shirts many athletes wear, proclaiming, "No Pain, No Gain!".

7) I remember as a teenager just *wishing* that some adult would care enough to put limits on me because what I was doing was hurting me, but there was nobody to stop me and I couldn't stop myself. Have you ever felt like that? Discuss how training and discipline contribute to limits and security for children.

CHAPTER 16

Keys to Parenting: Affection

§

Theresa called back sooner than I expected, just three weeks later. It was evening and I was sitting on the floor in the family room, playing a game of War with Jason and Jocelyn. I reached back onto the table by the sofa and grabbed the phone as it rang.

"Katie, remember what you said about keys to parenthood? I'd like to know more about that. When can we get together again?"

"Hey, girl, hello there. Hang on a moment; I'm playing a game with the twins, just a sec, okay?" Holding the phone away from my ear, I mouthed, "Guys, it's Theresa; I'll just be a minute."

They both groaned and flopped back on the floor.

"So, when can we get together?" I thought for a moment. "Uh, how about next Thursday morning at ten?"

"Great. My place or the Coffee Spot?"

"Come on over here; we can talk and Addie can play."

"I'll be there. Go back to your game. I'll see you then."

"Sounds good. Bye." I hung up the phone. "Ok, guys, who's winning now?"

*   *   *   *   *

"Gosh, it's weird that I lived here for five months. Seems so long ago." Carrying baby Addie, Theresa strolled into the living room later

166

that week, gazing around as if she'd never seen the place. She looked happy, wearing skinny jeans and a close-fitting green sweater; her hair curled in a pony tail. I smiled, thinking of the contrast to her old self on the day she arrived.

"Coming here. . .wow, seems like that was a lifetime ago. I feel like a different person now." After laying the baby on the floor and digging in her diaper bag for a few toys for her to play with, she flopped on the sage-green couch and reached for the cup of tea I handed her.

"You *are* different, girl. You've made a complete u-turn with your life; plus, you've has a baby. Both are life changing experiences."

"Yeah, I *am* different. I can feel it. Anyway, I wanted to ask you about keys to parenting. Remember you began to talk about them the other day when we were walking Addie around the park? Can we talk about that some more?"

"You mean the day I talked about the four-legged stool of parenthood?"

"Yeah, but I'm not sure I remember what each leg stands for. Refresh my memory, will you?"

I settled myself on the end of the couch opposite her, kicking off my shoes and folding my legs under me. Running my fingers through my wild-as-usual hair, I breathed a quick prayer for wisdom.

"Let me see. . .the four legs are discipline, affection, prayer and example."

"Hmmm. Discipline and affection, prayer and example. I'm gonna try to memorize those." Setting her teacup on the coffee table in front of her, she dug in her bag for her notebook and a pen.

"You'll remember them when you put them into practice. We discussed discipline the other day; let's talk about affection today." I leaned back, watching her, loving her.

God, she sure has changed, hasn't she? What a transformation!

Yep, and I'm loving it.

Me, too.

I smiled.

"So, why is affection so important? Because affection binds our children's hearts to ours. Our affectionate love makes them feel like they have a special place in our hearts that no one else can occupy. Every kid needs to feel that."

"Boy, don't I know it! I didn't feel like I had a special place in *anybody's* heart when I was growing up."

"Which is why God gave you to me," I said, grinning.

Making a face, she kicked at my shin, missing. I tucked my legs out of her reach.

"Okay, wise one, I don't have time to play with sassy people. Gimme the goods." Poising her pen over her paper, she looked at me expectantly.

I looked out the window, thinking.

Help me put this into clear words, Lord.

"Affection binds us and our children together. It begins with the attachment I was talking about when we took that walk around the park last summer, remember? When we talked about enjoying our babies? When they know we take pleasure in them, they feel loved, and they *want* to please us, *want* to be with us, *want* to listen to us. If our children, deep down, aren't sure that we delight in them, they're not going to listen to us. They'll shut their hearts and turn away emotionally."

"Sounds familiar." Her cheerful mood was momentarily overshadowed as if by a cloud.

"I know and I'm sorry. Your mother couldn't show you the kind of affection I'm talking about. Some people are so broken and bruised that they find it hard to show love. But as a healthy parent, it is our job not only to love our kids but also to nurture *their love* for us so they'll *want* to listen to us and obey us."

"Hmmm. Nurture their love for us. Never thought of it that way."

"A person who's never been taught to love, who has no love for anybody but himself, will use other people only to satisfy his needs, which leads to selfishness and sometimes appalling evil. God's given us parents the job of teaching our children *how to love*, probably the most important skill a human being will ever learn."

"Yikes. Sometimes the responsibility of all this begins to get to me." She began to pull a strand of hair out from her pony tail, but stopped herself and patted her hair back in place.

"It should, sometimes. That's when we realize what an essential job parenting is and how much we need God's help with it."

"It's a little staggering, if you ask me. What if I don't even know what to ask for?"

"God's already thought of that. Did you know that He's given us everything we need to live a godly life?"

I picked up my Bible from the end table, flipped it open to **2 Peter 1:3** and read: *". . . His divine power has given to us all things that pertain to life and godliness, through the knowledge of Him who called us by glory and virtue."*

"Wow. Is that ever cool. *All* things—like everything, every single thing that we need for a godly life? He's already given them to us?"

Holding her warm cup of tea against her cheek, Theresa let her eyes dig into mine. Really? Is this true?

"Absolutely. If His word says it, it's true."

"Wow, that's so awesome."

Taking a sip, and shaking her head in wonder, she looked out the window. The late November fields looked drab and dull after the blazing gold of fall.

"Give me specifics, Katie. How do you do all this? I didn't have the best example in the world, remember."

"Well here's something you can remember easily: the five "t's" of touch, time, tradition, tease, and talk. We're talking about affection and how to use it to knit you and your child together, right? So here are some ideas."

"Fire away. I'm listening." She looked up at me from her end of the couch, her pen ready.

"Touch is fairly obvious. Affectionate touch conveys love and connectedness. I watch a dad at church who has a thirteen year old daughter and every time she comes near him, he puts his arm around her and gives her a squeeze. She's not going to ask for a hug at her age and she may never give one in return but she's getting plenty of affection anyway. Look for ways to touch your child affectionately, especially as she gets older and might not be comfortable with the typical hugs and kisses. Give each other facials—"

"Good grief! I'm no good at that kind of stuff!" Theresa looked at me, horrified.

"Hey, I'm not either, but my girls and I have a lot of fun acting as though we are. Mainly, it's just a way to spend time together. They give me the most gosh-awful hair-do's and makeup jobs, but we love every minute of it.

"Give back rubs, and foot massages; have tickle sessions. Molly loves to tickle me until I gurgle with helpless laughter. Of course I grab her and tickle her too. She laughs; I laugh. I love it; we feel all warm and connected. Wrestle with your child; they love that kind of contact, especially when they're little. As a mom, you really can't wrestle with boys after a certain age, but you can let them show off their strength to you. When the two older boys got big enough, they loved to pick me up and carry me around. I pretended to struggle, but I loved the fact that they still wanted physical contact with me."

"I can't remember a single time when my mom touched me just for the fun of it, or just because she loved me. Wrestling, giving facials and back rubs. . .it all sounds pretty foreign to me. But fun!" She added quickly, looking up at me hopefully.

I reached over and squeezed her toe. "It is fun."

"Okay, time together. Obviously this overlaps with touch, because you can't touch without spending time together. Reading to AdaLayne, even as young as she is, is a great way to snuggle and spend time together. I know a young mom who reads a Bible story every night to her eighteen month old, and though he just grabs the pages and tries to chew them, he's getting cozy time with mom."

I paused to let her catch up as she wrote.

I wonder if this all seems like a foreign language to her?

"There are lots of ways to spend time together. Do things together. Take her for a walk and talk to her, even if all she's saying is 'Dah-dah-dah'. Point out the postman, the flowers, the birds overhead. Wave bye-bye to the school bus. Watch the trash truck with her. Sit on the floor with her and play blocks or roll a ball. Let her help you with your work. A friend of mine sits her little grandson on her lap while she's at the sewing machine, quilting. Little kids love to help Mommy and Daddy; it makes them feel big and important, and best of all: loved."

"What can a six month old help me with?"

"She won't be much help just now, but the point is, you're not just shooing her away while you get your work done. You're including her, putting that arm of love around her, letting her know she's important enough to spend time with. Maybe she's just in her high chair, watching you, but you can still talk and connect with her."

I hope she's getting this.

"I have to dig this idea of connecting down into my brain, I can tell. As a kid, I just did my own thing, trying to stay out of my mother's way so she wouldn't hit me." Theresa ducked her head, writing in her notebook. I finished my tea and watched her.

Lord, I love this girl.

Me, too.

"I know you did, and that's sad. A lot of kids are like that. That's why I'm trying to teach you that there's a better way."

"Keep teaching. I'm learning." She looked up at me with tear-bright eyes.

"As AdaLayne gets older, let her help you put clothes into the dryer, or collect the wastebaskets on a Saturday morning. In a few years, maybe she can put the toast in the toaster while you cook the eggs. Maybe she can help you dust or sort laundry. Make it fun to work together. She'll love doing the things Mommy does.

"When our kids were younger, I made bread every week and when it came time to knead the dough, I'd give each kid a chunk of dough for them to "knead". Of course, the boys made ropes out of theirs, hitting each other with them or throwing them up to the ceiling to see if they would stick."

"Gross!"

"Don't worry; I threw their chunks away!" I laughed, remembering. "By including the kids, kneading the bread took me half an hour instead of the ten minutes it would have taken me by myself, but I figured it was worth it. They may not have learned how to make bread but they did get one more time with mom tucked in for that day."

"Cool memories. I wish I had some memories like that with my mom."

"You may not with your mom, but you can make ones like these with AdaLayne."

"I'm listening. Soaking it all in."

She looked at her notebook again, reading off the next categories.

"OK, so we've discussed time together, and touch. What's next?"

"Tradition. Traditions are just things that families get in the habit of doing but it's good to examine them occasionally. Do they draw the family closer together? Does everyone enjoy them? Because, remember our goal here: to do things to weave our family closer together."

"I remember. This is all new to me, but I'm writing it all down. I'll go over it again later on."

"Traditions can be anything. They don't just have to be for holidays only. They can be as simple as snuggling in bed on Saturday mornings or telling stories before sleep time or making a kind of food you both like. Traditions give a child structure to her life; fun things that remind her that you two belong together. For example, whenever we were sick as kids, my mother used to feed us milk toast: toast in a bowl covered with warm milk."

"Ug. Sounds awful." Theresa stuck out her tongue and pretended to gag.

I laughed.

"It might be awful to you. But to us that dish meant Mom taking care of us when we were sick. It meant security, warmth, and tenderness.

"Here's another tradition we've done with our children since they were little: going around the table on their birthdays and saying what we love about them. They still ask for that, big as they are."

"That sounds cool. Maybe I'll do that with AdaLayne as she gets older."

"And do it however *you* want, since your traditions should be special for *your* family; a way to bind you two together. Discard the ones you don't want. I gave up baking Christmas cookies simply because I didn't like doing it; I wanted to concentrate on other parts of the holiday, and I didn't want to bake cookies just because I had to. So I don't."

"Wow! I don't think I know *anyone* who doesn't bake cookies for Christmas. Even my mother used to do that. Not that it made much difference. I'd rather she'd have paid some attention to us instead."

"That's exactly my point. You need to do what's good for *your* family, not what you think other people are expecting of you. Remember, you're *creating a family where you love each other*. If baking doesn't draw you closer as a family, don't do it. Read to your kids instead; make hand print place mats as gifts; act out the Christmas story from the point of view of the donkey or do something else you love."

"There's a lot to think about in that department. Just doing stuff to enjoy my family. . .making my own traditions. . .wow. I think this might actually be fun." She tapped her pencil to her chin thoughtfully.

"What's the next step?"

"Before we start on those, you want some more tea? Or crackers? Look at me, I'm still serving you tea with graham crackers! You'd think I could get a little more elegant, wouldn't you?"

"I like you just the way you are, Katie, graham crackers and all. More tea is fine, thanks," she said, holding out her cup, "but then I want to know about the last two categories here. If my notes are right, we have teasing and talk to go. Right?"

"Right. Back in a sec."

Pushing myself up off the couch, I uncurled my legs—stiff from sitting cross-legged so long—and hobbled out of the room.

God, please help me show her how to build a strong family, even as a single mom.

Just be yourself, girl. You're doing fine.

I want this to be You and not me, God.

Keep going.

CHAPTER 16

Keys to Parenting: Affection

Questions for Discussion

§

1) Have you ever thought about the concept of knitting your child's heart to yours? (Most of us seem to assume our kids are born loving us. . .)

2) What do you think about Katie's statement about 'teaching a person how to love, one of the most important skills he will ever learn'? Why is it so important that a person be taught how to love?

3) In your family of origin, did you have any family traditions that you enjoyed doing? How did it make you feel when your family did them? If your family was broken and some of these special traditions were lost, how did that make you feel?

4) What was touch like in your family of origin? Did your parents touch you lovingly, harshly, or not at all? Some families are the "huggy" type; others are more stand-off-ish. Which was yours? Did you wish it was different from what it was?

5) What about affection in your current family, if you have one? Do you hug and touch your kids much? What about some of the other things Katie describes: back-rubs, facials, tickling, and wrestling? Do you ever do any of those?

6) What about time together? Do you ever deliberately spend time with your family, just enjoying hanging out together? (Some families have this down to a fine art; others would rather all scatter to their individual rooms when they're in the same house.)

7) Discuss ways that make sense to you to knit your children's hearts to yours. Be specific and creative. Have fun!

CHAPTER 17

The Power of Words

§

"Okay," I continued, coming back into the room a few minutes later holding our refilled cups, "let's talk about these last two: teasing and talk"

I gave her a cup and settled myself on my end of the couch, facing her.

"The next one I call tender teasing. Teasing can be fun or it can cut deep. You know that nursery rhyme, '*Sticks and stones will break my bones, but words will never hurt me.*'? Not true. Words can leave permanent scars."

"You don't have to tell me! The only teasing I ever heard when I was growing up was the mean kind. *Is* there any other kind?" Her birthmark flared, even beneath her foundation.

"Actually, yes. We need to watch what we say and only use teasing to make family members feel loved and included.

"For example, when I was a kid, my brother gave me a nickname—don't ask, it's way too embarrassing—which reassured me that even though I was an awkward wallflower at school, I belonged to my family. They were the only ones who called me this goofy name and every time I heard it, I realized I was part of a family who loved me. I had a place where I belonged."

"That must've been cool." Her voice caught and she swiped at her eyes.

She cleared her throat, giving her head a hard shake and I handed her a Kleenex.

"It was. My school-days were not all that fun."

Taking a sip of tea, I went on.

"Here's a story to illustrate my point. My dad's mother died when he was two and until he was seven he had several different nannies. None of them understood his aching, little boy heart. He was a sickly child and they had no motherly love for him; in fact, one of them beat him with a hairbrush so hard it broke."

Theresa looked at me, her forehead wrinkled with concern.

"Ouch."

"Right, major ouch. So, when his dad married a loving, warm woman who had three kids of her own and she nicknamed him Old String, my father adored her for life.

"Nobody else was Old String—just him.

"That touched the heart of that love-starved little boy more than anything else she could have done. That nickname meant he was one of *her* kids."

"I always thought teasing was just plain hurtful." Putting her notebook down and drawing her knees up against her chest, she pulled the afghan around her shoulders and held it tight under her chin.

"It *can* be mean, so we have to do it tenderly. No hidden jabs or cutting remarks; no guilt trips or stabbing in the back allowed. Just loving teasing that knits us together."

"Give me an example. I have no idea what you mean."

"Little kids love to laugh at obviously silly stuff, like, 'Do you want to eat a snake for lunch? Or maybe a tree?' And then you can slap your forehead and say, 'People don't eat trees! Silly Mommy!' and both of you can laugh at silly Mommy.

"As your family gets older, collect funny family stories—best told on yourself for starters! For example, the story of the Eraser Cake is one of our family's favorites and my kids love to laugh at me because of it."

"And of course you know I want to hear it." Snuggling herself back into the corner of the couch, she pulled the elastic off her ponytail and shook it out, looking up at me, ready for a story.

177

"The summer I was eleven, we vacationed on an island in Maine. Our only connection to the mainland was a boat that picked up mail and supplies once a day.

"One day I decided to bake a cake. We had no baking soda or baking powder in the summer cottage, but I only needed a smidgen of each, so I figured they couldn't be *too* important. I didn't want to wait until the next day when the boat could bring them over, so I baked the cake without them. Amazingly enough, it didn't rise. Actually, it was the consistency of an art gum eraser: heavy and chewy. Of course my brothers had to try it out, and it bounced and even erased! Each time my family hears that story they love to laugh at me."

"And you don't mind?" she asked, incredulous.

"Of course not! It's part of being a family that loves each other. I laugh at myself too, and if it makes good memories for them, I'm happy. It's all about connecting us together."

Theresa just shook her head, staring at me in amazement.

"Okay, the last category is talk. The Bible says to fathers—and I think this applies to mothers, too—'*do not provoke your children to wrath, but bring them up in the training and admonition of the Lord*' (Eph. 6:4)."

"What's that supposed to mean?"

"*Do not provoke your children to wrath. . .*don't be unnecessarily harsh with your children, but use your words carefully, remembering that even if they need to be corrected, kids can get their feelings hurt if they're not reassured of your love."

"Nobody seemed to care about *my* feelings getting hurt when I was growing up!" she muttered, letting her hair fall in front of her face like a curtain.

That anger isn't far below the surface, is it, Lord?

"I know, girl. That's true for a lot of people, so all the more we need to be tender with our children. Now, I'm *not* talking about being so afraid of hurting our children's feelings that we never correct them or speak sharply to them if necessary. Sometimes children need to be corrected. I'm talking about *how* we correct. Do we yell at them and tell them they're stupid?"

"Well, yeah, if my mother is any indication. But I'm sorry to keep bringing her into this; I want to do things differently."

"And remember, you've forgiven your mother, so now you need to practice letting go of the resentment you have toward her. Deliberately change the way you talk about her. Ask God to give you a new example of how to be a mother."

"Like you?"

"If you want. Just remember I'm not perfect either."

"You're a whole lot closer than she was."

"Thank you." I smiled gratefully at her, reaching over and squeezing her foot. "Anyway. Where was I?"

"How to correct your kid."

"Right. We need to do it so they don't feel put down or stupid. We never want to make them feel like a failure. Satan does enough in that department; we don't need to add to his garbage.

"When I have to correct my kids—which is often—I always try to distinguish between *them* and their *behavior*. Even if their behavior is rotten, I still want them to know that *they* are precious to me."

"The way my mother yelled at me, I knew I was a failure, so why try? That's why I did so many dumb things with my life." Putting her tea on the floor, she scrunched the afghan into a ball and hugged it against her chest, rocking a little.

"That's why we need to be tender and encouraging with our children. The Bible tells us to *'be kind to one another, tender-hearted, forgiving one another, even as God in Christ forgave you'* (**Eph. 4:32**). So let our words be tender, gentle, full of love and encouragement, even when we have to correct them."

"Say my kid does do a stupid thing. How do I correct her without telling her it was a stupid thing?"

"You tell her that it was a bad choice. Tell her what was wrong with her behavior—that she was disobedient, for example—but don't say things that would make her feel even more stupid and bad about herself."

"Things like, 'You're such a jerk; can't you do anything right?'?"

"Exactly. See how one response tears the person down and makes her feel miserable, while the other simply lets her know her *behavior* was wrong? And incidentally, her behavior will often be wrong. Kids make bad choices all the time."

"I'll have to remember all this when I get to correcting AdaLayne."

"Here's another thought about the power of our words. Have you ever heard of the parable of the sower that Jesus taught?"

"Can't say I can bring it to mind if I have."

"Well, this farmer scattered his seed around fairly liberally. Some of it fell on rocky ground where it withered and died, some fell in the midst of thorns where it was choked out and some of it fell on good ground where it took root and grew, producing a sixty- or hundred-fold harvest. Jesus was making the point that words are like that seed. If they find receptive ground, they will take root and grow and produce a harvest *(Matt. 13:3-9)*."

"So? Go on."

"It's the same with the words we speak, to ourselves, our children, our friends, whoever. But it's especially true about our children when they're little: their hearts are like good soil, receptive to anything we plant in them. Our words bear fruit just like seeds do; bad words bearing bad fruit and good words bearing good fruit. So let's make sure we plant loving words that will grow into a harvest of self-confidence and joy in our children's lives.

"Make your words tender and encouraging but straightforward. If you need to correct, do it with a quiet authority. Remember, your authority comes from God, so you don't need to yell or criticize. Simply correct in love."

"Okay," Theresa said, uncurling her legs from under her and looking at her notes, "I've got to go in a sec, so let me summarize what we've talked about. I'm trying to knit AdaLayne's heart to mine, trying to wrap that cord of love around the two of us to make us into a family, and here are five *t*'s to remember.

"Touch and cuddle my child, even when she gets older, keeping my hands for blessing and never for smacking or hitting.

"Make sure we have time together, doing stuff we think is fun.

"Develop traditions for our family that are just for us, however goofy they may be.

"Use teasing in a way to let AdaLayne know that she is special to me, with nicknames just for her, and fun teasing and play.

"And use my words and talking in a way that is both tender and tough. Tough because it comes from God and I don't need to take any nonsense about it, but tender because it comes from Jesus, who leads us tenderly, like a shepherd caring for his sheep who are with young *(Isa. 40:11)*."

"Theresa, I swear, you'll be teaching this stuff yourself one day! As usual, you've said it better than I could."

She blushed, ducking her head, her birthmark flaming again.

"You're a good teacher, Katie. And I learn as much from watching you as I do from what you say. I saw you put all these things into practice when I lived with you guys."

"Well, from living with us, you also know that we are far from perfect, so you've had plenty of chances to see us repent to our kids as well!"

"That's what I mean; you model what you teach. For the first time, I'm seeing adults act like grownups. I'm thinking I might like to be an adult too." She stood, folded the afghan and laid it across the back of the couch.

"Next time we'll talk about marriage," I offered mildly, gazing at her over the top of my glasses.

"Okay, I'm outta here on that note! Don't call me, I'll call you when and *if* I'm ready to hear about marriage!"

Hopping up off the couch, she gathered AdaLayne—who had long since fallen asleep—off the floor, gave me a quick kiss, grabbed her purse and zipped out the door.

I called after her, "You just might want to learn about it *before* you contemplate it!"

"And that'll be never! Thanks for the time together. See ya!" And she was gone.

Oh Lord, heal her heart. She's so gun-shy, but I know she'd blossom under the love of a good man. Please bring her one. A really good one, Father, please. And thank You.

I have it all under control.

I know You do and I'm glad. I sure couldn't work all this out.

CHAPTER 17

The Power of Words

Questions for Discussion

§

1) Have you ever experienced teasing that hurts and sometimes even leaves lasting wounds? Have you ever done it yourself? (It's usually called bullying today.)

2) How did it make you feel to be the teaser or the one teased? What was your reaction to the person who did it? Did that kind of teasing happen in your family of origin? What about in your current family? If it happens among your kids, what do you do about it?

3) Have you ever experienced the other kind of teasing, the kind that draws you in and makes you feel loved and included? Do you have nicknames in your family? (My husband still has one for each of our children, even though the kids are adults now.)

4) We've all heard the phrase, "It's not *what* you say, but *how* you say it that makes the difference." Do you consider the effect the tone of your voice and the sound of your words has on the people around you, especially children? Can you say the same words, just in a quieter, more loving tone, and have the same effect?

5) Have you ever thought about the difference Katie brings up between a child's behavior and that child's self? Do your words reflect that difference?

6) Katie says, "Remember, your authority comes from God, so you don't need to yell or criticize. Simply correct in love." Discuss what this means. Why does having your authority come from God help you to be calmer?

CHAPTER 18

How Does Prayer Work?

§

"Hey, Katie, I need to talk to you."

"Well, hello to you too, girl. Usually when you call someone, you say hi and ask how they're doing before just jumping in. So, how are you doing?" Holding my cell phone, I pulled my head out of the cedar chest where I was getting out our winter clothes.

"I'm fine, thank you and I hope you are too because I really need to talk to you. Soon."

"Is there some crisis?" I asked, sitting down on the bed, a smidge alarmed.

"No, nothing like that. I just miss you and want to talk to you. That's all."

"Okay. I can handle that. When's good for you?"

"How about tomorrow? Here? I don't have to go to work until 3:00 in the afternoon; you want to come for lunch?"

"It's a deal. I'll be there at noon."

"Thanks, Katie. I can't wait to see you."

*   *   *   *   *

As I drove the next day I talked to God.

Lord, there's gotta be more than just her wanting to see me all of a sudden. Please give me Your wisdom about whatever it is.

183

Do I ever hold back wisdom from you when you ask for it?
No, You don't, Lord, but I just need a little reassurance now and then. I don't have much wisdom of my own, You know.
I know. I'll give it to you when you need it. Always.
I'm so glad, God. I couldn't do this without You.
And that's probably a good thing.

* * * * *

I climbed the rickety iron steps to her apartment twenty minutes later. At the top, Theresa waited for me in the chilly air, grinning like a kid on her birthday. I was immediately suspicious. She wore a hip-length teal sweater over black leggings with a turquoise necklace that hung down to her belly button. He hair had new strawberry blond highlights in it and skillfully done makeup completely hid her birthmark. Wow!

After I'd huffed my way up, she opened the door with a flourish, kissing me on the cheek as I squeezed into her tiny kitchen, newly painted yellow.

"We have company, I see," I murmured as I rounded the fridge.

"Yup, we do," she grinned.

A man of average build with deep smile wrinkles and thinning sandy hair stood up from the kitchen table and stuck out his hand, giving me a broad and genuine smile.

"Jim Schipper. And you must be the Katie I hear so much about?" He gripped my hand with his hard callused one and looked straight into my eyes.

"Yes, I'm Katie. How do you know Theresa?"

"I get to service her car pretty frequently. She drives quite the fixer-upper. So as time's gone on, I've gotten to know not only her car, but her too."

"Well, this is quite the occasion." I began to pull out my chair but Jim reached over and pulled it out for me.

Okay, Lord, pretty good so far.

Unzipping my red fleece jacket, I hung it over the back of my chair back and sat down. Blue place mats and flowered blue paper napkins gave the table a festive look and a bunch of holly and dry grasses in a green glass bottle decorated the center of the table

"Jim brought me that bouquet," Theresa said, blushing.

"I didn't have time on my lunch break to go buy flowers, so I brought her those. I think she likes wild ones better anyway," Jim said as he pushed my chair in and sat down with his eyes on Theresa.

"Can you imagine? Someone noticing, or caring, about whether I like wild flowers better than store-bought?" Theresa shook her head, her eyes averted.

I made a mental note. Interesting.

"So," I said brightly, "what brings us all together here today?"

"Um, I wanted you two to meet each other. You're the two most important people in my life just now—except for AdaLayne, and she's asleep—so I thought. . .I mean, well, I've been telling Jim about you, Katie, and the stuff we talk about and he said he wanted to meet this person who's been influencing my life so much—"

"And I thought if I was ever to get married to anybody, I'd need to know some of the same things Theresa is learning, that's all," Jim broke in, smiling broadly.

"Not that *we're* thinking about marriage or anything, Katie! He's not talking about *us*." Theresa leaned over from where she was fixing the plates at the counter and bored her eyes into mine to make sure I got that message clearly.

"Oh heavens, no! Why would I even think such a thing?"

"We're just friends, right, Jim?" she stared hard at him with eyebrows raised.

"Absolutely. Just friends. Nothing more. Basically buddies. You know, she makes a mean lasagna and I fix her car. Totally platonic," he nodded soothingly, gazing at Theresa.

"Good, now that *that's* settled, what *do* you want to talk about, girl?" I asked, stifling a smile.

She placed a plate with an egg salad sandwich on it in front of me and one in front of Jim. Bringing one to the table for herself, she took a bite and mumbled, "Could we talk about prayer? Either that or example, as those are the two legs of the parenting stool we haven't talked about yet." Seeing Jim bowing his head before taking a bite, her hand flew to her still-full mouth. "Oh, I'm so sorry! Speaking of prayer! Let's thank the Lord for the food. Katie, would you ask the blessing?"

$$* \quad * \quad * \quad * \quad * \quad *$$

"Prayer's one of my favorite topics," I said, trying to keep from dropping in my lap the globs of egg salad that oozed out the side of the sandwich with every bite, "and is certainly something we need a lot of as we raise our children. Speaking of which, Jim, do you have any children?"

"I have a son from a short marriage a long time ago, but it's been years since I've seen him. His mother has custody. . .it's a long story." The set of his jaw and the hardness in his eyes told me that door to his past was slammed shut.

I glanced away, embarrassed to have asked, and turned my attention back to Theresa.

"As you remember, Theresa, I've been using an example of a four-legged stool to illustrate four important aspects of parenting: affection and discipline, example and prayer. We need all four elements to be balanced and effective parents. Theresa and I have discussed affection and discipline, Jim, so now we're onto prayer.

"So, guys, what is prayer? What do you two think?" I looked from one to the other.

"Um, what we do before bed and meals and when we need help? I don't know; I never did it much. What about you, Jim?" Theresa mumbled through a mouthful of egg salad.

"I don't have the greatest prayer life, but I do talk to God—about little stuff mostly, like, 'Please, God, help me fix this transmission.'" Jim tilted his chair back and gazed steadily at me.

"That's exactly what prayer is; just talking to God about the stuff in our lives."

Theresa pushed aside her plate, opened her notebook and started to take notes, taking bites of her sandwich in between writing.

"But I'm sure we've all experienced prayers that seemed to go no further than the ceiling. Sometimes it seems that God is deaf, or maybe He just doesn't care." I looked from one to the other.

Jim nodded slowly, his smile gone and his eyes suddenly bleak.

"So what turns prayer from hopeless begging—not really believing God's even listening— to confident asking that moves God's heart to action on our behalf?"

I looked at each one in turn. Both faces told me that to their knowledge, their prayers had rarely even reached the ceiling.

"I say it's the relationship we have with God. Imagine, Theresa, if AdaLayne asked you for a piece of bread, would you give her an old sock to chew on?"

"Gross! Of course I'd never do that; what kind of a mother do you think I am?" She reddened with indignation, glaring at me.

"God's the same with us. He cherishes each one of us and has our best interest at heart, so if we pray with no faith in His love, He could ask us the same question: 'What do you think I'll do when you ask for help or wisdom, give you an old sock?'"

"That *would* be an insult to God, wouldn't it?" Theresa looked toward Jim and he nodded slowly.

"Yup. It would be." He stroked his chin thoughtfully, looking steadily from Theresa to me and back to her. "But it's hard for us who've had rotten parents to understand that God actually loves us," he said, clearing his throat hard and looking away.

"I couldn't agree more." I nodded. "I know it's taken me awhile to get it through my head." I looked from one to the other.

They're both so hurt, God. Will they ever feel Your love?

I hope so.

"So," I continued, "believing that God loves us and *wants* to give us what we need is the first step to successful prayer. We have to believe there's a two-way relationship between us and God. He loves us, we trust Him; He promises to take care of us, we pray to Him; He provides for our needs, we thank Him. Back and forth it goes.

"Over and over, Jesus tells those who come to Him not to be afraid, but only to believe. Check out the story of the man named Jairus who beseeched Jesus to heal his daughter. It's in ***Luke 8:41-50***, Theresa, if you're writing these down.

"This man Jairus, a ruler of the local synagogue, found Jesus and begged Him to come to his house to heal his daughter who was dying. But before Jesus could get there a messenger came from the house to tell Jairus that his daughter was dead. Jesus responded to this news by saying to him, *'Do not be afraid; only believe, and she will be made well'* **(v. 50)**."

"So believing that God will answer our prayers is the key that unlocks His power to work in our lives?" Theresa finished writing and looked up at me thoughtfully.

"Kind of like putting the key into the ignition of a car," Jim observed drily. "It won't go far without that."

I tipped my head in Jim's direction, looking at Theresa.

"Listen to this fellow, girl. He's getting it."

She kept her head down, but a small grin played around her lips and her birthmark blazed red even under her make-up.

"Okay, besides faith, another part of prayer is getting to know the Father and His will. I don't believe He grants us our desires if they're out of His will, except for the stubborn prodigal who's determined to do His own thing. I think eventually God says to him, 'Go ahead and do your own thing. I'll stand by and watch.' But I don't think it brings Him any happiness."

"Been there, done that," Jim muttered into his fist.

"So the more we get to know God and the more we read the Bible, the more we'll understand what's important to Him, and what prayers He will always answer with a yes. For example, I've prayed for years that all our children would love God and serve Him wholeheartedly. I know that's a prayer He'll say yes to, since the first commandment tells us to '*Love the LORD your God with all your heart, with all your soul, and with all your strength,*' **(Deut. 6:5)**. That's a request that I know is in line with His will.

"On the other hand, if I blow my grocery money for the week on a new dress and pray for Him to send me more, He probably won't miraculously expand my money to cover the groceries we need that week. He may let me experience the logical consequences of not managing my money well. He's a very practical being, you know."

"I love that about God." Theresa broke in, laying her pen down and looking at me eagerly. "Sometimes He's the most down-to-earth thing in the whole world and then other times, He seems far off and mysterious. We can never really get to know the whole guy."

She stared off into space as if she could almost make out the shadowy form of the God she was describing.

"You're right, Theresa, we can't ever get to know the whole guy, as you say. And that's probably a good thing!

"Okay, here are some of the ways we can use prayer to help and bless our families.

"Did you know that we can affect the fates of future generations of our families, hundreds of people, by prayer? We are connected to all the people who have gone before us, and all the people who will follow us.

"Look in **Genesis 24:60**, Theresa, for an example of what I mean. Abraham had sent his servant to find a wife for his son Isaac. The servant has found Rebekah, a relative in a distant land, who God seems to have picked out for Isaac as a perfect match. Rebekah's family is putting her on the camel and giving her their final blessing as she and the servant are leaving to return to Abraham's homeland. The Bible says that *'they blessed Rebekah and said to her: "Our sister, may you become the mother of thousands of ten thousands."'* They knew that she wasn't just going to be the mother of her own children, but of thousands and thousands of people resulting from her and Isaac's union. They got it; they knew Rebekah was part of a line of people stretching on for generations."

"Wow. . .the mother of thousands of ten thousands." Theresa shook her head slowly. "Gives motherhood a little different perspective, doesn't it? I mean, I had no idea I might be affecting that many people by my prayers. I just thought it was just AdaLayne and me and that's it."

"Kind of awesome, isn't it?" I agreed. "I'm positive that I follow Christ today because some ancestor of mine prayed for his descendants to love Jesus. Ever since I realized that, I've been praying for *all* my descendants, born and unborn, to follow Christ."

Jim spoke up. "How do you pray for them? What kinds of things?"

"I pray that each one will make a personal decision to love and serve Jesus. I pray for protection from evil. I think persecution of those who follow Christ is going to get worse in the not-so-distant future, so

I pray for faithfulness and steadfastness in the face of suffering for my children and all my descendants."

"Anything else?" Theresa asked, furiously scribbling.

"I pray for protection from depression, despair, discouragement and addictions of all kinds. I pray they'll marry godly spouses and have life-long, happy marriages, raising healthy, god-fearing families. I pray they'll read and obey God's instructions as found in His Word, the Bible. I pray they'll have a sense of humor and enjoy their children, their spouses, their lives and their Lord. I pray they find work God's called them to do and that it satisfies them. I pray their homes will be havens of joy, peace and love."

"Wow. You don't ask for much, do you?" Jim tipped his chair back and laced his hands behind his head, filling the doorway behind him. "What if we've already screwed up and don't see any way to fix the mess we've made of our lives as parents? I don't even know where my son is, much less how to pray for him."

"It's never too late to repent and ask God to forgive you of your failures as a parent. Then, start praying for your son, even if you don't know where he is. God knows where he is, and He can influence your son's life through your prayers in ways you may never know until you get to heaven. Remember I told you that I'm convinced I'm a believing Christian today because of the prayers of some ancestor? Obviously that person never knew me, but his or her prayers turned me away from being a lost, depressed college student to being a fulfilled and happy follower of Christ."

"So you think God can do the same thing in my son's life, huh?" Jim ran his hand across his eyes but not before I saw the hungry ache smoldering there.

"I know He can. He's in the business of answering the prayers of those who love Him, especially the prayers of parents for their children."

"Coffee, anyone?" Theresa got up and cleared the plates from in front of us. "And I actually made cookies for dessert. They're not the best, but here they are."

She set a plate of lumpy cookies down in front of us. Jim and I both stared at them.

I tried to suppress a grin. "Wow, Theresa. . .they look like every homemade cookie you ever ate in my house."

I helped myself to one and took a bite. It was rock hard.

"But good! Yum." I tried not to be obvious about the effort it took to chew it.

"Would you be more comfortable in the living room, Jim?" Theresa asked, pointedly ignoring me.

"I don't care where we sit. I'm gonna have to go back to work pretty soon, so can we finish up with this session? I want to hear all you've got to say on this topic, Katie. There's a lot I need to think about and I want all of it."

"Okay," I said, taking a sip of my water to wash down the dry mash in my mouth, "we'll finish up in here then. It's easier for Theresa to take notes on the table."

"Clue me in the next time you ladies get together, okay? I've never heard this kind of stuff before and I could use more of it." Jim took one bite of his cookie and laid the rest on his plate.

"Hear that, Theresa? You make sure to let this fellow know."

"I will, I promise." She kept her face assiduously on her notebook, her hair falling forward, but not enough to hide the blush that crept up from her neck.

"So, we were talking about the power of a parent's prayers. God has put parents in authority over their children, to care for them and watch over them, and that includes spiritual authority. So when we pray a blessing over our children, it has special strength and effectiveness. The Old Testament is full of stories about the blessing that was usually bestowed on the oldest son, and I believe that we, even as modern-day parents, can bestow a similar blessing on each of our children.

"We prayed such a blessing over Jeff as he graduated from high school last May and I anticipate doing it for each of the other children as well. It's a prayer that's carefully thought out—maybe even written down—asking God's specific blessing on that child's life. It can become something of a road sign, pointing a child in *'the way he should go'*, to quote **Proverbs 22:6.**

"God has a specific plan for each person's life, and such a prayer is a parent's way of committing their child to that plan and to God's care along the way. It's a beautiful custom, and I wish we celebrated it today as they did in Biblical times."

"Wow. Wonder where I'd be if my dad had prayed such a prayer over me." Jim muttered.

"You can pray a prayer like over your son, even though you don't know him. Ask God to give you the words and the specific things He wants included. He'll show you, and you have no idea how it will impact your son, wherever he is."

"I'll sure have to think about all this. I never heard this kind of stuff before." He fished a neatly folded white handkerchief out of his back pocket, shook it out and blew his nose loudly.

"Okay," I said, pushing my chair back as far as the cramped kitchen would allow, "to finish up, I'll share two of my personal prayers that I've used over the years with my kids. The first, my 'shark-cage prayer,' comes from a story I once read in the paper of a young woman who tried to swim from Florida to Cuba through shark-infested waters. To protect her from harm, her team built a floating steel cage for her to swim in as they towed it behind the safety launch. She still had to experience the wind, the waves and the exhaustion as she swam the full distance but she was protected by the cage from the man-eating sharks.

"My prayer for kids going through a rebellious time is that God will put a spiritual shark cage around them, protecting them from the man-eating spiritual sharks out there, like falling away from God, suicide, depression, bad marriages and broken families, alcoholism, despair, murder—stuff that can derail your life for a long time. There's nothing God can't rescue us from if we call out to Him, but the devil can sure do a number on us in the meantime, worming his way into our minds and planting his poisonous thoughts there.

"So I pray God lets them go through whatever they're determined to go through, but with His protection in the background. They'll still have to flail their way through the messes they've made and pay the consequences, but God won't let them be eaten alive by the sharks."

"Hmmm, shark cage prayer. I think I'll be able to remember that one," mused Theresa.

"And my last personal prayer is this, again for a rebellious child, *'Dear God, please don't let this child* waste *one day in rebellion.'* That way, either God protects the child from rebellion, or He uses what the child learned through it at a later date to bless someone else, so either way, the experience is not wasted and God gets good out of it.

"So that's it for today, guys. You've been great listeners and I've loved talking with you. I hope it blesses you. Theresa, thanks for the lunch. Jim, great to meet you. Hope to see you again sometime."

I began to push my chair back but before I could finish, Jim leaped up and pulled it all the way out. Thanking him, I gathered my red fleece and my purse. Theresa squeezed out from her spot between the table and the fridge and followed me out the back door.

"Thanks, Katie. I really appreciate you coming." She pecked me on the cheek.

"And yes, Theresa, I do like him. So far, so good."

"Don't go getting any ideas in your head!" She hissed at me and closed the door.

CHAPTER 18

How Does Prayer Work?

Questions for Discussion

§

1) Have you ever stopped to think that where you are and what you are doing today has been influenced by the prayers—or lack of them—of the people who have come before you?

2) Have you ever stopped to think that you can affect the lives of hundreds of people that will come after you, simply by praying for them?

3) When you pray, do you believe that God loves you and that your prayers are going right into His ear? Or do you feel more like Jim and Theresa, that your prayers don't even make it to the ceiling? If you do feel frustrated, can you think of any reasons why your prayers don't feel more effective?

4) How much does our early experience with our parents affect how we relate to God as a spiritual parent?

5) What do you think of the concept of the "blessing" as Katie described it? Could you have benefitted from a parent praying such a blessing over you as you left home? Have you ever thought of praying such a blessing over your children?

6) Do you wish someone had prayed a "shark cage prayer" over you if you went through tough times as a teenager? (I sure do!)

7) Have you seen any instances in your life where God has taken rotten experiences you've had and later on in life used them to

make you a better person: more compassionate or more understanding of others' struggles and hurts?

8) Discuss the idea of parents' prayers having extra power to them as they pray for their children. What do you think of this idea and why is it so?

CHAPTER 19

Communication 101

§

Christmas came and went. Twice I called Theresa to invite her to join us but she never called back.

Finally, in March, she called.

"Katie, it's Theresa."

"Hey, girl, what's up? It's good to hear your voice! I was beginning to think I'd never hear from you again. You okay?"

"Yeah, I guess so. It's been a rough couple of months. I wasn't sure I was going to make it there for a while." The voice on the other end was so low I could hardly hear it. Was this really Theresa?

"Why, what's going on? You should have called me! That's why I'm here, to be your sounding board, mother figure, and friend. You don't have to go it alone, girl."

"I know. . .I guess I figured I knew what you'd say. . .and I didn't want to hear it, and. . ." her voice trailed off.

"You crying, honey? What's going on? You wanna get together? I could come over and bring you and Addie over here. Or take you out for a salad or something. Talk to me, girl."

Muffled sobs choked the line.

"Okay, sweetie, take your time. Tell me when you're ready. I'm in no hurry." I bowed my head on the scratched kitchen windowsill and prayed.

Whatever it is, Father, please bring good out of it and please bless them.

"Oh, Katie, I've blown it! I mean we have. . .everything's ruined!"

"You talking about you and Jim? Is that it?"

"Yes! And everything's over between us. I've ruined the whole thing!"

More sobs. Hiccups. Sniffs.

"You at home, honey? I'm coming over. Don't go anywhere, okay?"

"I won't. But Katie, don't yell at me, please?"

"I won't. I promise. I'll be there in twenty minutes."

*   *   *   *   *

I left a note for the twins, due to arrive home in about an hour, and took off. Twenty minutes later, I took the rusty stairs two at a time and let myself in Theresa's kitchen door.

I found Theresa lying curled on the couch, her eyes shut, while AdaLayne sat on a quilt on the floor, playing quietly. The apartment looked reasonably orderly.

I sat down on the end of the couch and put Theresa's feet in my lap. Rubbing them, I talked softly to AdaLayne and prayed inwardly.

Theresa finally stirred.

"You gonna ask me what's wrong or what?" she asked in a thick, congested voice.

"I figured you'd tell me when you're ready."

She sat up, pulling her feet out of my lap and pushed the hair out of her eyes. It was flat and greasy and hadn't been brushed in a while.

"Katie, we had sex, and now he doesn't want anything to do with me. It's over." Her voice was as flat and dull as her hair.

"I'd be surprised if it was that simple. Tell me what happened."

She hugged her knees to her chest and rested her forehead on them. Her hair fell forward like a curtain, muffling her voice, and she began talking in a monotone.

"After you saw us last fall, we continued seeing each other—he'd come over for dinner on nights I didn't work. He'd help with the dishes and read to AdaLayne before bed, and I began to actually like him. That was scary. I wasn't sure I wanted to go in that direction, so.

197

. .I don't know, maybe I subconsciously decided to mess things up a little. Well, not a little—a lot.

"We'd cuddle on the couch after the baby went to sleep. Cuddling led to finding ourselves in bed one night. Of course we made love. After it was over, Jim got up, mad, saying he was disappointed in both of us. He said things would be different from now on."

She wiped her nose on the back of her hand.

"I haven't heard from him since. I'm so afraid I've ruined our relationship, and I was just starting to trust him, too!" she wailed.

She grabbed fistfuls of her hair as if to pull it out and began crying the gut-wrenching sobs of a child aching for love. I knelt on the floor in front of her, wrapped my arms around her and just held her.

Still holding her, I began gently rocking and humming. AdaLayne watched silently, sucking her thumb, her eyes wide.

Finally, Theresa stopped sobbing and sat up, shaking me off.

"So what do I do now?" she asked, sniffing hard, running the back of her hand under her nose and wiping it on her jeans. Uncovered, her strawberry birth mark flared deep red against her pale skin.

"You think Jim would be willing to talk? I'd be happy to be here, if that would help."

"I don't know if anything will help. But we can try. You call him," she mumbled in a thick, congested voice.

"I will, sweetie, and I'll let you know what he says. Will you be okay here by yourself if I go now?"

"I've survived on my own for quite a while; I'm sure I'll make it a few more days. It's a good thing Addie's here, otherwise I don't think I'd even get out of bed in the mornings."

Slowly she pushed herself up off the couch and headed for the kitchen, shuffling like an old woman, head drooping. In a minute she returned and without looking up, handed me a slip of paper with Jim's phone number scrawled on it. I took her in my arms and held her for a moment.

"I know you're gonna make it, honey. God hasn't lost track of where you guys are or what you're doing. There are no surprises for Him, and He can make good out of whatever messes we make."

"I'll take your word for it, Katie. I don't have a lot of hope right now, but you can hope for me."

"I will. I'll call you after I talk to Jim."

"Thanks." She swiped the back of her hand across her nose and down her cheek, not making eye contact with me at all.

I kissed her on the cheek, squatted down and kissed AdaLayne, checked to make sure she had food in her fridge, and left.

*　　*　　*　　*　　*　　*

God, I need your wisdom. I don't want to play matchmaker, but Lord, they did seem to be right for each other. Show me what to do, please!

*　　*　　*　　*　　*　　*

"Jim, Katie here. Theresa's friend. How are you?"

"Terrible. Not much to live for at the moment. Why do you call?"

"Uh. . .I talked to Theresa."

"And?" Jim's voice was more curt than I'd expected.

Had I misjudged him after all?

"And she thinks it's all over between you two and she's devastated." I blurted.

"*She's* devastated? She's the one who said it was all over between us after we had sex. She did tell you about that little indiscretion, didn't she?"

"She did, and she feels terrible about it. She feels as though you hate her for what happened and she thinks you never want to talk to her again."

"She's got it backward! I'm angry at myself. I should have been the leader and I wasn't. We're trying to live this Christian life and this is what we do? Like a couple of copulating teenagers, we didn't wait, and now we've wrecked the first relationship for either of us that might have actually worked out!"

"Why don't the two of you talk it over, Jim? You're both assuming it's over, and you're both dying inside. Talk to each other."

Jim mumbled so quietly I had to strain to hear him.

"Do you think she'd even talk to me? I mean, after how I've let her down?"

"I can be there as an intermediary if you want. The sooner the better, judging by the condition you're both in."

"Is she bad off, too? Does she want to see me? Really?"

Raw, painful, hope surged through the line so palpable I could almost feel it. My insides tightened.

"When I arrived at her apartment today, she was curled up like a little wet kitten on the couch. She couldn't even talk for about twenty minutes. Then she cried for another twenty. Does that tell you anything?"

"Yeah, maybe. When do you think I could see her? Tonight?"

"I can't make it tonight; what about tomorrow? I'll call her."

"If she doesn't want to see me, don't call me. No, do. I don't know what I'll do if she doesn't want to see me."

"Jim, I'll call you either way. Now get some rest."

"Can you call me back tonight?"

"I'll call you as soon as I know anything. Now try to sleep. I don't think things are as bad as you think they are. Remember, God's watching over this whole situation."

"Thanks, Katie. Call me as soon—"

"You're welcome. Good night."

*   *   *   *   *   *

Two days later, we met in Theresa's tiny living room. Jim hunched on a stool against one wall, elbows on knees, cradling his head in his hands and staring at the floor. Theresa perched on the couch five feet away, twisting a kleenex in her hands. Head down, she hid behind the flat, greasy hair that covered half her face and almost hid the birth mark flaring red against the pale skin of her neck. The old cut-off sweatshirt she wore hung halfway off her shoulder but she didn't bother to pull it up even though her bra strap was showing.

AdaLayne slept down the hall.

"Okay, guys. You screwed up. As well as the sexual sin, which you're well aware of, you've also created a breakdown of communication with each other and with God. Now's your chance to work it out and hear each other's side. Jim, you go first; what's on your mind and in your heart?"

In an almost inaudible monotone, Jim began to speak to the floor.

"I feel like a jerk to have made a mistake with sex like this. I knew better, I didn't want it to happen, and then—boom!—we messed up and went too far like a couple of out-of-control teenagers. I'm mad at myself and truthfully, I'm mad at Theresa too. I'm even mad at God. Just when I thought maybe I was getting my life in order. . . I fail again!" He pounded one fist into the other. "What a *jerk* I am!"

In a lower voice, he continued, "I'm not sure where I stand with God or Theresa either, for that matter. Is God angry at me? Does she hate me? Am I a failure in her eyes? A screw-up? Is she laughing at me behind my back, and going on to the next guy?" His head sank even lower in his hands as he spoke.

"Jim!" Theresa blurted out, brushing her hair aside and staring at him. "How could you?"

An angry blush stained her pale, teary face.

"How could you say that? You make me so mad! You think I'm the kind of girl that would laugh at you behind your back? I guess you don't know me as well as I thought you did!"

"Hold on, girl." I reached out and rested my hand on her shoulder.

"This is Jim's chance to air his side. Listen to what he's saying—not just the words, but also the feelings behind them. You'll get your turn to talk. Go ahead, Jim."

"I hope you give me another chance, Theresa. Not just me. Us." He lifted his head and stared steadily at her, his color rising.

Theresa stared steadily back.

"Are you done, Jim?" I asked.

"For now," he answered, eyes still riveted on Theresa.

"Okay, it's your turn, Theresa, to tell Jim how you feel."

"Well, I'm mad and sad and I know it was mostly my fault but you should have stopped too, Jim. I was beginning to think our relationship might work out righteously, like the Bible says, and now we've fallen into the same old patterns I've been in all my life."

"What kind of patterns?" I asked.

"Screwing my life up. I thought I was on a better track, but no, here I am, same old failure girl I've always been." Theresa dropped her head into her hands, letting her hair fall forward to hide her face. Her shoulders shook.

"Hey, baby, in my book you aren't a failure girl. You never have been." Jim offered quietly in a steady voice.

"Right. You're just saying that to be nice. Forget it, Jim. I'm not good enough for you and I never will be. You might as well look somewhere else." She refused to meet his eyes.

"Listen! Don't you tell me what to do. If I want you as my fu– . . . I mean, if I want to have a relationship with you, I will. So don't go telling me to look somewhere else. Cripes' sake, Theresa!" He half rose from his stool.

"Hang on, guys," I put out a hand toward each of them, "we need to sort this out and not get all riled up here. We're working on communicating with each other and laying all this to rest, so why don't you start by acknowledging what went wrong and forgiving each other. Jim, do you need to forgive Theresa or acknowledge your wrong?"

"Forgive? Uh, yeah, I guess I do. I mean, you forgive someone when they've done something bad to you, right?"

"Right."

"Well, I think I'm the one who's in the wrong. I've royally messed things up with a girl I care a lot about. Do I ask forgiveness of God or what?"

"Do you need to forgive Theresa or ask her to forgive you?"

"Theresa, I'm sorry. I did a wrong and stupid thing. You know I don't come from a religious background so I'm not sure how to do this, but I want to make it right between us. Will you forgive me for messing up our relationship?"

"Theresa, to forgive someone means to let it go, forever. When God forgives us, He says He removes our sins as far away as the east is from the west (**Ps. 103:12**). So if you forgive Jim, you're letting go of this situation. You'll never bring it up again or hold it over his head."

"Jim, I want to start over and do it God's way this time. So, yes, I forgive you. I'll never bring it up again and never to blame you for it. You're forgiven." She sniffed, pushing her hair out of her face and giving him a wobbly smile.

"Jim, what about you?"

"Huh?" With some effort, Jim pulled his eyes off Theresa and glanced my way. "What? What about me?"

"Do you need to forgive Theresa? Theresa, do you want to ask Jim to forgive you?"

"Jim, I'm sorry for screwing up and for assuming you hated me for it and for not calling you. Will you forgive me?"

"Yeah, I forgive you. I don't want this to come between us any more. Look, I'm letting it go." He opened his hand as if releasing a helium balloon. "I'm never gonna bring it up again. It's gone."

"Now, you both seem like people who beat yourselves up over your mistakes. Can you forgive yourselves? Jim?"

"I never thought about forgiving myself. I figured I messed up and I'm stuck with that fact. But if you're talking about letting go of it, yeah, I'd like to forgive myself. How do I do it?"

"Just the way you forgave Theresa. Tell yourself you're letting go of it, it's in God's hands now, and neither you nor the devil can ever bring it up again."

"Well, this seems weird, but I'll give it a try. Here goes." He bowed his head. "Self, you old screwball, I forgive you for almost losing this girl. I'll quit blaming you, an' you do better from now on. We're startin' on a new page now, you hear?"

He looked up. "Did I cover the waterfront, Katie?"

I couldn't help but smile.

"I believe you did, Jim. I've never heard a prayer quite like that, but it was clearly your spirit telling your mind, will and emotions where to line up. Theresa, do you need to forgive yourself?"

"Yeah. I'm so down on myself I can hardly see straight so maybe if I forgave myself, I'd feel better. Will you pray for me, Katie?"

"You can do it yourself, Theresa, from your own heart."

"Well, Theresa, you've made a mess of things *again*, but you know what? I love you and I forgive you. I know you can do better next time. I don't hold this against you. Go on now, you're free."

"You know, that sounds like what Jesus said to the woman caught in adultery. He forgave her, and then He said, *'Go and sin no more* (**Jn. 8:11**)*.'* And that's what He says to you two: 'Go and sin no more'."

"Don't we need to ask God to forgive us, Katie? Isn't He the one we're really sinned against? Do you think He'll forgive us?

"All you have to do ask Him, and He will.'"

"Can I do it right now?" Jim wanted to know.

"Go ahead."

"Well, um, God, I know You must be irritated at us for messing up like this when we should have known better, so would You please, please forgive us and help us to do better in the future? Thank you, God. Katie, do you think He's forgiven us yet?"

"I know He has. It's like I tell our children: *whenever* you come to God with a truly humble heart, asking His forgiveness, He will *always* forgive you. He doesn't ever hold grudges against those who love Him and are trying to follow Him. Ever."

Done playing referee, I sat down next to Theresa.

"Okay, guys, let's look at what you've done here. Communication is a skill you'll need as you deepen your relationship. I learned what I'm passing onto you guys from a seminar I attended years ago put on by Gary Smalley and his team and it's proved to be invaluable for Craig and me over the years. You can't go too wrong if you can talk out the things that arise between you.

"So, the first thing to do when you have a disagreement is to cool down enough so that you can talk to each other. As you realized, it's easy to assume, often wrongly, that you know what the other person is thinking and feeling. You need to really *listen* to what the other person is saying while he shares his point of view. We didn't do it here, but it's helpful to repeat back to them what they've said in your own words to be sure you understand it. It's amazing how often what we *think* we're hearing isn't what the other person means at all.

"For example, Jim, you might say, 'I hear you saying, Theresa, that you're mad at me because I let you down.' And then Theresa might say, 'No, I'm saying I'm mad at both of us, not just you.' Then Jim would say that back to you, in his own words, until you both knew he understood you. Then you'd repeat the process from your side, Theresa, making sure Jim understood you.

"Communication is tricky; we need to work on both the sending *and* receiving parts of it and keep working on it until both parties are satisfied that they're being understood. Make sense?" I looked from one to the other. They nodded.

The storm was over.

"Yeah, it makes sense. It's like when I write down the customer's orders at the restaurant to make sure I have them straight and I say them back to the customer if I'm not sure."

"Good example, Theresa! Jim, this lady's got the gift of teaching. God's going to use it someday, just you watch."

"I'll keep watching; believe me. I'll keep watching for as long as it takes." He stared straight at her. She ducked her head and hid behind her hair.

"Then the next thing you two did was to apologize for what you did wrong and ask the other person to forgive you. That's a crucial step too, because you can talk things out all you want, but if you don't apologize and forgive, you keep dragging this ugly baggage with you."

"Like a big ol' chain draggin' along behind," Jim said, straightening up and rolling his shoulders as if shucking the weight pulling him down.

"Exactly. Well, all that's left for you two is to kiss and make up and I bet you can do that just fine without my help."

"I believe I can handle that part, Katie," Jim said levelly, looking at Theresa, who ducked and looked anywhere but at him. "Thanks for rescuing us. Here I was about to lose the best thing that's ever happened to me. Thanks. I'm so glad you didn't leave me and Theresa by our own sorry little selves."

I slipped out the door. They had some making up to do, and I needed to start supper.

As I drove home, I prayed: *Please bless them, God. Please help them, when they blow it again, to remember that You forgive Your children. Please help them rest in that forgiveness and love. I don't get the impression they've had much of it in their lives. Thank You, Lord.*

CHAPTER 19

Communication 101

Questions for Discussion

§

1) When I was growing up, my father lost his temper occasionally and yelled at us. However, once he'd cooled off, he always came back and asked us to forgive him for yelling. Was that kind of repentance practiced in your family of origin? Or were hurts and wrongs swept under the rug to stew and fester but not to be forgotten?

2) What about in your current family? Do you, as a parent, (if you are one), ask your kids to forgive you when you've lost your temper or otherwise done something wrong? Or don't you think that is a good idea?

3) Do you think a parent asking his child to forgive him decreases or increases that child's respect for the parent?

4) An argument can be like a fire that quickly rages out of control if people aren't careful. Emotions run high and things can be said that are regretted later. If there is a layer of resentment and hurt under the surface, a small disagreement can escalate into a huge blow-out. According to what Katie told Jim and Theresa, how can this kind of escalation be avoided?

5) Why is it so important to listen to the other person and repeat, in your own words, what he or she is saying until you're both sure you understand each other?

6) Have you ever been in a situation where what you thought a person on the other side of an argument was thinking and feeling wasn't

accurate at all? If so, how did you find out and what did you do about it once you found out?

7) Discuss the benefits of "talking out" arguments and disagreements like this, versus just letting them "blow over" without really resolving anything.

CHAPTER 20

Example, the Last Leg of the Stool

§

Theresa called about a month later. The April day was warm enough that I was vacuuming with the windows open and almost missed the phone, grabbing it on the last ring. I could hear joy in her voice as soon as I answered.

So good to hear her cheerful, Lord!

"Hey girl, what's up?"

"Things are better, Katie. Thanks so much for rescuing us a while back. We almost lost each other and over something that stupid, too."

"It's the little stupid things that trip us up. Believe me, I know. What's on your mind today?" I pushed sweaty hair off my forehead and leaned on the vacuum handle as I listened. My back ached from vacuuming the family room, the living room, the stairs, the kids' rooms, our room. . . I massaged my lower back.

"You up for more talking? I was going over my notes with Jim last night; we've got three legs of the stool of child-rearing, but not the fourth—the one about example. Doesn't sound like an area I'm going to shine in, but, oh well, it's all about learning, right?"

"Right, and don't for a minute think that I've got it all together either. I have to keep learning and re-learning these things too." I slid down onto the floor to rest my back as we talked, stretching my legs out and leaning against the wall.

"Well that's encouraging! You mean I'll never come to the place where I have all this down pat?"

"Nope. But that way we have to keep turning to God for help and guidance."

"Hmmm. . . there's something to be said for that. Anyway, when can we get together?"

"How about this afternoon—or do you work? I've got some free time if you do. Will that work?"

"Today's my day off; yeah, it'll work. Can I come over there? There's more space for AdaLayne to crawl around, and I always like coming to your house; it's peaceful."

"Sure, come on over. I'll be here."

"See you in about half an hour."

I rushed through the vacuuming, sending up quick little prayers for wisdom, and was just putting the machine away when she knocked on the door.

Wow, that was fast!

*　　*　　*　　*　　*　　*

I got us each a glass of lemonade, and we settled in the family room as it was more kid-friendly than the formal living room. A box of our kids' old toys stashed behind the couch provided entertainment for AdaLayne. I shoved a chair in each of the doorways to barricade her in as she was crawling now. Once she got her settled, Theresa, wearing tight jeans, pink lipstick and a cute ruffled plaid pink and green shirt, tucked her legs under her on the couch and got out her Bible, notebook and pen.

"Fire away, oh, teacher of mine," she said, grinning up at me. Her hair, curled, shiny and tied in a pink ribbon bounced in a high ponytail; a few curls softened her face. Her birthmark barely showed through her skillfully applied make-up. I couldn't help but smile.

She looks happy. Thank you, God. Now, please give me the wisdom I need. I haven't had any time to prepare, and I'm hot and tired, so help me remember all the things I want to tell her. Thank you.

Giving myself time to think, I combed my fingers through my thick, sweaty hair and pulled it on top of my head. Fanning my neck and looking for something to hold my hair up, I slid a stray scrunchy off the wooden arm of the couch and wrapped it several times around the unruly mess. At least it was off my neck.

I don't look near as good as she does, but oh well.

I settled against the couch, closing my eyes for a moment, letting the rush of the day fall away.

"I want to emphasize that this is not a to-do list I'm going to give you. The best way we can be good examples to our kids is by loving God with all our hearts, asking forgiveness when we blow it and doing our best to live righteously *because we love Him and want to please Him*, not because we want to earn brownie points. I'm not going to give you rules to follow, but rather principles to think about. I don't want you to fall into legalism, thinking you have to do everything I say to be a good Christian. Got that?"

"Got it," she said, writing. "No legalism. . .soak up ideas. . .not requirements."

"Perfect.

"Now, we can't do anything to *make* God love us more (remember, we're not racking up brownie points). Any attempt on our part to be good is simply our grateful response to God's love for us; our way of showing Him we love Him."

I brought my legs up and sat cross-legged on the worn leather couch; my bare feet were getting cold now that I'd stopped rushing around.

"So you mean we try to be good to *show* Him our love, but not to *gain* His love? Kind of like when Addie does something just to see me smile?" she said, glancing fondly at the chubby baby sitting in the middle of the room.

"Seriously, Theresa, I hope you take your gift for putting truth into clear language and use it someday for more than just talking to me. That's exactly it; we want to make God smile, to gladden His heart, and to bless Him. Then, with that attitude, we can be good examples for our children."

She hugged herself with a sudden shiver and I tossed her the brown and tan plaid blanket lying on the back of the couch. She snuggled up in it and rearranged her notebook and pen.

"What example are we in how we obey God? We've discussed training our children to obey us, but are we obeying God? Remember, children learn by watching what we *do* more than hearing what we *say*."

"Well, that's comforting. If she's gonna watch how I've lived my life, she doesn't have much of an example to follow."

"That's where you're wrong, Theresa. By chucking your old way of life, turning around and following God, you're giving her the best example you could."

"Thanks, Katie."

"Let's look at the Ten Commandments: God's basic instructions for us. Starting with the first one, do I make sure God has first place in my life? Has my love for Him grown stale and old, or is it vibrant and alive? Do I give Him time in my day? Do I listen to and obey His voice? Have I checked lately: do I love Him more than anything else in my life?"

"So this is ongoing, huh? We never arrive?" She looked at me thoughtfully, her pen pressed against pursed lips.

"Yup. We only arrive when we get to heaven. For now, we need to do spiritual housecleaning once in a while."

"Wow." She shook her head as she bent to write that down.

"Next commandment: *'Observe the Sabbath, to keep it holy,'* **(Deut. 5:23).** Do I take one day a week to rest and renew my body, my soul and my spirit? Do I worship God and spend time with Him; do I relax, and do things that provide recreation for me on that day, or is it just another work day?"

"So what's that mean, Katie? Spell it out for me."

"The Bible says that God rested on the seventh day *(Gen. 2:2),* and He tells us to do the same. We are to take one day a week to worship Him, play and have fun, be with family, do things we don't do all the rest of the week. It's a day to draw away from the pressure of our lives, and to spend time recharging our batteries with the ones we love—God, our families, and our friends. Imagine having a God who cares enough about us to provide rest and relaxation for us!"

"Hmmm. . .never thought of it that way." She snuggled herself closer into the corner of the couch, laying a pillow over her lap to form a writing surface.

"We don't need to get legalistic about it and do nothing but read our Bibles and study our Sunday school lessons but neither are we supposed to disregard the blessing of a rest day. God gave us a day of rest so we wouldn't burn out. He knows our bodies, minds and spirits need to be renewed each week."

"I always used Sunday to catch up on my housework and laundry."

"I know a lot of people do, but I don't think that's what God designed it for. Maybe we need to change our thinking."

I looked at her, eyebrows raised. These had been new thoughts to me too, not too long ago. Theresa looked off into space, thoughtful.

"The next commandment tells us to honor our parents *(Deut. 5:16)*. We've talked about that before and I encourage you to keep working on it with your mom. You don't need to carry on your bitterness and anger toward her. Nor, for that matter, does AdaLayne."

"That's easier said than done, Katie, but I'm working on it. I'm still trying to think of one good thing about her per day. It's tough; there's not a lot to work with. Besides, God's gonna have to change my heart to make me even *want* to think good things about her!"

She looked up at me with suddenly blazing eyes.

"Girl, that's where you're wrong. Honor is a decision, not a feeling. You can talk about her respectfully even while you're asking God to heal your hurt and anger. What example do you want AdaLayne to see and follow: respect towards parents or disrespect and anger? Don't forget, the way you treat your mother is the only example Addie will have as how to treat you when she's older."

"Yikes! Put the fear of God into me, why don't you!"

"We need to have the fear of God, because too often we take God's commandments lightly. I know I do, and I'll bet I'm not the only one."

"Well, yeah. Whaddya think I've done my whole life?"

"The rest of the Ten Commandments are pretty self-explanatory. Don't take the name of Jesus in vain, meaning use it respectfully and never as a careless swear or slang word. I don't believe He cares much for that.

"Don't kill; don't lie; don't steal; don't commit adultery, which means, as we've already talked about, don't have sex outside of marriage. Pretty straightforward. Don't covet your neighbor's goods; be content with what you have, not always yearning for more, especially when you see your neighbor enjoying the things you want."

"C'mon! I thought we were all supposed to be upwardly mobile in this culture, always striving for more, bigger and better. What gives?" she challenged me.

"You're right, that is what our culture tells us. The problem is, even though we as followers of Christ live in this twenty-first century culture, we're not supposed to conform to its ideas of *how* we should live. That's what I'm trying to get across to you: we live by what the Bible says, regardless of what the culture around us says.

"It's not wrong to improve your life, especially if you want to give your children a better life than you've had, but it goes back to the heart attitude. Do we *have* to have bigger and better things? Do we crave what other people have? Are we always dissatisfied with what we have? Bottom line: do we trust God to love us and provide for our needs?"

She leaned back and pursed her lips; I could almost see the wheels turning in her head.

"My English teacher once told us about marching to a different drummer—listening to the beat in your own heart instead of the noise all around you. Is that what you're talking about?"

"You got it. Only we don't just listen to our own hearts. Our hearts are deceitful and corrupt *(Jer. 17:9)*, so in order to live righteously we have to listen to what God says—in the Bible or as He speaks to our own hearts.

"Here are a few more points to think about. Do my kids see me loving and honoring Craig, working together with him to raise our family, with the *'incorruptible beauty of a gentle and quiet spirit,'* as it says in **1 Pet 3:4**, or do they see me being bossy and controlling? Look in Ephesians chapter five for some good advice on this topic. Also read **Colossians 3:18-21** and **1 Peter 3:1-7**."

"I can see I've got a lot to learn. It's a little overwhelming, to be honest, Katie."

"I know it is, and that's why we have to keep coming back to God to get encouragement. It's a life-long process.

"Now, here's another area where we consciously have to work to be a good example: our tongue and the words we speak. The Bible has tons of verses about it; just do a word search on the tongue sometime and you'll see pages of verses about our mouths and the words we speak. God must've known we'd need a lot of help in this department!"

"What do you mean? I've cut out swearing and I don't call AdaLayne names; what else is there?"

"What about negative talk, complaining, or whining? Do you ever put yourself or someone else down? Do you harp about your boss, the government, the speed limit, or the weather? Did you know that each time we speak or think negatively the body releases chemicals that actually make us feel bad? Did you also know we have the power to release chemicals that make us feel good by saying and thinking positive things?"

Thank You, Lord, for bringing to mind some of the information I picked up at that conference given by Dr. Aiko Hormann so many years ago. At the time, all that material seemed a little overwhelming, but if it helps Theresa, it was all worth it.

I continued on as Theresa scribbled in her notebook. "We can train our mouths not to *say* negative things, and after a while, that begins to affect how we *think*. We can actually re-train our brains by re-training our mouths. If we intentionally cultivate an attitude of thankfulness and cheerfulness, our brain will catch on after a while and start thinking that way on its own. If we're really in a slump, we can always start by simply thanking God for being our Father."

"So you mean I always have to put on a happy face and think sweet thoughts, even if I don't feel like it? What if I really am upset about something? What do I do then?" she challenged.

"There's nothing wrong with telling God you're upset. David did that all the time in his psalms. If you notice, though, each time David poured out his heart to God in complaint, he ends up by praising Him.

"*Psalm 139:4* tells us that God knows our words before we speak them. He knows what's on our hearts even if we don't tell Him, so there's no point in trying to hide anything from Him. Coming to Him with our genuine complaints is different, though, from spewing our anger and dissatisfaction all over the people around us.

"Our words are powerful and they affect people even if we don't mean them to. We can tear others down with our words or we can build them up. We can change the atmosphere of the room just by our words. I'm sure you've seen that with AdaLayne."

"Actually, now that you mention it. . . any time I'm cross or grouchy at her, she sure picks up on my mood and the whole place seems darker and life seems more hopeless."

"Right. And although your actions and body language affect her as well, it's primarily through your words that you communicate with her. Loving, encouraging words can be like hot chocolate that warms and soothes us; on the other hand, cruel words are like a knife going into a child's heart, leaving scars and wounds." I leaned back, smiling at my own fanciful language.

"I see what you mean about words. And, yeah, I think the ones that cut like a knife are the ones I'm the most familiar with. My mother used to always–uhhhh. . . I mean my mother had a lot on her plate and tried her best with us kids."

"Hey, way to go, girl! Tell me, how do you feel about your mother this instant?"

"Umm, maybe a teensy weensy bit more compassionate towards her?"

"Exactly! See what the power of words can do? They can actually change the way you think and feel. Is that cool or what?"

"Definitely cool, Katie. Definitely cool."

"That's what I'm talking about; words can change how you feel. If AdaLayne hears you talking compassionately about your mother, she'll form a more positive image of her, and she'll start talking and thinking positively about her as well."

"Okay, got that. I can see that I'm going to have to start painting AdaLayne a more positive of my mother, and hers. Next topic?" She glanced at Addie, who was holding one of the kids' old books up in front of her face as if she was reading it except that the book was upside down. Watching her, we both smiled.

"Here's another area of example: my devotional life. Do my children see me spending time with God? Time is a precious commodity and how I spend it indicates what's important to me. Do I have a vibrant and grace-filled relationship with God? Does His love permeate my life in ways they can see and experience?"

I waited while she wrote that down and went on.

"Here's another topic: am I being a good example in how I take care of myself?

The Bible tells me my body is the temple of the Holy Spirit *(1 Cor. 3:16)*; am I taking good care of it? Do I dress like a slob, or do I wear clothes that bring glory to God by appropriately showing the figure He gave me? God created women to be beautiful; do I believe that and am I acting that way?

215

"Do I exercise and eat healthy foods? Do I get enough rest? Do I love myself and consider myself worth spending time on? God tells us we are to love others *as we love ourselves (Matt. 22:39).* If we don't love ourselves, we can't love others very well."

"Wow, that's a lot to get out of taking care of myself."

"I know, but do you see how loving yourself leads to loving others? I notice you put yourself down a good deal; it doesn't sound like you love yourself when you do that. Honestly, when we dislike ourselves our attention is turned inward, focusing on ourselves, but when we love ourselves and feel loved by God, we can reach out to those around us. The love just spills over. If Addie sees you loving yourself in a healthy way, she'll be better able to love herself."

"Hmm, good point. I'll really have to think about that one. Anything else?"

"Just one more and then we'll stop. What about my willingness to forgive others? Do my children see me making the effort to forgive when I've been wronged, or is my side of the story—sometimes angry, sometimes inaccurate, but always one-sided—all they hear? Do I exhibit a quiet and gentle spirit? For the Bible say that **a *'gentle and quiet spirit . . .is very precious in the sight of God'* (1 Peter 3:4).** Do I make a consistent effort to make that my *modus operandi?*"

"I don't know what kind of *operandi* you mean. All I know is that I'm starting to feel a little overwhelmed. I think we'd best stop before I totally give up." She snapped her notebook shut.

"Fair enough. And remember, these are all lifetime goals. Nobody's going to reach them all perfectly. They're sign posts, pointing the way we should go, not things to beat ourselves over the head with!"

"And you'll love me even if I never attain any of them?"

"You know I will, girl. And so will God. Always."

"I'm glad to get that settled!"

She threw off the blanket and got up. Folding it up and laying it over the back of the couch, she said, "Come on, Addie girl, we've got to get going. Mommy needs to put away your toys."

CHAPTER 20

Example, the last Leg of the Stool

Questions for Discussion

§

1) Have you ever thought about how much of an example, both positive and negative, you are to your children? (If you don't have
children, think of the example you set for the people around you,
especially if you're known as a follower of Jesus.)

2) Have you ever noticed the difference words can make in an environment? In a workplace or a home, think of the effect that griping
and negative words have on everyone. Can you change the atmosphere of a place simply by the words you speak?

3) Speaking of words, how do you use the names of Jesus and God?

4) Have you thought about Sunday as a day of rest—even in our day
and culture? How do you spend your Sundays or whatever day of
the week you take for a rest day? (If you take one; many people
don't.) Have you ever thought that your body, your soul, and your
spirit all need recharging on a weekly basis? Have you ever thought
about how amazing it is that we have a God Who cares that we get
enough rest?

5) What is your current attitude and practice of exercising and eating
healthy foods? Is that something you're conscious of or has it
never crossed your radar screen? Does it seem to be too much of
an effort to change current habits?

6) Many of us have come from childhoods of hurt or neglect. How do
(or don't) you live out the commandment to honor your parents?
Have you ever thought about the difference between love being an

emotion, and honor being a decision to act in a certain way? Why is it so important to honor your parents? (Hint: read **Deuteronomy 5:16.**)

7) Discuss the idea of how loving yourself can lead to loving others, and vice versa. How does hating yourself keeps you wrapped up in yourself and unable to love others fully? Likewise, how does loving yourself enable you to love others more fully?

CHAPTER 21

What about Marriage and Divorce?

§

"So, Katie, tell me about divorce, will you?"

"What?" Brushing the flour off my hands from the bread I was kneading and propping the phone between my shoulder and my ear, I leaned my elbows on the counter and tried to clear my head. As usual, after a hiatus of several weeks, Theresa had jumped into the purpose of her call without much introduction.

"What do you mean? Is someone you know getting divorced? By the way, hi, girl. Good to hear your voice. How are you?"

"Oh, Katie, sorry! I want to know the answer about something and I know you'll have it, so I call you without thinking about asking how you are and all that good stuff. You doin' okay?"

"Thanks for asking. Yes, I'm fine; Craig's fine; we're all fine. Now, why did you want to know about divorce?"

"Can I come over? AdaLayne could play and we could talk?"

"Sure, honey. I'm making bread, but I can talk and do that at the same time. Come on over."

Twenty minutes later she was at the door. I'd finished kneading the bread and had just enough time to put two cups of water into the microwave for tea when the doorbell rang.

She swept in and went straight for the kitchen. Setting AdaLayne down on the floor, she pulled a hand-made wooden train from her diaper bag and set it in front of the sturdy baby. Seeing me eyeing it, she explained.

"Jim made it. It's her favorite toy. I have to lug it everywhere. Good thing is, though, it'll keep her quiet for at least half an hour." She smiled down at the chubby baby.

"Perfect. That's actually about all the time I have today anyway. So you want to know about divorce. May I ask why?" I pulled out two stools at the bar and set our cups of tea in front of us, giving her a spoon and the sugar bowl as well.

"Well, it's like this, Katie. If I marry Jim—and notice I said *if*, not *when*—if I marry Jim, I want to know what kind of an escape clause I'll have if things don't work out," she said, hopping up onto a stool. I took the one across from her. She wore sweats and an old tee shirt, her hair pulled up into a messy ponytail, but despite her casual dress, she looked healthy and happy, more so than I'd seen in a long time.

"And what makes you think you'll have an escape clause at all?" I asked, holding the warm cup against my cheek and letting the tension drain out of my shoulders.

"Well, 'cause there's always divorce if things really get bad, but I just wanted to know what you thought of it. Have you and Craig ever talked about it? Have things ever gotten bad between the two of you?"

"Well, now that you mention it, yes. We've had our bad spells. I think most people do, somewhere along the line."

"So did you ever consider divorce?" She asked without looking up as she stirred her normal four spoonfuls of sugar into her tea.

"Actually, no."

"Never?" she looked up at me, her spoon in midair. "Jeesh, Katie, what are you, a saint or something? Everybody I know, if they haven't been divorced, has at least talked about it. What's up with you?" She stared at me, incredulous.

"When we got married, we figured we'd made a promise before God for keeps, until we die. So we closed the door to divorce from the get-go. It's not even an option for us. When things get bad, we *have* to work them out." I answered, looking at her levelly. She ducked her head.

"So what are you supposed to do if things *don't* work out, and you have to get out of the marriage? Don't you need some back door to escape from?" she asked in a small voice.

"Let me take those questions one at a time," I said, stirring my tea, thinking.

God, I need your wisdom here!

You've got it. Always.

"You say, 'if things don't work out' as if 'things' had a mind of their own. 'Things' as you say, don't just work or not work. We have to work *at* them. To make a marriage work, you have to put your time— one of the things we're the most selfish with—and your effort into it. You have to be completely committed to making it work, whatever it takes.

"Love changes over time, and the *feelings* of love may come and go, depending on what's going on in your lives at the time. Exhaustion, stress, worry, not apologizing when you're wrong and not forgiving when the other person's wrong, looking to other relationships for satisfaction—all these things can destroy the *feelings* of love. Our emotions are fickle and unreliable and you can't base a marriage on them alone."

"I forgot to bring my notebook, but I'm going to have to remember this stuff. Nobody ever told me anything like this before," she said, staring at me intently, absently swirling her tea in her cup. Addie sat at our feet, playing quietly with her train, putting little wooden people in the cars and taking them out again.

"What holds a marriage together over the decades is the commitment to see it through to the end in such a way that you're both happy. Marriage is sacred and worth fighting to preserve." I sipped my tea thoughtfully, looking at her, hoping she'd get what I was saying.

"Sacred? How? I thought it was just a relationship between two people for as long as they feel like they love each other."

"It's sacred, Theresa, because it's a commitment made before God. Actually, it's His idea in the first place, which is what makes it sacred. It's a solemn vow we take before God with our family and friends as our witnesses and as such, should never be broken. It's a holy, three-way partnership with us, God, and the spouse we've committed ourselves to."

"Wow. You make it sound like a whole lot more than I ever thought it was." Resting her elbows on the counter, she held her chin in her hands, looking at me.

"I know. Many people don't get the sacred part of it, the part that originates with God. In the Bible, Jesus is often referred to as the Bridegroom and the Church as His bride, so marriage is sacred because it's a picture of the marriage between Jesus and His Church."

"Well, as usual, you're broadening my thinking. So marriage is bigger than just the two of us living together as long as things go well? It's kind of like a holy place we enter into?" Staring at me, she leaned her cheek on her hand and crossed her legs, jiggling her foot up and down.

"That's an excellent way to put it. Kind of like a holy place we step into. I wish more people had that concept."

"But how do you stay there? I mean, what if it gets miserable in that holy place?" The pace of the jiggling increased.

Addie held up one of the train cars full of little people to show her, and Theresa blew her a kiss. "I see it, baby. Now play like a good girl."

"Well, before you step in, as you say, knowing a few truths about marriage will help you count the cost before you say 'I do'."

I sipped my tea thoughtfully.

Lord, I need a crash course here. What's the most important thing I can tell her?

Intimacy. Into me see.

"Okay," I said, setting down my tea, still too hot to even sip. I propped my elbows on the counter and continued, "here's the most important thing I can think of to tell you about marriage.

"I've heard the word 'intimacy' defined as 'into-me-see'. In other words, intimacy is letting another person see into your most vulnerable mind and heart, the deepest parts of your spirit, and your naked body. It's this privilege of knowing another person intimately that husbands and wives give each other when they get married; a gift for the other person and no one else. That's why adultery is so devastating; it's allowing a third person to enter a space once reserved for two people and no others."

"Kind of like a part of my heart is for AdaLayne? Nobody else can have that part of my heart, 'cause it's just for her?"

"Exactly. So, giving a man other than your husband access to the private parts of your body, the deepest parts of your spirit, or the most vulnerable parts of your mind will be off limits as long as you're married. Unburdening your heart and your deepest emotions to another man opens the door to trouble. I can't tell you how many affairs start because intimate confidences, hurts or passions have been shared between two people of the opposite sex who are married to someone else. Emotional adultery can be just as devastating as physical adultery and one often leads to the other."

I leaned forward across the counter, looking right into her face.

"Please understand what I am saying, and what I am *not* saying. I am *not* saying that a male doctor can never examine you or that you can never go to a male counselor. I am *not* saying that men and women can never work side by side and be excited about what they are working on together. Those are professional roles, with safeguards in place to protect both of you. I'm not even saying that you can never have male friends. What I am referring to is contact that goes beyond professional limits; contact that is private, unsupervised, and has no safeguards in place."

"Give me some examples of what you mean. I haven't had too many healthy friendships with men, if you recall," she said, glancing down at Addie and back at me.

I took a sip of my tea.

"Okay, here are two examples, one good and one bad. The good one is Craig's work situation. He works with an office full of women, and as the boss, he's the only man. That could be a situation ripe for disaster, except for the fact that Craig and all the women there clearly understand the boundaries. His office door has a window, so no matter who is in there with him, the meeting is clearly visible to anyone else in the office. He never rides alone in a car alone with any woman other than me, nor does he go out to lunch with one female co-worker at a time. They all know he's happily married to me and I know all of them. Within those boundaries, they can all tease and laugh and work together without worrying. And I don't worry."

"And the other example?" Theresa wanted to know, pulling a strand of hair out of her ponytail and flicking it back and forth against her cheek, still watching me.

"The other example's a little embarrassing, since it's about me. Several years ago, Craig and I were having a rough time in our marriage. He was extraordinarily busy at work and I was busy with home school and the kids, so neither of us had much time for each other. It's easy when you're both busy like that for hurts and miscommunications to pile up without talking about them and working them out. In addition, my parents had divorced and my dad had recently remarried, which I was still pretty upset about. I felt lonely and sad; distant from and neglected by both my husband and my dad."

I sighed, remembering. Talking about it still brought back painful memories.

"In the midst of this mess, with me in a needy and vulnerable state, I got a part-time job offer from a friend, asking me if I would write a monthly newsletter for his company. He knew I was a good writer, he said, and was sure I'd do a good job. Feeling low in general and pretty unappreciated at home, I was flattered by his confidence and without really checking it out with Craig, I accepted. After all, he was a good family friend. What harm could it do?"

I looked away, remembering that painful period of my life. Theresa's eyes locked onto me like a cat stalking a nest of baby mice. I squirmed on my stool, looking anywhere but at her.

Is it hot in here, or am I having a hot flash?

"So go on; don't leave me hanging," she demanded. "What happened?"

"I was a good writer, but my computer skills were sadly lacking, so he had to teach me. The best time for us both to work on this was the evening and we spent a good deal of time together, sometimes late at night, working on the newsletter. Craig was not at all happy about the situation, but he and I weren't really talking about it. But then I began having dreams about me and this man—nothing indecent—just dreams about the kind of tender love that I was so lacking at home during that the time."

It is definitely *hot in here.*

I ran my finger around my collar at the back of my neck.

"You? Can't imagine it." Theresa murmured, almost mesmerized.

"Yup. Me. Late one evening," I went on in a rush, wanting to get this over with, "we were printing our first run of the newsletters. The first one came out of the copier looking terrific—better than we expected. Spontaneously, out of joy over a job well done, I threw my arms around my friend's neck and gave him a hug.

"That was it. I suddenly knew this relationship was getting more intimate than God—or I— intended, and that we were about to cross a dangerous line. It scared me when I realized how gradually it had happened and how needy for this man's approval I was. In tears of shame, I told Craig about it later that night and the next day I resigned as editor of the newsletter. Needless to say, our friendship with that man came to a end," I finished in a rush.

"So, can you see how meeting in a private and unsupervised place with no safeguards to protect you can lead you into a heap of trouble?" I asked her, meeting her eyes at last.

"Yeah, I am seeing that. Never really thought about it before. . ." She nodded thoughtfully, looking off into the distance.

"So, Theresa, once you get married *your heart is off limits to any other man,* and you need to protect it. It's your husband's territory and no one else's. You don't invite other men in there. The same goes for your body. For example, I never kiss any man but my husband, and except for him, I don't kiss anyone on the lips—not even the kids. Any time I hug a male friend it's warm but brief. To other men, I give the message that I am no longer in circulation; I belong to Craig and no one else."

"So I have to say good-by to flirting with other men if I want to get married, huh?"

"Yup. That's not to say you can't tease and have fun, but you can't give out that unspoken message of 'I'm available' any longer."

"Hmmm," she turned away from me on her stool, glancing down at AdaLayne but not seeing her, pursing her lips and thinking.

"I'll have to think about this. I think I'm beginning to see what you mean. It is a big commitment, isn't it?"

"Probably the biggest you'll ever make, aside from following Jesus.

"And here's another major thing: once you get married your spouse's needs are just as important as yours, sometimes more so. It's often said that marriage is a fifty-fifty deal, with each person giving half, but I say, in order to make a marriage work well, each person needs to give 100 percent to serving the other, caring for the other, taking the other's needs into consideration."

"Sounds like a lot of work to me."

"It is, but it's worth it since you love the other person. Look for ways to keep that love alive: respecting, communicating with, blessing, and serving your spouse. Keep working at it; keep forgiving and repenting; keep spending time together; keep having fun! Ignoring your marriage will cause it to die just as surely as any living thing will die without care, food and water."

225

"So you have to keep in mind that you're married? Don't just forget about it and go on with your life as if it didn't matter?" She swirled the remains of her tepid tea in her cup, looking thoughtfully down into it and then up at me.

"That's exactly it, Theresa. It seems like some people just go on living as if they weren't building a relationship meant to last decades and affect generations to come. Because don't forget, your marriage doesn't affect just you; it affects your whole family for generations."

"Wow. That's a lot to live up to. What about people who are already divorced? Have they just blown it?"

"I'm not here to judge anyone who's been divorced. Many divorces happen out of ignorance about the very things you and I are talking about. I've heard more than one person say, 'I have no idea why we got divorced. We just did.'

"And then there are people suffering from abuse or infidelity, which is the one thing that Jesus mentions as an acceptable reason for divorce."

I pulled down my Bible from the shelf above the counter and opened it to the New Testament.

"Look with me here in **Matthew 5:32**, Theresa. Jesus is teaching the people about what God thinks of marriage and divorce. Remember, they've never heard most of this stuff before."

"I can relate there," she murmured, still swirling the sugary tea syrup at the bottom of her cup.

"Jesus says, *'But I say to you that whoever divorces his wife for any reason except sexual immorality causes her to commit adultery; and whoever marries a woman who is divorced commits adultery.'*"

"So Jesus says sexual immorality is the only grounds for divorce?" she asked, looking up at me. "You can't divorce your husband if you, say, just don't love him any more? What about people who have just grown apart? Or those who have irreconcilable differences? Or people who find out that they don't like each other? What about all those people?"

"Theresa, all I can do is to point you to the Bible and what Jesus says. He says that the only legitimate ground for divorce is unfaithfulness; cheating on your spouse. Anything other than that the Bible calls adultery. God doesn't totally *forbid* divorce, but He says that He hates it, because it brings violence into the hearts and emotions of those experiencing it, and because God's plan for marriage is that the man and wife join together and raise up godly offspring *(Mal. 2:14-16)*. That's not to say that divorced people can't raise godly children, but divorce sure adds a lot of complications.

"And now, flip over here to *Ephesians* where Paul discusses marriage *(5:31-32)*. First, he explains that a man needs to leave his father and mother when he is joined to his wife in marriage, and the two shall become one flesh—intimately, inextricably joined. Then he says that the mystery of marriage is profound because it refers to the marriage between Christ and the Church; a relationship of laying down one's life for the other."

"Wow. . .that's a pretty tall order! Laying down my life for another person. . .that sounds pretty heavy to me. I'm not sure I'm up to all that."

"Well, you're right. It is heavy. But, if you think about it, you're doing it already for AdaLayne. And you do it 'cause you love her, right? It's the same with marriage. God never asks us to love solely in our own strength, but He sent His Spirit to fill us with His love for the other person."

"But what about when I fail?!" She wailed, leaning her elbows on the counter and her head in her hands. "'Cuz you know I will, don't you?"

AdaLayne looked up, alarmed and whimpering at the sound of her mother's wail. Theresa turned her head, still in her hands, and said, "It's okay, baby. Mommy's okay. You can play."

"Of course you'll fail. I fail too. So does Craig. So does everybody. That's why it's so important to repent and forgive each other. Forgiveness and repentance are the tools God's given us to dig ourselves out of the messes we make when we fail."

"Once again, I'm getting the impression that this whole thing is bigger than just what makes me feel good," she said, letting her shoulder sag and looking at me bleakly.

"You're right; it is. And so many times people use just feeling good as the guide for their behavior, almost as if they were saying to themselves, 'This is fun and it makes me feel good, so I'll embrace it. But over here, this is hard and discouraging so I'll discard it.' Marriage doesn't make you feel good all the time; in fact—like any time we love another person—it has its share of heartbreaks. Not everything we encounter as we follow Jesus is going to be fun or make us feel happy. The standard we need to use for our marriages is not our feelings but what God says in the Bible: *'What God has joined together, let not man separate* **(Matt. 19:6)**.'"

"You always get back to the Bible. Any subject I ask you about, it's always, 'What does the Bible say?' Don't you ever look elsewhere for advice?" She crossed her arms again, staring at me and jiggling her foot up and down.

"Sure. As long as that source doesn't contradict God's Holy Scriptures. There are plenty of excellent Bible teachers, and lots of books that teach us how to follow Jesus in our daily lives. But the Scriptures are God's love letter to us, His instruction book, His guide to living life, since—in case you haven't notice—it doesn't come naturally to live life His way."

"Hmmm," she twirled around on her stool, and gazed thoughtfully at Addie, who was now trying to stack her wooden people into a tower. She could get two stacked up, but the tower always collapsed with the addition of a third person. "I'll have to think about all this. Most of it I've never heard before."

"Think all you want," I said, hopping off my stool and collecting both cups, "and I'll be happy to talk about it more with you anytime. But for now, the twins'll be home in a minute, so I need to stop. I just want to say one more thing before I scare you off from marriage altogether. It's worth it, Theresa. There's nothing better than finding a man who will love, cherish, and take care of you. Yes, marriage is a lot of work, but knowing that there's someone in the universe who loves you with all his heart, and whose heart is yours alone, makes it all worth it. Go out and find that man, girl."

"Oh jeesh, Katie! Now you've got me all scared."

I wrapped her in a quick bear hug and kissed the top of her head.

"Don't worry. God'll be with you every step of the way. Just ask Him. I love you. Now get along with you, I've got to punch this bread down and start supper."

She gathered AdaLayne and the train and whooshed out of the house. I'd never noticed before how much energy she took with her as she left. I ran my fingers through my hair and watched her out the window as she strapped the baby into the car seat, hopped in and took off.

CHAPTER 21

What about Marriage and Divorce?

Questions for Discussion

§

1) How do you regard marriage? Do you see it as "a holy place we step into" as Theresa said, or as something two people do together as long as it's fun, or as something in between?

2) What do you think about what Katie said about how she and Craig decided in the beginning of their marriage that divorce wasn't going to be an option? How does a decision like that affect a husband and a wife when things get tough?

3) Have you ever thought of marriage painting a picture of the relationship between Jesus and His church?

4) If you are married, or considering it, did anyone talk to you ahead of time about counting the cost of marriage and the necessity of closing off access to your innermost heart, spirit, and body to all other members of the opposite sex besides your spouse? If not, do you wish someone had? What is the danger of not closing off these parts of your self? (This is not to say that we can't have deep friendships with members of the opposite sex; there are just places that are privy to a marriage partner alone.)

5) Why is this exclusivity so important? Does it seem to be important in today's culture?

6) What are some of the strains on a marriage that can lead to divorce? Can we do anything about them?

7) Discuss the fact that, by some estimates, divorce is just as rampant in the church as out of it. Is there anything, to your knowledge, that can change these statistics, at least in your own life, and hopefully the lives of your children?

CHAPTER 22

Appreciating Our Husband's Competence

§

I called Theresa a few days later.

"Just wanted to follow up on some of the things I said to you the other day. How're you doing and how's the baby? Got time for a quick phone chat?"

"Yep, about twenty minutes before I need to start getting ready for work. What's up? I took notes on all that stuff and I've been thinking about it. It sure is a whole new slant on the marriage bit."

"Good, I'm glad you're thinking about it. Sometimes it takes us a while to re-program ourselves, especially if we haven't had the best start in the world. But I wanted to add some stuff for you to think about."

"Fire away. I've got my pencil and paper out."

"Okay, here's what I've been thinking. I said to you that it doesn't always matter how you *feel* in a marriage; you shouldn't go by emotions alone but by your commitment to your marriage and to the word of God. Here's what I want to add. You *should* be paying attention to how your husband feels. You'd be amazed at how easy it is for women to put their husbands down and not even know it. We can belittle our men, make fun of their faults, and make them feel like they're always messing up; in general we can make them feel pretty bad about themselves. And half the time we don't even realize it! It's just the way we talk. We've discussed the power of our words before, remember?"

"Yeah, I do. And I've been noticing it more lately, too. Of course I never heard my mother say anything good about my fa—woops! Sorry. There I go with the negative talk again! I listen to the girls at work, and they're always putting their husbands down, like they're the dumbest things that ever lived. And it's always a big joke."

"Exactly. You hear that kind of talk a lot. Somehow, it's always the woman who is portrayed as the smart, together one, and the man is the doofus, the jerk. There's often little or no respect for him as a husband or as a man. This is a subtle message that permeates our society; you'll even see it in some of our kids' books. Start noticing as you read to AdaLayne how the father is portrayed in modern books pretty much as if he were one of the kids. This is a far cry from the way fathers were portrayed a few generations ago, not to mention how the Bible speaks of men and fathers.

"I even caught an example of this kind of belittling of dad in a radio drama broadcast by a well-know Christian ministry that I admire. In this dramatization, as the family was getting ready to leave on vacation it was the mother who was organized, competent, and ready and it was the father who was trying, but failing each time, to fix the engine or pack the car. He was the dumbo; the incompetent one.

"So, this is what I wanted to tell you. A friend lent me a CD of a sermon by a preacher named Andy Stanley the other day. It was a mother's day message, I think, and he was telling wives about how to build their men up and not tear them down. He said that men are naturally drawn to the person or situation where they feel the most successful and competent. He said it's a strong pull that most men—as well as their wives—are unaware of, but it's the reason so many men take refuge in work or hunting or sports or even other women. They feel capable and appreciated in those situations or with those people."

"So don't put your guy down, huh? Is that it?"

"Yeah, but it's more than just that. It's also deliberately building him up; letting him know you admire him; letting him know that you trust him to care of the family. It's all part of acknowledging his competence and making him feel like a respected man at home. That kind of appreciation will go a long way toward making him *want* to spend time at home and with you.

"I know I have a constant voice inside my head telling me I'm no good, that I'll never make it and I'm sure men have that same nasty little voice in their heads. It comes from Satan, after all, and he is no respecter of persons. The last thing I want to do as Craig's wife is to add my critical voice to Satan's!"

Propping the phone next to my ear with my shoulder, I opened the drawer beneath the counter, and pulling out a pad of paper, began doodling as I spoke. I drew a picture of a little devil with horns and a pitchfork tail and a megaphone. Then I drew a little man with huge ears and a downcast face. Lastly, a heart appeared, trampled under the sharp feet of the devil. I smiled to myself at my artwork. But where was the woman?

I continued talking to Theresa.

"You know, so often we women want to fix whatever we think is wrong—including our husbands if we're not careful. We want to fix their eating habits, how often they exercise, what they watch on TV, how they should put away their clothes, how they should be the spiritual leaders of the home. We're pretty sure we have all the right answers to these problems—which our husbands may not even see as problems, by the way—and we're *sure* they're just waiting to hear our solutions! The thing is, most of the time, they don't want our solutions. They want to figure it out themselves. Ever tried to tell a man to ask for directions when you're in the car and you're lost?"

"I don't generally drive around with men in my car, Katie."

"Sorry, you're right. Anyway, it's kind of funny to watch a man drive and drive and not be willing to ask directions just to save his pride. It illustrates the principle I'm talking about: men don't like to feel incompetent. In general, I think, they want to make their own way, figure things out on their own, and most of the time, they sure don't want their wives' unsolicited help!"

"So what should I do on the off chance I'm ever in a car with a man who won't ask for directions, and we're lost? I do have a good sense of direction; do I just sit there?"

"Well, think about it for a minute. If you have a good sense of direction and he obviously doesn't, how do you think it's going to make him feel if you jump in and tell him where to turn and how to get where you're going?"

"Pretty dumb. But what if he *is* being dumb? Or what if he *is* just plain incompetent? What do I do then? Play the little dumb female? No way!"

I could just see her tossing her head and sticking her chin in the air.

"Take it easy, girl. All I'm saying is that men are not attracted to people or situations where they feel incompetent. I think this is probably true of us women, too, if you think about it. Nobody likes to feel stupid. So if you care about how your man feels you won't make him feel stupid. Do whatever it takes, but don't make him feel foolish. Men are built to conquer, to create, to provide and to protect, and feeling foolish tears all those things down and makes them feel insignificant and small. So, on the off chance you should be riding around in a car with a man who is obviously lost, think of ways to encourage him that don't make him—or you, for that matter—sure that you think you can find your way better than he can."

"Something like, 'I know you'll find our way. I've got all the time in the world and I just like being with you, so take your time.'?"

"That's a great line. I'll have to remember it for the next time I'm out with Craig and we're lost. Because between you and me, I do have the better sense of direction of the two of us. But I'd never tell him that."

A woman stick figure appeared in my doodle. She had a big head and a wide-open mouth and she was pointing right at the man with her stick forefinger.

"Well, this seems to be just another way that we women are told to put ourselves down so that men can be lifted up. What's the deal here? Why do we always have to be the ones that are put down?" I could hear the frustration in her voice, a sound I could identify with all too well.

"Because it goes both ways. You're not putting yourself down so much as building him up. If you have the kind of marriage where you each want to bless the other person, you'll both look for ways to build the other up. It's not that one always gets the raw end of the deal; it's more that each one honors the other so that you both feel loved and appreciated.

"That's why I wanted to call you about this, since I had said the other day that how you *feel* isn't always as important as the commitment you've made. That may be true, but how you make your *spouse* feel is very important; it can make or break your marriage, in fact."

"Yeah, like I'm even married. Or about to be. I don't know if it will ever happen. Or if I even want it to."

"Anytime you want to talk about all that, just give me a call. For now, I've got to run. Love you, girl."

I hung up the cordless and stood there for a minute looking out the window. The field behind our house was once again covered with those tiny purple flowers that up close were just weeds, but all together created a royal covering bursting with beauty and vibrancy.

So beautiful, Lord. Thank You.

You're welcome, My daughter.

CHAPTER 22

Appreciating our Husband's Competence

Questions for Discussion

§

1) This is an interesting concept that I heard in a sermon by Andy Stanley: the pull of the male desire to be seen as competent. It's true for all of us, actually, not just men. Can you think of examples in your own life where a man has been attracted to a place or person where he feels competent and admired? This is one major cause of divorce.

2) A jilted wife may be appalled at the "other" woman who has stolen her man's heart right out from under her. The abandoned wife may feel that she is far more beautiful, capable or intelligent than this imposter. But often men will say (if they'll talk about it at all) that the mistress or lover "may not be beautiful, but she makes me feel like a prince." Why does that kind of admiration have such a strong draw on men?

3) Infidelity can take many forms. It can be emotional, physical, or spiritual, and is not limited to just being with another woman. If a man feels competent and respected at work, but nagged and belittled at home, where do you think he'll want to spend the majority of his time?

4) Can you think of examples in our popular culture (TV, books, DVDs, etc), in which the father is put down and made to look foolish, while the mother runs the family ever so capably? What message is this giving to little boys and girls?

5) There's a popular little saying (usually said by wives), "I have four children—my husband and my three kids". We laugh, but what is

this remark really saying? (Is it any better when the husband says it?)

6) Think back a generation or two. Has this belittling attitude always been around? How have men been portrayed in books and stories from the 1950's back? (Think of Pa in the Little House series, by Laura Ingalls Wilder.) Who or what do you think is responsible for it?

7) Discuss ways in which you can show respect and admiration to the man in your life. (It may take a conscious effort!)

CHAPTER 23

What Is Submission?

§

Near the end of May, I called Theresa. I'd been thinking about the things we'd last discussed, and I wondered how she was incorporating them into her life.

"Theresa, how're things going? You and Jim doing okay? Haven't heard from you in a while."

"Oh, Katie, I'm sorry I haven't called! Jim and I've been kind of stuck since we last talked, like we don't know where to go from here. We want this relationship to succeed, but we don't know what step to take next. Think you and Craig might have time to talk to the two of us sometime, maybe over pizza? We'll treat. I think Jim would really like to hear a man's perspective."

"Sure. The kids can watch themselves these days, so I don't need to worry about getting a sitter. What night works for you?"

"Tuesday night okay? That's my only night off."

"Let me check," I glanced at the calendar on the kitchen wall. "Ummm. . .yeah, next Tuesday's clear for both of us."

"Can we meet at the Red Hot Pizza Kitchen, say, about six?"

"We'll be there. Bring your notebook and pen and your Bible. I look forward to it."

"Thanks, Katie. See you then."

*　　*　　*　　*　　*　　*

We ordered a large supreme pizza and four salads. Jim and Theresa arrived a few minutes later and slid into the booth across from us, Jim on the outside. He crossed his arms and leaned back, looking at both Craig and me. He glanced sideways at Theresa and leaned forward, resting his elbows on the table and holding his chin in his hand. He smoothed his hair and rubbed his nose. He scratched his neck. He leaned back and ran his fingers through his hair. He turned sideways and crossed his legs in the aisle.

I finally laughed.

"You look nervous as a cat, Jim! We don't bite, you know."

"Much." Craig added helpfully.

"Okay, so I'm a little nervous here. I've never done anything like this before. Talk about marriage, I mean."

"If it makes you feel any better, neither have we," Craig said, looking me up and down. "I just met this girl."

"Oh Craig, now you're embarrassing *me!*" I protested, punching him.

"So the great giver of advice on marriage and all things Christian should never be embarrassed?" he asked. He looked at Jim, wide-eyed, and shrugged.

"Okay, enough, you two," Theresa broke in. "You guys can goof off later, but right now I want to pick Craig and Katie's brains about marriage."

Craig leaned forward and held his head in his hands, offering it to Theresa.

"Here it is, pick away. What do you want to know?"

"Katie, c'mon, give me a hand here." Theresa looked plaintively at me. "Aren't we here to discuss marriage and all that stuff?"

"Maybe we should let these guys eat first. Men can always think better when their stomachs are full. Here, Jim, have a piece. Craig? Theresa?"

"Uh, what about praying? You guys do that in public?" Jim's face reddened as he asked, looking at Craig.

"Go for it, man."

"Not here. You do it."

Glancing at me, Craig bowed his head. "Lord Jesus, we thank You for this food and this time to be with Jim and Theresa. Please guide our discussion, and give us Your wisdom. In Your name we pray. Amen. Okay, everybody, dig in."

Around a mouthful of pizza, Jim asked, "So what's the most important thing I need to know about marriage, just in case. . .uh. . . Theresa and I decide to. . . uh. . .?" Turning red, he looked helplessly at my husband.

I looked at Craig, who had just taken a big bite of pizza. I could see vestiges of a grin.

He chewed and swallowed. "The first thing God told Katie and me, before we were married, was not to be yoked to an unbeliever."

"Yeah? What's that mean?"

"Well, at that time, neither of us had any kind of a relationship with God, though Katie was further along that path than I was. I was an atheist, searching for some kind—any kind—of meaning to my life. Then along comes this lovely young woman who was all excited about getting to know Jesus. I admit, I was attracted to her, so I began asking her about her discoveries about God and the Bible and such. Out of curiosity to see what was really in it, we began to read the Bible together. It seemed like every other verse we read was about not being yoked to an unbeliever—not being in a relationship with someone who doesn't want to get to know God—as if God Himself was saying, 'The first thing you need to do is get to know Me, and then We'll see about you two being in a relationship with each other.'"

"Can you give me a Bible verse about that?" Theresa asked, her pen poised.

Craig riffled through the concordance at the back of his Bible. "Here: **2 Corinthians 6:14:** *Do not be unequally yoked together with unbelievers. For what fellowship has righteousness with lawlessness? And what communion has light with darkness?*"

"Knowing God and following what He says in His holy Scriptures has to be step one," I chimed in, "or none of what we'll tell you now or in the future will make any sense. Any advice we give will be based on the Bible, so if you don't see it as the source of all wisdom for your life, we might as well stop here."

"Well, I think we have that point covered," Jim said slowly, looking at Theresa.

"Both of you have confessed to God that you're in need of a Savior and have accepted Jesus' death in place of the one we each deserve?" Craig's eyes rested on Jim and then Theresa and back to Jim.

"I did with Katie a long time ago," Theresa nodded slowly, looking at me.

"Theresa and I talked about this the other day and I asked Jesus to forgive my sins. I told Him that I accepted what He did for me by giving up His life for mine, so I think we're okay on that score," Jim answered, steadily returning Craig's gaze.

"What do you think, then, Katie, shall we bring up that dirty word: *submission*?"

"We'd better tackle it sometime."

Craig jumped in: "Okay, guys, this is how it works. The wife does what the husband says; the husband does what God says, and everybody's happy—end of story. It's a pretty good deal for us guys, Jim." He grinned and leaned back, winking at his counterpart. Jim, not prepared for this sudden shift in mood, lifted a questioning eyebrow at me, not sure what to make of my husband. I knew the feeling.

"Maybe you'd better tell them the second half of the verse. . ." I nudged Craig.

"Grab your bibles and look in **Ephesians 5:22-24**. It's in the New Testament, Jim, right between Galatians and Philippians, just a tiny little book, but, boy, does it pack a whallop! Got it? Here it is: *'Wives submit to your own husbands, as to the Lord.'*

"Sounds pretty good, huh? So, going on; *'For the husband is head of the wife, as also Christ is the head of the church; and He is the Savior of the body. Therefore, just as the church is subject to Christ, so let the wives be to their own husbands in everything.'* And I used to stop there and think I had it made in the shade. She had to submit to me as if I was the Lord. Wow. Not bad for this new little Christ follower."

"But then. . ." I looked at him with eyebrows raised.

"Okay, okay. But then my bubble burst when I read the next verses. Look down in **verse 25**: *'Husbands, love your wives, just as Christ also loved the church and gave Himself for her.'* And further on down, in **verse 28**: *'So husbands ought to love their own wives as their own bodies; he who loves his wife loves himself.'*

"So, I realized that, yes, God wants our wives to love and obey us, but what He asks of us men is even harder; we're to lay down ourselves for our wives. I understand that to mean I'm supposed to be good to her, listen to her, support her, care and provide for her and protect her in every way I can. Kind of a tall order, as it turns out. One that I can't do without God's help, that's for sure."

"I'm not even sure I know what all that means," Jim muttered, resting his chin on his fist, eyes riveted on Craig.

"Well, let me give you a quick run-down on God's order for families, set up for our protection and our marital harmony."

He began sketching on a paper napkin as he spoke.

"God's at the top. Under Him, yet somehow equal, are His son, Jesus, and His Spirit, often referred to as the Holy Spirit. Although Jesus has been with God as part of the Godhead since before creation, He became human and laid down His life here on earth to bridge the gulf between us and the Father that's been caused by our sins. The Spirit is the part of the Godhead that dwells on earth with us now, giving us wisdom, teaching, leading, and guiding us. Got all that?"

He looked from Theresa, who was busily writing all this down, to Jim, who nodded soberly.

"Likewise, there are different roles in the family. The father is the head; the buck stops with him. God created the man to be the woman's protector, providing the strength and covering she needs. The woman, under the man, yet somehow equal, is different; she's softer, more nurturing, more attune to feelings and relationships, the things that make the interior of a family function well. So her role is not the head; but rather, she's the heart of the home. Or, as I'm always telling Katie, if our home is a wheel, she's the hub. Without her, it all falls apart. It's kind of a mystery, because there's equality between husband and wife and at the same time different roles for each one.

"And of course the kids are below both parents in terms of authority. They have to obey either parent, and wise are the parents that provide a united front to their children, since the little buggers learn pretty fast how to divide and conquer."

"Craig!"

"C'mon Katie, you know they can be little buggers. Get real. You can't give these poor people the impression that family life is all peaches and cream, 'cause it sure ain't. Not in our house anyway."

"Well, that's good to know. I was starting to think we had an impossible example to follow." Jim shook his head in relief.

"I could have told you a few stories to ease your mind on that score, Jim. Don't forget that I lived with them for five months," Theresa stage-whispered to him behind her hand.

"So, to put it in a nutshell," Craig continued, ignoring their remarks, "submission works like a see-saw. You lay down your life for her, she loves and obeys you, and the whole thing balances on an even keel— most of the time. Except when she's got PMS."

Unable to protest because I had just taken a bite, I jabbed my elbow into Craig's ribs, smiling sweetly at Jim and Theresa all the while.

"Hang on a sec, I'd like to add one more thing," I said around my mouthful, afraid that if I waited to swallow it, Craig would be on to other topics.

"Look at **Ephesians 5:33**. It says, *'Nevertheless let each one of you in particular so love his own wife as himself, and let the wife see that she respects her husband.'* Note that God is directing the husbands to *love* their wives, which includes tenderness and affection and attention, and is telling the wives to *respect* their husbands, which includes admiration, appreciation and affection."

"Commonly known as sex," Craig helpfully added.

"Yeah, but you guys need more than just sex. You need our admiration, our affection, and our appreciation of who you are as males. You need to be appreciated as men, not just oversized women."

"Huh?"

"Come again?"

Obviously, I'd lost both men.

"In our current culture, there's a huge pressure to blur the sexes. Boys and girls are taught there's no difference—except biological— between the sexes. They dress pretty much alike; they're taught they can have identical careers and anyone who teaches otherwise is politically incorrect. While some of this is important—women have been underrated way too long—I think we've taken it too far when men are supposed to be like women and women like men. God made us different for a reason, and He wants us to enjoy and appreciate the differences, not blur them.

"Men need to be appreciated as *men*, and not just as another species of woman. They need to be admired for the work they do, for the way they protect and provide for their families, for their strength, for their masculinity, and for their position in God's sight.

"They need the room to be *men*; maybe bold or loud or sometimes a little crass, not always worried about the things that we women think are important, like clean floors and good manners. In short, they need our respect to be the men God created them to be. And in turn, we women need to be appreciated as *women*, with all our emotions, our intuitions, our needs for tender love, understanding, and encouragement.

"The couple that gets a handle on this truth—that we both need love, but that love looks different for each gender—is a long way ahead in having a successful marriage," I finished, looking first at Craig and then at Jim and Theresa.

"Well, whaddya know?" Craig said, turning his body to look full at me, shaking his head in wonder. "That's quite an insight."

"Yeah, and I wish I could remember it all the time. It's too easy to fall back into my default mode, thinking you and I think and feel the same way when we don't. I think and feel like a woman and you, foreign creature, think and feel like a man."

"*I'm* not the foreign creature! You know, Jim, there are times when I don't understand this wife God gave me. Sometimes I think she might as well be from another planet. We're that different."

"Yeah, and I think God made us that way so we'd have to work at loving and understanding each other. Otherwise, it might be too easy." I winked at Theresa. "But seriously, I have had to work at it. Take submission, for example. Craig doesn't always do things the way I do and once in a while I've just had to swallow that fact and go along with it."

"What are you getting at, honey? You mean you haven't always wholeheartedly embraced my enlightened leadership? I think they're as confused as I am here."

My husband looked at me, innocent and wide-eyed, incredulous.

"Take family devotions, for example." I looked at Theresa, pointedly ignoring the creature at my side. "I always believed we had to have at least twenty minutes of prayer and Bible reading with the kids before school, praying for a different area each day—government, church, our extended family, crises in the news—you get the idea."

"Man, was that ever a hassle!" Craig broke in. "We're trying to get six kids out the door for school, and she wants us to pray these lengthy prayers for things the kids hardly even understood, much less cared about. I didn't care much either, not at that time of day, anyway. It never worked, but I gotta hand it to her—she kept trying!"

"Yeah, I did, getting more and more frustrated, until one day I got so exasperated that I finally exploded at Craig and asked him why he wasn't cooperating with my efforts to train our children spiritually? He calmly told me he taught the children godly truths when they needed them, like it says in the Bible, when you're out walking, or sitting in your house, or whenever the occasion arises. Check it out in **Deuteronomy 6:7**, Theresa.

"Of course it's more helpful to explain God's truths to children when they need them and can understand them instead of forcing them to sit still and pray each morning just because I say it's time. Once I cooled down, I could see that his way really did work better than mine.

"So that was an area where I learned to submit to my husband and his way of doing things," I ended, holding my hands palms up in resignation.

Theresa pushed away her plate and leaned back, staring at Craig and me. "Okay, so what if the husband doesn't want to be the leader? Or what if the wife is better at it? What then? I mean, I think I'm further along the path of following Christ than you are Jim, no offense, so shouldn't I be the one to lead us spiritually?"

"Excellent question, Theresa, and one that a lot of people struggle with, including Katie and me, obviously. Look with me at **Genesis 3:16** for a clue to the answer."

He riffled through his Bible and waited while they found the place before continuing.

"After the fall, God cursed Adam and Eve, saying to Eve, *'Your desire shall be for your husband, And he shall rule over you.'*

"Now, flip over to the next chapter, **verse seven**, and you'll see the only other place in the Bible where that version of the word *desire* is used. God is rebuking Cain for bringing an unacceptable sacrifice, and he says, *'Cain, sin lies at the door. And its desire is for you, but you should rule over it.'* I looked it up in the concordance once: the word *desire* there means 'stretching out after; a longing.' *(Strong's Exhaustive Concordance of the Bible; Riverside Book and Bible House.)* God is telling Cain that sin is longing for him, almost like fingers reaching out to him, longing to reach him. He must master sin and not let it rule over him."

He glanced up at his audience to make sure they followed him.

"So part of the curse is that Eve will feel that longing to rule her husband, in the same sense that sin longs to rule us. Yet God makes it very clear that the husband, with Christ-like love, shall overrule his wife's longing to run the show when He says '*And he* [your husband] *shall rule over you'* (Gen 3:16). He makes it very clear that the husband shall be the one who rules over his wife. But, keep in mind—I can see your hackles rising, ladies—the husband is to rule like Jesus did, as a servant-leader, willing to lay down his life for his bride."

"Couldn't longing in that context refer to sexual or emotional longing? That makes a whole lot more sense to me," protested Theresa.

"I know what you mean, but then why would it be part of the curse? I don't think there's anything sinful about god-given emotional or sexual longing. Why would God have used the same word—that's never used again in the whole Bible—for both situations, if He didn't want to connect the idea of longing for control with the idea of sin?"

"I'll have to think about it," Theresa said doubtfully, frowning.

"The point I get from all this," I broke in, "is that even though the woman may long to take over—since she's sure, in her heart of hearts, that she could run the show better than her husband—God clearly says that the man should be the head of the house and the woman is to be under his care and protection."

"So," Craig took over, "the man and woman are both supposed to do their part in the marriage, regardless of what the other half does. God never says, 'Wives, if your husband doesn't care to be the spiritual head of the house, you must jump in and do it yourself.' No, instead He tells wives, 'Step back and give your husbands the space they need to be the leaders in their own homes, *even if they aren't doing their part.* Respect them; I made them to be the leaders in their homes.'"

"Wow," Theresa mused. "This isn't going to be easy. . ."

"For either of us," Jim finished her thought.

"That is, of course, *if* we get married."

"Right. *If.*"

"But, guys, here's the good news." Craig went on, leaning forward eagerly. "If we each do our part, fulfilling the role God's given us, God, in turn, does His part and fills in the gaps. As we obey Him, He blesses and takes care of our families." He leaned back, studying Jim and Theresa.

Were they taking all this in?

"One more thing and then I think we'd better stop and let you guys go home and absorb all this." I said, wiping my mouth with my napkin and leaning forward from my corner to make my point.

"If the wife takes over and runs the show, reducing the man to nothing more than a breadwinner, what is that teaching her children about God? Is she teaching them, by her example, that God can be trusted, regardless of the family situation? Or is she showing her children that if her husband won't or can't be the spiritual leader of the home, that it's wise to take matters into her own hands, regardless of what it says in the Bible? As I've told Theresa numerous times, attitudes are more caught than taught, so what attitudes are our children catching from us? Remember that our husbands need our respect in order to feel our love. Are we showing respect if we take over the spiritual leadership in our homes?"

I looked at all present. No comments at the moment, so I went on.

"That's not to say that if the husband is not a believer or has perhaps turned away from a faith he once had, that the wife cannot teach her children to love and honor the Lord—and their dad as well. So much of it rests on her heart attitude, and I think it boils down to this: is she trusting God to take care of her and her children, even in the face of an unbelieving husband or is she determined to take things into her own hands?"

"Okay, Katie. It's time to let these people go home and relax for a bit. The mind can only take in what the seat can absorb." Craig was getting restless: I could tell.

"Can we make another date? You want to, Jim?" Theresa looked eagerly at him.

"After I get a chance to work through all I've heard today, sure. You name it, Craig and Katie; you're busier than we are."

"Yeah, but I'm the one working evenings. The only evening I'm free is Tuesday for this month. How about two weeks from today; same time, same place?" Theresa glanced hopefully at me.

"Sounds good to me," I said, pulling my pocket calendar out of my purse and checking it.

Craig pecked at his BlackBerry, "Yup, me too. And you know, I admire you guys for wanting to educate yourselves like this. When Katie and I got married, we didn't have a clue."

"Neither do we, and that's why we need all the counsel we can get," muttered Jim as he slid out of his seat and held out his hand for Theresa.

CHAPTER 23

What is Submission?

Questions for Discussion

§

1) Is the concept of submission a familiar one to you, or have you never heard of it? If you have heard of it, what images does it conjure up for you? To many people, both men and women, it has a negative connotation of the woman being a doormat. Is this what it means to you? Or does it mean something else? Have you learned anything new about submission from this chapter?

2) Craig tells Jim and Theresa that the order God set up for families—with the man at the head and the woman as his helper, "under the man, yet somehow equal"—is for their protection and harmony. How could this structure provide protection and harmony?

3) What kind of an example of submission do we see in Jesus?

4) Often, as Craig did at first, men stop at the verses about wives submitting to their husbands, as if this were the most important aspect of husband-wife relationships from a Biblical point of view. What is the equally important other half to God's instructions in this department?

5) What do you think of Katie's claim that men and women are completely different, and that men should "be appreciated as men, not just oversized women"? What do you think she meant by that?

6) What about this idea that our culture is trying to "blur the sexes"? Do you think this is happening? In what ways? Should gender roles be interchangeable? Should men and women be required to do the same jobs, because the sexes are equal? Is being capable of

doing the same jobs the same thing as being identical in all ways except biologically?

7) To answer Theresa's question about whether a wife should take over as the spiritual head of the family if the husband won't, Craig reminds her that God told Eve that as part of the curse, *"your desire shall be for your husband,"* and then in the next chapter tells rebellious Cain that *"sin lies at the door. And its desire is for you,"* (**Gen 3:16, 4:7**). In both cases, according to Strong's concordance, *desire* means longing for, or reaching for. Discuss how a woman might (and often does) have a longing to run the show. Does our culture reinforce this concept that women are better able to run the show than men?

CHAPTER 24

The Nagging Wife

§

The next two weeks were awful around our house. I wanted to jump out of my skin; Craig and I couldn't get along; the kids were crabby and I couldn't even find time to read the Bible and have a quiet time with God. Could I really have PMS for two whole weeks? Or was I pregnant...?

*Not now, Lord, **please**! Not another pregnancy...*

One night I walked into the bedroom once again seeing socks, newspapers and a sweatshirt on the floor on Craig's side of the room. His bedside table was overflowing with books and papers and three out of four of his dresser drawers were left halfway open. Craig himself lay on the bed, peacefully listening to the ball game and reading the paper.

Conveniently ignoring the towering pile of books on my own bedside table and the outfits from the previous three days strewn across the chair on my side, I stopped in the doorway, put my hands on my hips and huffed. No response. Fuming, I walked a few steps into the room. He kept on reading, oblivious to both me and the mess on *his* side of the room. I walked up to the bed with lips pinched tight, lifted my eyebrows and glared at him, jerking my head in the direction of the dresser.

Of course he can see it! He's just trying to irritate me by lying there!

When he didn't respond, in the most godly and mature voice I could muster I hissed, "Don't you even *think* about putting your own stuff away? Or am I just the *maid* around here? For your infor-*mation*, we don't *have* a maid around here." At that, I bent down and began throwing all his stuff into a pile.

"Hey, wait a minute! I haven't finished with that paper yet! Don't throw it away!" He rolled off the bed and confronted me, face to face. "What's your problem, girly-girl?"

"Don't call me girly-girl! My *problem* is you not helping out around here! Why can't you ever put away your *own* stuff?! I have to pick up after you all the time. I'm. Sick. Of. It!" I said, slapping the bed with a rolled up newspaper to emphasize each syllable. My voice was rising and the kids could probably hear every word from their bedrooms down the hall, but I couldn't help it nor did I care.

"Now that I'm thinking of it, why don't you ever clean out the garage, either? We've been needing to do that for months now and all you do when you come home from work is just *sit around*!" Boy, was I was on a roll.

"Wow. If Theresa could see you now."

"Oh, shut *up*!" I hissed and stomped out of the room, leaving his stuff in a pile.

I spent the rest of the evening sulking in Theresa's bedroom in the basement, reading old magazines and trying not to think about anything. Especially Craig.

When I dragged myself up the stairs a few hours later, exhausted, all the lights were off and everyone was asleep upstairs. Including Craig.

Wonderful. He could *have waited up for me. He could have been waiting with open arms to tenderly wipe all my irritation away.*

But no. He was snoring.

*   *   *   *   *   *

· For the rest of the week, I was irritated with everyone. For some reason, I just couldn't find my normal equilibrium. Conversations between Craig and me were strained. We were approaching the last weeks of school and I went through the required field trips, permission slips and end-of-year assemblies with robotic precision. I knew our next session with Jim and Theresa was coming up and I felt inadequate to say anything of use to anybody.

Not that I cared.

We got in the car on Thursday night and headed for the pizza joint.

"So," I broke the cool silence, "what are we going to talk about tonight?"

"How about nagging?" Craig asked agreeably. Way too agreeably for my taste.

Not that I cared.

I scrunched over as close as possible to the passenger door and stared resolutely out the window, trying not to dislike my husband intensely.

*   *   *   *   *

"Hi, guys!" Craig slid into the booth across from the two of them. I perched on the edge of the bench, thinking I could slip out and go to the ladies' room if the conversation got too difficult. I had no idea what my husband had in mind tonight.

Not that I cared.

"Hi, Craig. Hi, Katie. Boy, you look awful; is something wrong?" Theresa looked at me, her brow wrinkled with concern.

"Oh, she's fine. It's been a rough week and she's tired. End of school and all that, you know." Craig explained cheerfully.

"Well, no I don't, but I guess I will someday. You sure you're okay, Katie?"

I tried, and failed miserably, to smile at her in thanks for her concern. "I'm fine, honey, thanks," I murmured through lips stretched tight in a flavorless smile.

"Everybody got their notebooks? We're gonna jump right in, and the topic we're discussing is nagging. Husband to wife; wife to husband." Craig was evidently in charge tonight.

Not that I cared.

Would anyone notice if I just shut my eyes and went to sleep?

"Oh jeesh, I don't think I need any teaching on this topic! This is what I grew up with!" Theresa exclaimed.

"No, I mean doing it God's way."

"Oh." Theresa and Jim both settled back and looked at my husband expectantly. They each had a notebook open on the table and Theresa had her hand poised, ready to write.

Not that I cared. At all.

"First, a definition. Nagging is one person's effort to manipulate another person to do what the first person wants, especially in the husband-wife relationship. Call it manipulation if you want. Got that?" He waited for a minute while they both wrote.

I gazed around the restaurant, totally uninterested in anything going on at our table.

"Next; a story. Have you ever heard of Sarah and Abraham in the Bible?" He looked from face to face; they glanced at each other and back to him, shaking their heads.

"Here it is in a nutshell. God told Abraham—one of the first Hebrew patriarchs—that he would have multitudes of descendants, as many as the stars in the sky. It's in **Genesis 15**; look it up if you want.

"The only problem was that Abraham had no kids, and he was no spring chicken. Nor was his wife. In fact, they were both closing in on one hundred years. Yet God had promised him a son from his own body. Sarah actually laughed when she heard about it."

"Can't say as I blame her," Theresa interrupted him.

"Sarah didn't believe God could do what He said He'd do, so she thought she'd take matters into her own hands. She said," here Craig pitched his voice into a quavery falsetto, "'Abraham, honey, I know God told you we'd have a baby, but it's not happening through this old body. So, look, I have an idea. Take my maid—she's a pretty young thing and I'm sure *she's* still fertile—and sleep with her and let her have the baby. Then we'll raise it as our own, and—voila!—God's prophecy will come true! No one will be the wiser.'"

I couldn't help but snicker at his rendition of the ancient Hebrew Sarah, but I pretended to wipe my mouth with my napkin so that no one would hear.

"That's exactly what they did, and nine months later the maid had a baby boy named Ishmael. Jumping into the story at this point, nothing happens for thirteen years, except a lot of strife in the camp. Hagar,

254

the maid, is smug because she has a baby, and Sarah is still resentful because she doesn't."

Craig glanced over at me. I glared back, stony-faced.

What?! I'm listening.

He looked back at Jim and Theresa and continued with his story.

"Finally, God appears to Abraham and tells him that within a year, Sarah will have a baby boy. This is when she laughs, eavesdropping behind the tent door. I mean, think about it: thirteen long years have gone by since God had told them they'd have a baby—and nothing. Year after year. That's 156 monthly disappointments. Nada. Zip. Zero. And then God shows up again and says, 'Okay, now it's time.' I think I would have laughed, too."

Not me. I would have been happy as a clam just the way I was.

Keeping a straight face, I continued gazing at my husband, who, I did have to admit, was doing a great job of explaining all this.

Not that I cared. . .much.

"But it happened just as God said: Sarah had a baby twelve months later. From the time that boy was born, there was nothing but anger and resentment between those two women and their children. Hagar—who, after all, did have the firstborn son—looked down on Sarah as second best, and Sarah—who, after all, did have the son of God's promise—looked down on Hagar as a mere maid. Ishmael, no doubt feeling displaced by this somehow superior child, mocked Isaac and Isaac probably whined and tattled on Ishmael. It got so bad that old Abe finally had to send Hagar and her teenage son away into the wilderness so he could get some peace in the camp."

"Been there, done that," Jim muttered low. Craig glanced his way but continued on without commenting.

"God found them out there, about to die of hunger and thirst, and made a nation from Ishmael and his descendants, what we know today as the Arab nations. The descendants of Sarah's son Isaac became the Jewish people whom God calls His chosen ones. And wouldn't you know? There's still just a little bit of strife between those people today."

Craig dug into the pizza, which had arrived during his narrative, as if that was all that needed to be said on that topic.

I lifted an eyebrow and glanced from Jim to Theresa and back again. They both shrugged and looked blankly back at me

"And that relates to nagging, how?" I asked Craig, turning to look straight at him, hoping to skewer him somehow.

"It's obvious," he explained cheerfully, waving his pizza in the air for emphasis. "Nagging is one person's efforts to manipulate another person to do what the first person wants. In this story, Sarah wanted to have a baby, and even though God had promised that it would come from her and Abraham, she couldn't wait, so she figured she'd take things into her own hands and manipulate Abraham to give her a baby one way or another. And look at the mess she made."

"So you're saying that when I nag you to pick up your socks and papers—heaven forbid I should do a thing like that but on the off chance that I did—it's manipulating you and getting in the way of God's plan? I think, personally, that's a bit of a stretch," I pronounced primly.

"No. I think I see his point," Jim said slowly, talking around a bite of pepperoni and onions.

"Well, please educate the rest of us, 'cause I sure don't see it." I was beginning to regret my snotty tone, but Jim didn't appear to notice.

"Well, I think it's like this: You nag Craig about something, and then it's *you* trying to change him, not God. If God wants Craig to change, He'll tell him. Maybe you should leave Craig alone and let God work on him."

"Yeah, but–" I blustered.

"No buts, Katie. Hear the man out. He may be onto something. Go on, Jim." Craig laid a restraining hand on my arm but I flinched it off.

"Well, I'm no expert in this area, but I'm learning that I can't *make* another person do what I want. I can yell at Theresa 'til I'm blue in the face about not being late, but it doesn't make her change. Maybe if I said it nicely it would help, but nagging sure as heck doesn't get anywhere."

"I've noticed," Theresa remarked drily.

"Maybe you could say that nagging is trying to play God, trying to shape another person to your specifications?" I asked, squirming about the direction this conversation was going.

Craig looked over at me and nodded, lips pursed thoughtfully. "Maybe it would help to revisit God's order for the family. Katie, would you care to tell us how it goes?"

I felt like kicking him under the table, but I knew he'd be sure to ask—ever so innocently—why I was kicking him, and I'd have to explain and no doubt we'd get into what a miserable witch I'd been all week and I did *not* want to go there.

"Be glad to, dear." I answered, giving him a saccharine smile.

In a sing-song voice, I recited: *"'The husband is the head of the wife, as also Christ is the head of the church. . . and gave Himself up for her'* **(Eph. 5:23, 25).** Is that what you meant?"

I knew I was going to get it once we got back in the car, and besides, I was getting the impression that even the Lord was losing patience with my attitude. I decided I'd better *try* to be civil and cooperate with my husband. So I continued, forcing myself to be more pleasant, "And a little further back, it tells wives to submit to their own husbands as to the Lord **(Eph. 5:22).** I guess if I thought about it, I wouldn't nag the Lord to pick up his socks and put away His clothes."

"Now that you put it that way, jeesh, I wouldn't either!" Theresa exclaimed.

"You know the only thing nagging accomplishes?" I said, finally warming up to this conversation.

"Do tell us, Katie." Craig prompted, with a bland smile and innocent eyes.

I wanted to gag—or hit him.

"It just puts me between you and God." I muttered.

"And once I'm there," I blundered on, knowing I was heading for a fall but not being able to stop myself, "you don't want to listen to *me*, but you can't hear God's voice either, so I'm defeating my own purposes. If God wants to deal with you, I'm sure He'd rather do it directly, without me in the way."

"Well," Craig said benignly, folding his arms and gazing straight at me, "That's quite the insight, especially for someone who's had the kind of week you've had."

I still wanted to kick him, but the desire was fading.

Moving on, Craig opened his Bible.

"Okay, now look with me at **Galatians 6:7-10**, guys."

Jim flipped open his Bible and Theresa peered over his shoulder.

"It says here:

'Do not be deceived, God is not mocked; for whatever a man sows, that he will also reap. For he who sows to his flesh will of the

257

flesh reap corruption, but he who sows to the Spirit will of the Spirit reap everlasting life. And let us not grow weary while doing good, for in due season we shall reap if we do not lose heart. Therefore, as we have opportunity, let us do good to all, especially to those who are of the household of faith.'"

Jim looked up. "How does all that relate? You gotta remember, Craig, I'm a brand-new believer. Translate for me, will you?"

"Scripture's very down-to-earth, but you gotta dig beneath the surface. Okay, here's my Craig version. Look at the first line: *'Do not be deceived, God is not mocked.'* In other words, don't think you can pull anything over on God, 'cause you can't. Then it says *'whatever a man sows. . .he will also reap.'* Not too hard to figure that one out; it's 'garbage in, garbage out.' You sow discord, you reap discord. You sow selfishness into your marriage, wanting your own needs met and not caring about the other person's, whining and complaining—well, that's what you're gonna get from the other person in return: more selfishness, more strife. It'll be an escalating mess that only leads to *'corruption'*, as the Bible says, which means death and destruction."

"Been there, done that, have the tee-shirt," muttered Jim. Theresa just stared at Craig, slowly nodding her head.

"But, there's hope. If we *'sow to the Spirit,'* as the Bible says; sowing good deeds of patience, kindness and generosity, (which we can only do by the power of the Holy Spirit), we'll reap a joyful and peaceful life. Now that's a prize worth working for, in my book!"

Theresa was busily taking notes. Jim had abandoned note-taking and was simply following along in his Bible.

"What about the next verse?" he asked, holding his place and looking up.

"It says, *'as we have opportunity, let us do good to all.'* In other words, don't give up doing good to the people around us while we have the chance. In due time you'll reap a good reward. So, while we have the opportunity—in this case, while we have our spouses with us, or our children, or even just other people—do good whenever we can. Keep short accounts. Forgive. Admit you're wrong when you've lost your temper or done some other stupid thing. Spend your time loving those around you, not nagging or criticizing them. Love can blossom and grow in an atmosphere of peace, but it wilts and fades in an atmosphere of carping and whining."

Feeling totally convicted, I began to flip through Proverbs; I knew there was an appropriate verse in there somewhere, if I could just find it. But Craig beat me to the punch and said, "Guys, listen to this from **Proverbs 25:24:** *'It is better to dwell in a corner of a housetop, than in a house shared with a contentious woman.'* Contentious is just a fancy word for nagging. And then flip over to **17:14** where it says, *'The beginning of strife is like releasing water; therefore stop contention before a quarrel starts.'* And then back in **16:24:** *'Pleasant words are like a honey-comb, sweetness to the soul and health to the bones.'* If that isn't straight talk to husbands and wives, I don't know what is," he finished, looking at Jim and Theresa and totally ignoring me.

I slid down a little further down in my seat.

Would anybody notice if I just crawled under the table and snuck away?

God, I am so busted.

I know.

"Guys," I finally blurted, "I've been an absolute *witch* all week. I've been the poster child for nagging; I've actually *enjoyed* nagging Craig. I've wanted to make him over into the kind of husband *I* think would be best—talk about manipulation! Old Sarah and I would have gotten along just fine!"

Craig nodded agreeably, looking from me to Jim and Theresa and back to me again.

Digging my fingernails into my palm, I looked at my husband, asking with all the humility I could muster, "Craig, will you forgive me for nagging you this week, not appreciating the person *you* are, but trying to make you into what *I* want? I've been wrong to treat you that way and I am sorry. Will you please forgive me?"

Ugh! I'd rather eat nails!

Craig kissed his fingertips and brushed them against my burning cheek. "I do, my love."

Red-faced, I looked up at Jim and Theresa, both intently watching us.

Theresa burst out, "Yay! Now I know there's hope for the rest of us! If *you* can blow it and be a bi—'scuse me, a witch—and get forgiven, I guess I can too."

"And if you can forgive so easily like that, Craig, I guess I can too," Jim smiled at Theresa.

"Hey, don't forget, it works both ways, buddy boy. Husbands nag at wives, too." Theresa nudged Jim with her shoulder, looking at him with mock severity.

"Yes, and wives can forgive husbands, too. Or friends, as the case may be."

"Right. Friends. Still just friends."

*   *   *   *   *   *

As we stood in the parking lot a little later saying our good-byes, Jim and Craig became engrossed in conversation so I pulled Theresa aside for a moment. I had just remembered something the Lord had showed me a long time ago and wanted to share it with her.

"You know, when I'm tempted to pray away some of Craig's faults, God reminds me of something He showed me once. I call it 'hands-off praying'."

I clasped my hands behind my back.

"He told me to keep my hands off Craig when I prayed for him so I wouldn't be tempted to pray like this: 'God, please fix Craig here and take off a little there. I wish he wouldn't watch so much TV, Lord. And look at the way he eats; he'll be dead before he's sixty! Can't You persuade him to exercise more, Lord? And God, his spiritual life. . .'

"You get the picture, I'm sure."

"Well, how *are* we supposed to pray for our men, then?" Theresa asked, glancing over at the guys and lowering her voice.

"Start by thanking God for the man you have. Thank God for his good qualities, and focus on them. When you're focused on what a wonderful guy you have, it's hard to get too negative about him. If we look for negative attributes, we'll find them, but it's also true that if we look for positive ones, we'll find those too. Develop an attitude of loyalty toward your man. If you have to, start from scratch and make a list of all the good things about him that you admire. Remember, the Bible tells us to *respect* our men, which means holding them in high honor. We can't respect them if we're always carping to God about their faults."

"Hmmm, good point. Anything else before I go?"

"Pray for him. Pray for him to be blessed, for a blessed man is a happy man. A blessed man has more energy with which to love you. A blessed man can grow spiritually, without us nagging at all. Imagine that!

"My favorite prayer for Craig is for God to give him wisdom and joy. Joy to make his heart glad and give him strength and wisdom for the day in front of him."

"I think I can remember that. Thanks, Katie. Thanks especially for being real with us and showing us your down side tonight. I have a lot more hope about myself now."

"Hey, I love you, girl. If I can't be real with you, well, I might as well give it all up."

"Theresa, we'd better get going," Jim said, coming over and taking her arm, "I've got to get up early in the morning. Same time, same place in two weeks, guys? That work for you?"

I looked to Craig before automatically nodding since I was still a little rusty on working together as a team.

CHAPTER 24

The Nagging Wife

Questions for Discussion

§

1) The title of this chapter is "The Nagging Wife." Are there other people, aside from wives, who nag as well? Are the people who nag at you only members of your family or do outsiders nag at you as well?

2) What do you think of the definition of nagging as explained by Craig? Is it pretty accurate or can you think of a more accurate one?

3) As Craig explained it, nagging is really manipulation, trying to make someone else do what you want them to do. Is this always wrong? Are there times when you need to make someone else do want you want them to do? If there are, are there ways to do this without nagging?

4) Why is nagging a bad thing to do? Why might it harm marriages? Is it harmful to families in general?

5) How does the story of Abraham and Sarah illustrate the concept of nagging, or manipulation? What were the results of Sarah's efforts to make God's promise of an heir come true? When we nag at others to do what we want them to do, what kinds of results do we get, in general?

6) Why would Katie's nagging of Craig get in the way of him hearing from God directly about how he should change?

7) Discuss the difference between nagging and giving someone guidance and direction.

CHAPTER 25

Where Can I Find Wisdom?

§

The next two weeks zoomed past in a blur. End-of-school activities came to a crescendo, ending with Rob's graduation, a houseful of company and a huge graduation party in the backyard that seemed to include most of his senior class and all their friends and families. And, I was sure, it also included every stray cat and dog in the neighborhood. They must have put out an alert or something: free food!

After making mounds of potato salad, piles of cut-up veggies and an enormous cake—and cleaning it all up afterwards, I was exhausted and didn't give our talks with Theresa and Jim a second thought until Craig and I got in the car Tuesday evening.

"I haven't the faintest idea of what to talk about tonight, do you?" I asked as I slid into the passenger seat.

"Don't have a clue. I'm hoping God'll show us something."

"Sounds good to me," I said, putting my head back and promptly falling asleep.

*   *   *   *   *

"We're here, honey. I think we're supposed to talk about wisdom tonight."

"Huh?" I looked at him, trying to force my heavy eyes open.

"Come on in, oh wise woman you. Just follow me."

I followed him, in a stupor.

God, You're gonna have to help us out tonight, 'cause I sure don't have any wisdom to impart.

Jim and Theresa were already there and had ordered the usual: the special with everything on it and four salads. I slid wearily into the booth, grateful ordering was one decision I didn't have to make.

"Well, guys, tonight we're going to tackle the topic of wisdom. How's that for light evening entertainment?" Craig looked expectantly from face to face. Theirs were about as blank as my own. "What's up with all of you tonight? Cat got your tongues?"

"No. It's just been a bad week. I got laid off from my job and have no clue what to do next. I'm bummed out, if you want to know the truth," Theresa answered glumly, her chin in her hands, staring at us.

"I always want to know the truth about what's going on with you. I swear, I'm actually starting to like the two of you. For real." Craig reached across the table and gave Theresa's arm a brief squeeze. She gave him a wan smile, not up for much teasing.

"I don't know where to turn or what to do. I don't know much except waitressing; I don't have many other marketable skills," she sighed.

"So, it looks like tonight's a good night to talk about wisdom and where to get it. You think?"

"Go for it," Theresa said, leaning her cheek on her hand and staring bleakly at us both. Jim just nodded. Craig launched in.

"Well, we can't do much without wisdom. We can't manufacture it ourselves and there's no point in looking for it from the world around us, so we might as well find it in God's Word."

"How did I know you were going to say that?" Theresa said testily.

She pulled a strand of hair out from her messy ponytail and fiddled with it restlessly.

"Because you're wise and you know to turn to the Bible for wisdom. So open your Bibles, everybody, and turn to **James 1:5-8**." While he waited for them to find the spot, he read:

If any of you lacks wisdom, let him ask of God, who gives to all liberally and without reproach, and it will be given to him. But let him ask in faith, with no doubting, for he who doubts is like a wave of the sea driven and tossed by the wind. For let not that man suppose that he will receive anything from the Lord; he is a double-minded man, unstable in all his ways.

The pizza arrived. Craig ignored it but I reached for a piece and sat back and to watch as my husband unfolded God's truths for Jim and Theresa. I'd never known he was so good at this.

"Let's take this verse apart and look at it. Step one, if you need wisdom, go to God. This isn't as obvious as it seems. What do we do first when faced with a challenge, like this job loss, Theresa?"

"Uh, cry?"

"Yeah, and then? What do you do, Jim?"

"Try to figure out what to do next, I guess." He put his arm around Theresa. She leaned slightly against him.

"Exactly. That's what most of us do, especially us men. We try to figure out a solution on our own. If you're like me, you stumble around until you find an answer that looks good to you and you run with it. But God says, 'Hey guys, if you're in a pickle and don't know what to do, come to Me and I'll give you the wisdom you need. I've got an infinite supply and I won't even make you feel dumb for asking for it.'"

"I love your Craig version of the Bible," Theresa murmured as she reached for a piece of pizza.

"Well, it's the only version I know. I'm just trying to make some sense of it in today's English. God goes on to say, 'If you ask for it, you'll get it. It doesn't matter what you've done to get where you are; if you ask for wisdom, I'll give it to you.' That's a promise."

"You mean, here and now, I can ask God what to do about my job? And He'll tell me?" Theresa asked around a mouthful of pepperoni and onions. Tonight she wore her old gray cut off sweatshirt over a tank top and her hair hung limp. Without makeup to cover it, her birthmark stood out on her neck.

"He'll tell you all right; we just have to watch and listen closely. He gives us wisdom however He chooses, just not always with an open door and a well-marked trail, the way we want. Remember, if we ask for wisdom, we get it, even if we don't see it at first. We have to believe God's guiding us—even if we can't see the signposts. Got all that?"

"It'll take time to sink in, but yeah, I get the idea," Jim said, nodding thoughtfully, jotting notes in his notebook. "It's hard to believe I'm getting something I can't grasp with my five senses, but there's a lot in this Christian walk I can't grasp with my five senses. But if God says it, that's a guarantee, huh?" He glanced up at Craig.

"Think about your shop. After you've fixed a car, you give the customer a guarantee, something like: 'If this repair fails in ninety days, we'll fix it for free,' right? You expect your customers to take that on faith, don't you?"

"Yeah, but we usually give them a piece of paper with the guarantee written on it."

"And that's just what God's done," Craig grinned triumphantly. "His guarantee is written in the Bible."

"I sure walked into that one," Jim admitted, smiling, laying down his pen and leaning back. He looked over Theresa's shoulder to see what she was writing, but gave up trying to make out her chicken tracks from where he sat.

"That brings us to the next point," Craig said, pointing with his slice of pizza for emphasis.

"He tells us to ask in faith, because if you doubt, you're like a restless wave: never settled in your mind, always seeking, but never finding *(Jas. 1:6-7)*. A wave washes in and washes out, eating away the shoreline a little at a time just like unbelief nibbles away at the shoreline of our faith until there's nothing left."

To illustrate his point, he swung his pizza back and forth in front of his face in a wave-like motion, taking a nibble each time it passed. Theresa rolled first her eyes back and forth, following it, and then her whole head, mesmerized. She began to giggle.

Mission accomplished. I knew my husband. Dear man.

"We have to settle it in our minds," he said, taking a big chomp of the pizza that was left in his hand, "God is a God of love. He hears our prayers and when He says he'll do something, He'll do it. No second guessing necessary." He popped the remaining corner of his piece into his mouth, and looked at us expectantly.

"When I pray," Theresa said, "I feel like a beggar way down outside God's castle walls, knocking on His big, heavy door, pleading, begging, hoping He can hear me in there. It sure doesn't seem like He's listening, most of the time."

I hear such hurt in her voice, Lord.
I do too.

"That's where faith comes in. We have to wrap our minds and hearts around what God says and practice believing it. If God tells He'll give us wisdom when we ask for it, we have to *assume* we have it, even if we can't see it." Craig propped his elbows on the table and leaned forward, gazing around at all of us to make sure we got his point.

"So if I'm trying to make a decision, say, in the repair shop or something, I can ask for wisdom from God and then just go ahead and make the best decision I know how to make, assuming that since I asked, God is actually guiding me?"

"That's the way I see it, Jim. That's exactly how I practice wisdom in my own life."

"Okay, guys, bring it down to earth for me. How can this help me find another job? I don't want any pie-in-the-sky stuff tonight." Theresa twirled a strand of hair restlessly, staring hard at Craig.

"We're getting there; hang on. Here, have some more pizza; you'll feel better." Craig scooped up a piece, and with a flourish, he laid it on Theresa's plate.

She smiled wanly. "Gee, thanks."

"Let's look at the characteristics of wisdom and how to get it. You guys ready? We're gonna do some page flippin'."

"Go for it, big guy!" She dared him to prove it to her.

Sparks sure are flashing tonight, Lord; Theresa wants the real thing or nothing.

"Point number one: all wisdom comes from God. It's our job to go to Him for it. We just covered that.

"Point number two: we want wisdom, but we want it our own way. Look here in *Genesis 3:5*, where the serpent—Satan in disguise—tempts Eve to take a bite of the apple. He tells her that her eyes will be opened and she will be like God, knowing good from evil. That temptation tips her over the edge and she takes a bite. She wanted to be wise like God, but she wanted it in her own way. That's a struggle we still have today: we want God's wisdom, but we don't want to go to Him for it."

"Yeah, it always seems easier to look elsewhere first, but it never really works out," Jim observed drily.

"A while ago," Craig went on, pulling a slip of paper out of his Bible and consulting it, "I looked up wisdom in my concordance and found some interesting things.

"Look in **Exodus 28:3**," he said, flipping to the front of his Bible, "where God talks about the *'gifted artisans, whom I have filled with the spirit of wisdom.'* And in **Exodus 31:2-4,6**, He says *'I have called by name Bezalel... And I have filled him with the Spirit of God, in wisdom, in understanding, in knowledge, and in all manner of workmanship, to design artistic works. . . I have put wisdom in the hearts of all the gifted artisans, that they may make all that I have commanded....* And in **36:1**, He refers to *'every gifted artisan in whom the Lord has put wisdom and understanding, to know how to do all manner of work for the service of the sanctuary.* What do you guys think this means?"

"I haven't a clue," I volunteered helpfully, picking out and munching on the carrots in my salad.

"Come on, Katie, look at it. God says He puts His spirit of wisdom into these people to do a particular task, in this case building and decorating the Temple.

"And that's point number three: when God gives us an assignment, He gives us the wisdom to do it well."

"I don't see what people building the temple in the Old Testament have to do with me finding a job. C'mon, get real." Theresa held her chin in her hands and stared hard at Craig.

"He'll do the same for you, Theresa. If He gives you a particular task to do, He'll give you the wisdom and the capabilities you need to do it. We just have to keep listening to Him—not to ourselves or the world around us—to get that wisdom."

"But what about finding out what that task is in the first place? How do we do that?"

"Look in **Proverbs 1:7**." He riffled through his Bible. I was impressed; I'd never seen him whip back and forth between scriptures like this before.

"'The fear of the Lord is the beginning of knowledge, But fools despise wisdom and instruction.' The fear of the Lord doesn't mean we're scared of Him, but that we honor and obey Him. So our first job is to get our hearts right with God. Do we yearn to be taught by Him? Do we want to hear what He has to say? Will we obey it?

269

"Now, look in the second chapter of Proverbs where it talks about wisdom. Here. . ." he ran his finger down the page, "here it is, **Proverbs 2:2**: *'incline your ear to wisdom, And apply your hearts to understanding'* —note that we have to do the inclining and applying—*' for the Lord gives wisdom. . .He stores up sound wisdom for the upright'* **(Prov. 2:6,7).**

"So here's point number four: God desires to give us wisdom, but we need to diligently seek after it. Sometimes that takes work, like reading our Bibles, studying, and praying.

"Point number five is that wisdom brings righteousness. **Proverbs 2:10** says that wisdom and knowledge that come from God preserve us from evil. To me, that means that God's wisdom will preserve us from making stupid mistakes that lead us into disasters. Want to stay out of the clutches of evil? Get wisdom. Ask God for it and search for it with all your heart. Have faith that He will give it to you and then depend on it as you live your life."

Craig sat back with a satisfied look on his face, crossed his arms and surveyed his audience. Surely this was as clear to us as it was to him, but like deer in the headlights we stared blankly back at him. Finally, I asked, "What are you telling Jim and Theresa that will help them make the decisions they need to make, here and now?"

"Don't you see, Katie? Without wisdom we can't function. We just wander about like one of those automatic vacuum cleaners on the bottom of a swimming pool that moves about at random. We never really know if we're serving God or even following His plan for our lives."

"So wisdom is what opens up God's plan to us," Theresa said slowly, the light dawning on her face.

"That's it, Theresa! And when we follow God's plan for our lives we walk in righteousness. In other words, we won't be screwing everything up all the time and making a mess out of our lives. God's way works."

"Well, this'll be a nice change, then," Jim remarked, pursing his lips and nodding slowly.

"You know," I chimed in, finally getting with the program, "think of the Wise Men at the time of Jesus' birth. They were learned scholars who'd heard that a great and wise King was to be born so they pored over the ancient books to find out when this would occur. Eventually they found prophecies foretelling that the birth would be announced by an unusual star. They searched the skies night after night, looking for that star and once they saw it, they embarked on a two year journey to find this amazing King. Talk about putting forth an effort to find wisdom! Can you just imagine what their friends and relatives must have said?

'You're going *where*?'

'Uh, we don't know, exactly.'

'And you'll be doing *what?*'

'Worshiping a King we've never seen.'

'And it's going to take you *how long* to get there?'

'We have no idea.'

'Are you crazy, or *what*?'

'No, not crazy, just determined to find this King.'

"With all their wisdom, they somehow knew that the pursuit of this King was the wisest thing they could do even though it seemed crazy to those around them. So they put all their time, money and energies into finding Him."

"So you're saying that the wisest thing I can do is to pursue Jesus with all my heart and somehow He'll guide me in finding a new job?" Theresa raised an eyebrow at me, skeptical.

"Exactly. I don't quite know how it works. . ."

"It's plain to me," Craig cut in. "God is the source of all wisdom. The closer we get to Him, the more we can hear His voice and the more we can dig His wisdom out of the Bible, finding the direction we need. It's kind of a 'duh' thing, if you ask me."

"Okay, so I need a new job. What do I do first?"

"Get with God. Read the Bible. Ask Him for wisdom. Assume you get it when you ask for it. Start brainstorming: 'God, what do You want me to do?' Remember, He gives us the wisdom to do the tasks He has for us. Maybe He wants you to go back to school or something. Ever think of that?"

"Hmmm, not exactly. I figured I lost my chances with that when I had AdaLayne."

"Well, there you go using what I'd call the wisdom of the world. 'I blew it so I don't deserve a second chance.' Nonsense! Think outside the box. God is a god of second chances and creative alternatives. Think big!"

"Here's one last scripture that fits in," I interjected. "Look in **James 3:17**: *'But the wisdom that is from above is first pure, then peaceable, gentle, willing to yield, full of mercy and good fruits, without partiality and without hypocrisy.'* In other words, God's wisdom is gentle, kind, and full of mercy."

"It sounds to me like God's wisdom is mixed in with His love. You can't get one without the other. He'll give you wisdom if you ask for it, but He'll also give you His love and care. Wow. Quite a package deal, I'd say," Theresa mused thoughtfully, chewing on her thumbnail.

"You've got it in a nutshell, Theresa! If we can count on His love for us, we can count on His wisdom as well." Craig turned to me, "Katie, this woman's smart!"

"Don't I know it!"

"Well, gang, that about wraps it up for tonight. Hope it's been helpful. Let us know what God shows you about a new job, Theresa. I know He's got something for you. Love you guys. C'mon, Katie, let's let these people get some sleep."

"Can we still meet together?" Theresa asked plaintively.

"Give us a call when you know what your employment situation looks like and of course we'll see you again. 'Night, all."

Grabbing my hand, he hauled me out of the booth.

CHAPTER 25

Where Can I Find Wisdom?

Questions for Discussion

§

1) Do you know someone who you think of as wise? If so, where do you think they get this wisdom?

2) Can you list—in your own words—the five points that Craig made about wisdom in this chapter?

3) Have you ever thought about the fact that if you ask for wisdom, you will get it, just because God said you would—even if you can't see, hear, taste, touch or smell it?

4) What do you think Craig meant when he said that God 'gives us wisdom however He chooses, but not always with an open door and a well-marked trail'?

5) Have you ever felt like Theresa when she mentioned that she often felt like a beggar, knocking at God's huge door when she prayed, and wondering if He was even listening?

6) What was the point that Katie was making with her story of the Wise Men?

7) Discuss the idea that God's love and His wisdom are intertwined, and we can't 'get one without the other', as Theresa said.

CHAPTER 26

Parenting the Older Child

§

Theresa called finally called again in late August. When the phone rang, I was in the basement, sorting the basket full of odd socks that accumulated every few months. I stuck the phone in the crook of my neck and continued to sort.

"Katie, it's Theresa. Hi."

"Theresa, hey, girl, it's good to hear your voice! How are you guys? I've thought of you so often lately! You guys okay?"

"Katie, we're fine. More than fine, actually. I, uh, I have some news to tell you."

"And you know I want to hear it."

"You're not going to believe this, but Jim and I got married."

"*Got* married?" I nearly dropped the phone. "As in, past tense? As in, the deed's already done and I didn't even know about it? As in, you never called to tell me? As in, I don't know whether to wring your neck or dance for joy? So tell me about it."

"It all stemmed from that talk we had about wisdom last June, remember? Craig told us that if we ask God for wisdom, He'll give it to us even if we don't feel anything. So, after you guys left, we asked God right there in the restaurant for His wisdom in our situation. Then we just went home, still not having a clue what to do."

"And?"

"A few weeks later, we were trying to think of ways to make ends meet and Jim mentioned what Craig'd said about me going back to school. My heart leaped, Katie! But how, I asked him, could I pay someone to watch AdaLayne while I went to school? Then Jim said that if I went nights, he could come over and watch her and it rolled on from there. Suddenly it seemed silly to have Jim here until late and have to go home every night. And then he said if we were married, he could support me while I went to school."

I couldn't stop grinning. Walking from the laundry room to Theresa's old room, I sat on the bed and listened, shaking my head and grinning at the wall.

"That was it, Katie. His offering to *support* me so I could do something *I* wanted blew me away. So I blurted out, 'Why don't we just get married, then?' You'd think I'd offered him a million bucks! He just kept asking, 'Are you serious, Theresa? Are you *sure*?' I finally knew this was the man I wanted to wake up with every day for the rest of my life. I *was* sure. Once that was settled, we just went ahead and did it. Neither of us has much family or much money so we just took AdaLayne, went before the Justice of the Peace and said our vows. Three weeks ago last Saturday. School starts tomorrow."

I flopped back on the bed, not knowing whether to laugh or cry. "Theresa, I couldn't be happier for you. Jim's struck me as a good man since I first met him. Oh, girl, I'm *thrilled!*"

Sniff. Quaver. I wiped my nose on the stray sock I still held.

Good grief, what's with me? You'd think this was my own kid getting married!

"Katie, don't cry. You'll make me start. I've never met a man like him before. He's kind and gentle and he adores AdaLayne. She's got him wrapped around her little finger; I can tell you that!"

"So when can we have you over for a celebration dinner?"

"Wait, there's more. All this talk about God's got Jim thinking about his son again. He hadn't contacted his ex-wife in years, but he finally decided to try to find his son so he called her. Long story short, Travis is coming to visit us for a week in December. Jim's so nervous about it he can hardly sleep at night. Looks like we're going to have to have some more talks with you guys about how to do the dad thing with an older child."

"Hey, we're on, girl. You know we love talking with you two. It'll be good to catch up. I can hardly wait to lay eyes on you as a *married woman!*"

"When can you do it?"

"Let me check with Craig and I'll call you back."

"I'll be waiting by the phone."

"I love you, girl. You married lady, you!" I heard her sputtering as I hung up.

Wow, God, I can hardly believe this. Married—just like that. Thank You that they finally had the courage to take the plunge. Please give them all the wisdom, love and patience they'll need.

Do you think that I wouldn't?

*   *   *   *   *   *

The weeks flew by with beginning of school activities. Each of the kids still at home was in a different sport and it seemed like all we did was go to one game or another. It was early October before I got my act together enough to call Theresa back. I was mortified; I'd told her I'd call her as soon as I checked with Craig about the date.

"Theresa, hey there! It's Katie. I am *so* embarrassed; I said I'd call you as soon as I checked the date with Craig, and here over a month has passed! I am *so* sorry! Do you still want to get together, or have you given up on us completely?"

"Ummm. . .who's this calling? Katie? Katie who? I don't think I know any Katies, at least not any more."

"Theresa! Give me a break, girl! It's been hectic. You know, school activities—"

"I don't know, actually. AdaLayne's still a little young for all that. I just wanted to hear you squirm. I *have* been waiting for your call, and I *did* wonder if you'd forgotten."

"Oh, girl! Make me feel lower than a worm, why don't you? I am so sorry. I never forget you; it's just that time flies by so fast. How's school going?"

"Fine, thanks. I'm just feeling a little homesick for some 'Mom-time,' I guess, and a little sorry for myself. Do you know that my mom doesn't even know that I'm married? Or going to school? Or if she has heard, she doesn't care."

"Theresa, I'm so sorry! Here you are in the middle of some of the biggest changes in your life with no mom to talk to about it all. Give me another chance, will you?"

"You know I will. I need you. Both Jim and I need you and Craig in our lives, especially now that Travis's coming to stay with us over Christmas vacation."

"Come on over to our place this Friday, and we'll have a celebration dinner for you—even if it is a little after the fact—and we'll talk afterwards. Deal?"

"Deal. I'm eager to see you. Can we bring AdaLayne? You should see how big she's getting. She can walk now. I'd love her to get to know her maw-maw."

"Girl! You're making me old before my time!"

"Better watch out. Your time will be here before you know it, so you might as well practice on AdaLayne. What time?"

"About six. And I'm sure the girls will be happy to watch the baby after dinner so we can talk."

"We'll be there. Thanks, Katie. You don't know how much this means to me and Jim both."

Lord, I love the way she's talking about "me and Jim both". That's a good sign.

*   *   *   *   *   *

"Okay, guys, got your notebooks? Let's take our coffee into the living room. Molly, can you and Jossie take AdaLayne upstairs for a while so we grown-ups can talk? Thanks, honey." I watched as the two girls walked the chubby little toddler toward the stairs, each holding a hand.

"Need a warmer, anyone?" I held the coffee pot aloft as we picked our coffee cups up and trooped out of the dining room after a tasty meal of pot roast and chocolate soufflé.

Theresa squeezed my hand as we filed out of the dining room. "Great meal, Katie, thanks so much. We didn't even have a honeymoon, so this is the first real celebration of our marriage." She kissed me lightly on the cheek as we made our way through the family room, cleaned of its usual kid-clutter in honor of the occasion.

We settled down in the white living room where Theresa and I first sat to talk so many months ago. I thought of how hurt and angry she'd been then, guarding her heart so fiercely.

Oh, God, I'm so grateful for all the changes in her life since then.
So am I.

Jim and Theresa sat down, holding hands, on the sage-green couch under the seascape with its blue, green and lavender waves; I sat on the love seat across from them, cradling my hot cup, and Craig sprawled on the recliner in the corner, setting his cup on the end table. Theresa unlaced her hand from Jim's long enough to pull the afghan off the back of the couch and spread it over their laps. She tucked a corner of it up around her outside shoulder and snuggled closer to Jim. He put his arm around her.

"So, Travis's coming to stay with you for Christmas and you're a little shaky about parenting an older child?" Craig asked, looking at Jim.

"Not shaky, petrified! Neither of us has ever parented an older child. I last saw Travis ten years ago; he was two then."

Setting my cup on the arm of the loveseat I kicked off my shoes and crossed my legs Indian style to warm up my toes as the room was a tad chilly.

"So, you need to get to know him, huh?" Craig asked Jim.

"Yeah, but how? I wouldn't blame him if he wanted nothing to do with me."

"He's coming to stay with you, isn't he? Whose idea was that?"

"I suggested it and he accepted the invitation."

"Let's assume he wants to know you. Maybe he's always wondered about you, so here's his chance. Of course, he may resent you for not being part of his life. He may be angry that you have a new wife and baby. When a kid feels displaced, he's usually gonna be angry so you might as well deal with that right up front."

"How? What do I say?"

"What do you think? What would you want your dad to say if the roles were reversed?"

"I'd want him to say, 'I love you, son. I've been a lousy father and I'm sorry. I left you and your mom and I haven't been part of your life for the last ten years. I haven't watched you grow up; I haven't gone to your ball games; I don't even really know who you are and that's my fault. It's wrong, even though I've thought of you every day. Every boy needs a dad to be present in their life and you haven't had one. I hope you can forgive me.'"

"Well, heck, what do you need me for? You've said it all right there. You've covered all the bases: you love him, you've messed up, you've never forgotten him and you're sorry. He may not want to answer back right away—I don't know what kind of a kid he is or what kind of a background he's had—"

"You and me both. I don't even know him." Jim interrupted, wiping his hand across his face as if to wipe away the pain.

"—so whether he's familiar with forgiveness remains to be seen. But at least you'll have made a start. Don't pressure him for a response. Let him think it over and take as much time as he needs.

"But, Jim, the main thing is just be yourself. Most kids can spot a phony a mile away so just be you. Let him see what kind of a man you are, good and bad. Let him see you loving your family, including him, and let him see you repent when you blow it.

"Don't worry; he'll be watching you and asking himself, *Is this guy for real? Is he going to be part of my life from now on? Can I trust him? He hurt me once; will he hurt me again? Does he love these new people in his life more than he loves me? Does he even* love *me?* But chances are, he won't ask you even one of those questions out loud. You'll have to answer them by your actions."

"So how come you know all this stuff?"

"Jim, I had a dad who walked out on me and never came back. Now I have three sons of my own. It doesn't take a rocket scientist."

"Sorry. I never knew your dad walked out on you. Here I am so worried about my life that I never asked about yours. You and Katie seem to have it so all together that I forget that you might have problems too."

"Yeah, well, it was a long time ago. I've forgiven him and he's gone now, but I do still remember that longing to know I was important in his eyes. So let *your* son know how important he is to you, will you?" Craig finished with an uncharacteristic catch in his voice.

"Yeah, I will." Jim looked at his hands.

"So," Theresa chirped, breaking an awkward silence, "you have anything for us to write down this time? We've got our notebooks, Bibles, everything. Go for it."

I stepped in. Craig fished his handkerchief out of his pocket and blew his nose loudly.

"Yeah," I answered her, "we wrote down some things about raising older children. You ready? I've got a list here." I opened my Bible and drew out a piece of paper.

"Here's the list of topics we came up with:
1) Respect, communication and discipline
2) Expressing affection to the older child
3) Order and the use of leisure time
4) Service and self-esteem
5) Being authentic
6) Garbage in, garbage out

"Just think, guys, in six sessions you'll be expert parents!"

"Wow." Theresa rolled her eyes. "Right."

"So, you ready?" Craig asked, clearing his throat and looking straight at Jim.

"Give me all you've got. I've only got a few more months before he arrives."

Craig kicked the footrest of the recliner down and sat up straight. This was stuff he was familiar with after raising four teenagers.

CHAPTER 26

Parenting the Older Child

Questions for Discussion

§

1) In your mind, how are the marriage of Jim and Theresa and their prayer for wisdom connected?

2) Do you think Jim and Theresa got married hastily or have they had enough time to get to know one another? Give reasons for your thoughts.

3) If you had to list several topics that you wanted to discuss about raising older children, what would they be?

4) If you have a parent who left you when you were a child, what would you want that parent to say if she or he walked into the room right now? What would *you* say if you were the parent who had left and you are just now seeing your child for the first time in several years?

5) Craig says that Travis will "be watching you, and asking himself, *Is this guy for real? Is he going to be part of my life from now on? Can I trust him? He hurt me once, will he hurt me again? Does he love these new people in his life more than he loves me? Does he even love me?* But chances are, he won't ask you even one of those questions. You'll have to answer them by your actions." What does this mean, and how can Jim answer Travis through his actions as a dad?

6) If you have a blended family, discuss the major challenges you've faced as you've brought the two parts together. What advice would you give someone contemplating a marriage that would create a blended family?

CHAPTER 27

Respect, Communication and Discipline

§

"Let's start with respect, communication and discipline. Travis is not a little boy any more. At twelve, he's becoming a man and he needs loving, masculine attention in order to develop a healthy sense of who he is as a male. Relying on mom's feminine version of love is no longer enough."

Jim nodded slowly, his eyes glued to Craig.

"Growing into manhood, he can best see himself through the image you portray of him. What you think of Travis and how you communicate that to him will greatly influence what he thinks of himself. He craves your love and respect."

"Wonder how some of us develop any kind of male self-esteem," Jim muttered.

"Know what you mean. I didn't have a decent dad either, but I've been a decent dad to my boys only because God works through me. He supplies what I don't have. In the beginning of our child-raising years, I was just as scared as you are."

He glanced at me. I nodded, remembering those years.

"So, Jim, how can you convey to Travis that you love and respect him, especially since you have no idea what he's really like?"

"Uh, by listening to him, maybe? By treating him like a half grown man instead of a kid?" he shrugged, clenching and unclenching his fists, his eyes bleak.

"Good idea. As you talk, ask Travis what *he* thinks. Let him know you value his opinion by listening to it."

Theresa, balancing her notebook on her knee, furiously scribbled away. Jim simply listened.

"What about not trying to be his buddy? Tell us about that," I interjected, feeling Craig could do a better job of explaining these things than I.

"She's right, guys," he said, putting his arms behind his head and leaning back in the recliner.

"Yes, respect him and his opinions, but more importantly, make sure *he* respects *you*. You're not his best buddy; you're his father, and that distinction needs to be clear. In the Ten Commandments, the fifth command instructs us to *'honor your father and mother. . .that it may be well with you* (**Deut. 5:16**). So, we're actually imperiling our children's lives when we act like their best buddy and not their dad. Kids don't want their parents to be their pals but mature adults they can look up to. They won't honor a dad who puts himself on an equal footing with them, just trying to be a pal. Fathers and sons can be best friends when the son reaches manhood but that relationship is earned over years of the dad being a dad: strong, kind, and a good disciplinarian."

"Give me some nuts and bolts. I need specifics." Jim stared at Craig, nodding slowly.

"If I was you, I'd sit down with him on the first day and explain the rules and expectations in your home, not as a drill sergeant, but as a loving father wanting to make his son comfortable in this new place. Tell him the reasons for the rules. Let him know that as your oldest son you're proud of him and you're confident he'll do a good job. Tell him that if he deliberately breaks these rules, there will be consequences and explain what those will be. Get his cooperation as much as possible, maybe asking him what it's like at his home. If a kid feels like he has some input into the rules he has to obey he's more likely to follow them than if they're arbitrarily handed down from above."

"Hmmm, never thought of it that way, but you're right. I see that at work all the time," Jim nodded.

"Don't get so hung up on the everyday rules that you forget the bigger ones like honesty, courtesy, integrity, loyalty and self-sacrifice. Most of these will be learned through your example—"

"Attitudes are caught, not taught, right, Katie?" Theresa looked at me, stage-whispering behind her hand. I nodded back at her.

"—but they're the ones that really count. You could call them character; something that's frequently lacking these days."

"Yeah, all you have to do is listen to the news to know that." Jim nodded somberly.

Craig nodded, agreeing, and continued. "The best way for Travis to learn these character qualities is to watch you modeling them. For example, as you open the door for Theresa, pull out her chair or help an old lady across the street you can teach him, *this is how you treat a lady, son.*

"Of course, the most important thing to pass onto him is a relationship with Jesus. Let him observe you praying or reading your Bible. But don't make a big deal out of it; just be real. If you come across as a phony, he won't have any desire to copy your lifestyle.

"As you do these things, you'll be creating a loving relationship between you and your son. As you may be finding out with Theresa, a love relationship takes work and consistency and many acts of kindness, honesty, loyalty, communication and affection, among other things."

"Katie told me about the four parts of a parent's love, kind of like the four legs of a stool, when she was teaching me about raising AdaLayne. She said they were—" Theresa flipped back through her notes, "—affection, discipline, example and prayer. Are these things still true for an older child, or is there a whole new set of things we need to learn?"

Craig propped his elbows on his knees and leaned forward, his face alight, as he responded. "Those four principles work for kids of all ages, Theresa. You just have to modify how you do them with older kids. Expressing affection to an almost-teenager will be different from how you express it to a small child. Discipline will be different too. You can spank a toddler, but to spank a junior-higher who has never lived with you? *Not* a good idea!"

"So what do we do for discipline?"

"Keep in mind the purpose of discipline: to restore the erring person to God and the love of the family circle. Allowing a child to stay angry only leads to bitterness on his part and resentment on yours, creating a wedge between you. Left to fester, those wedges can last a lifetime."

"You don't have to tell me," Theresa nodded.

"Consider his attitude. Is he trying to please you and just made a mistake, or is he deliberately testing you? Many children push the boundaries just to see if their parents actually mean what they say. Are you dealing with rebellion and anger or with a kid new to your house?"

"I can see this isn't going to be easy." Jim looked to Theresa for support. She shook her head, wide-eyed, spreading her hands out palms up.

"Don't look at me, babe. I've never raised a twelve-year old boy!"

Jim looked back at Craig, a touch of panic in his eyes.

"Relax, Jim. The main thing is just to love your son; take the time to talk to him, to teach him, to show him how to be a man. Just *being* with him will show him you love him. You don't have to be perfect or even an expert. Just be yourself, his dad."

"I guess I can do that," Jim said slowly, taking out his handkerchief and wiping his forehead.

"If he misbehaves, talk to him. Let him know that his character's too important for you to let him continue with bad behavior. Ask if he knows that his actions were wrong, (chances are he does). Remind him of what you discussed in the beginning about the consequences for bad behavior. Let him know his punishment and tell him that he needs to acknowledge his wrong, apologize and remedy the situation if possible. He may need some time and space to do those things since repentance requires humbling our pride—which is never easy—but don't let more than a few hours go by before he apologizes.

"When we had to punish our kids for misbehaving we taught them to say afterward, 'I'm sorry: I was wrong for (being rebellious, disobedient, disrespectful, etc). Will you please forgive me?' Saying out loud that you were wrong shows the other person that you're humbling yourself in front of them. It's pretty hard for a person to stay mad at someone who is being genuinely humble."

I jumped in the conversation.

"You know, it works both ways. When we parents do wrong, we need to admit it and apologize to our kids. Craig's a great example of this. I can't stay mad at him when he comes to me and sheepishly tells me he's been wrong and asks me to please forgive him"

"Wow. Wish my old man had talked to you before he raised me!" Jim murmured, the muscles in his jaw working in and out. Theresa looked at him, her eyebrows knit with concern, and snuggled closer.

"I know the feeling; believe me," Craig said, nodding.

I nodded thoughtfully, thinking of the many occasions we'd had to put all this stuff into practice.

Craig took a sip of his coffee and continued.

"On this first visit, Travis may feel more like a guest—both in his eyes and yours—than an actual member of the family. Give him a chance to get to know and trust you.

"Part of creating that trust is to be consistent. You can't punish him one day for something and the next day let him get away with the same thing. Your rules have to be fair and you have to enforce them consistently."

Jim nudged Theresa to make sure she wrote all this down.

Craig continued, "Sometimes consistency is the hardest thing in the world for me. When it's the end of the day and I'm pooped, I just want to sit in my recliner and read the paper. Then one of the kids mouths off to Katie and I have to respond to that disrespect, and I mean *now*. I have to get out of my chair, take that child aside, make sure he understands that what he did was wrong and punish him for it. If it's one of the younger kids, that also means I have to take the time to cuddle and love them afterwards and help them to repent to God and to their mom. If it's one of the older ones, I have to be sure the apology comes from the heart, at least within the hour, and I have to follow up on whatever punishment I've given. Sometimes, to be honest, it's the last thing I want to do!"

"Wow, you really have to put their welfare ahead of your own, don't you? I haven't had a whole lot of practice with this," Jim muttered.

"Looks like you're doing a pretty decent job of it with Theresa and AdaLayne," I interjected. He smiled at me gratefully, the wrinkles from the corners of his eyes almost meeting those from the corners of his mouth.

Craig went on.

"Remember that punishment for wrongdoing is training your son's character. To me, the sign of a truly great man is one who is big enough to admit his wrongdoings and apologize for them. We can all think of people we know, some of them public figures, who squirm every which way to avoid confessing their wrongs; they pass the blame onto others, and spout lie after lie. We can all see how disgusting that is."

"Boy, ain't that the truth!" Jim agreed, nodding.

"And you know, training our children helps them to live a better life. When we do the right thing we receive approval from those around us and we feel good about ourselves. On the other hand, when we're rebellious and angry we invite unhappiness and strife into our lives. It's our job as parents to steer our kids away from that kind of a miserable, messed-up life. So, never punish just because you're angry at your kid for the dumb thing he did; instead, you punish in order to right the wrong and steer your child back to a place of peace and approval."

"That sounds a little like conditional love to me, as if you're saying, 'I'll only love you if you do the right thing.' What about this uncon-ditional love I hear so much about?" Theresa challenged, looking up from her writing.

Craig took a sip of his coffee and made a face. "Ugh, lukewarm. Can you get me some more, lovey?" he asked, holding his cup out to me.

"Hold that thought; I want to hear what you have to say." I clicked an imaginary remote in his direction. He obediently froze. Theresa snickered.

We'd never discussed these ideas before and I wished we had. Why had I never tapped all this wisdom under the surface of my hus-band before?

Returning from the kitchen with the coffee pot, I waved it in each person's direction—no takers—before pouring Craig's cup and sitting down again.

Craig picked up his Bible. "That's a fair question, Theresa. Society tells us to love our kids unconditionally or we're not good parents, right? But what does God say? Turn to *Genesis 4* and the story of Cain and Abel."

He riffled through his Bible and waited until they'd found the place. I just listened as he paraphrased the story.

"Cain and Abel have been raised by Adam and Eve and they're grown men now, old enough to know that God requires the blood of a living animal as a sacrifice to cleanse them of their sins. This was a foretaste of what Jesus would do for the world, so it was a major point with God.

"But this time, Cain thinks he'll do it *his* way and not God's, so he brings vegetables and grains instead of an animal to sacrifice to God. He knew that God required the blood of an animal; he just didn't want to provide one. He tilled the soil instead of raising animals and he wanted to bring his produce instead of going to the effort of obtaining an animal. That's been our primary problem ever since: we want to do things *our* way and not God's. Rebellion in a nutshell."

"So how does this relate to unconditional love?" Theresa challenged Craig, pulling a strand of hair out of her ponytail and flipping it against her cheek, back and forth.

I was curious myself.

Craig held out his hands, palms up.

"Don't you see? Cain disobeyed, God didn't approve, Cain pouted and God responded: 'Hey buddy, why are you angry? I taught you how to do this sacrifice, but you did it your way instead of Mine. Are you surprised I disapprove? If you obey Me and follow My instructions, you'll have My approval and My pleasure. If you insist on doing things your way, you'll fall into sin, and believe Me, it wants to overtake you and drag you down. Master your own will and obey Me *(Gen 4:6,7)*.'

"It's not too much different from what we might say to our own sons. But note, He doesn't stop loving Cain; He just disapproves of his choices.

"Kids need to know that not all actions receive their parents' approval. Yes, we love our children. We want the best for them, we want them to grow into mature adults and we're willing to put in the time necessary to achieve that goal. But no, we don't accept selfish, rebellious behavior any more than God does. So, while we may love *them* unconditionally, we don't always love their behavior in the same way. Make sense?"

He looked inquiringly at Theresa. She nodded, still a little stormy.

"But, remember, our responsibility to let our children feel the weight of our disapproval over their bad behavior doesn't change our love for them; in fact it takes *more* love on our part to train and correct. It's much easier—in the short run—to let their bad behavior simply slide by.

"Our goal is to help our kids understand that bad behavior ruins relationships, separates us from God and the people we love and creates a load of guilt and anger. We are failing to truly love our kids if we let them drag that load around all their lives."

"Wish I'd experienced more of that kind of love when I was a kid." Jim muttered darkly.

"I know, Jim, me too. But the good news is that we can give it to our children and not let the cycle keep repeating itself."

"Not sure where I'm going to get all this wisdom and love from, but I'll try."

"Don't try to do it in your own strength. Ask God to give you the wisdom and patience to love and raise your kids and He will. Believe me, He will."

"It's getting late for AdaLayne and we need to go soon," Theresa glanced at Jim and leaned forward with her notes open. "So, let me see if I can summarize what you've been saying, Craig, and then we'd better go."

"Good idea. Got any more questions before we start, Jim?"

"Nope. Some praying to do, though. Go ahead, Theresa."

She cleared her throat and sat up a little straighter, throwing the afghan off.

"We need to make our rules clear with Travis from the beginning so he'll feel comfortable and we also need to let him know we value his input. We—especially Jim—need to show Travis affection and respect, all the while remembering that Jim's the dad and Travis is the son. They're not just equal buddies. For his own well-being, Travis needs to respect his dad.

"We need to be good examples ourselves, apologizing when we're wrong. We need to show him that bad actions on his part separate him from us and from God, but that asking forgiveness restores those relationships. We need to remember that when we punish our children, it's to train them, and that we're not just taking out our anger on them for the stupid thing they did. When we punish them, we need to make sure it leads them to apologize, confess their wrongdoing, and ask to be forgiven because that's what makes them feel loved and accepted again. That about cover it?"

"You've summed it up well. All I'd add is just enjoy him. Have a good time getting to know your son again. If you're genuinely glad to be with him, he'll pick up on that more quickly than anything else."

"Craig, Katie, you don't know how much we appreciate this. Just to know someone's in our corner. . .I can't tell you how much it means to us. Thanks." Jim cleared his throat and shook his head hard. Pulling his handkerchief out of his pocket, he wiped his whole face before blowing his nose loudly.

Theresa stood up and offered Jim a hand up.

"Thanks for the lovely dinner and a great evening, you guys."

CHAPTER 27

Respect, Communication, and Discipline

Questions for Discussion

§

1) What kind of discipline, if any, did you receive as a child growing up? If you had none, did you wish you had more? If you did receive it, was it harsh or fair? Can punishment be harsh and fair at the same time?

2) According to Craig, what *always* needs to follow punishment? What is the point of punishment?

3) What kinds of punishments did your parents use on you as a child? What kinds do you use on your children, if any?

4) What do you think about the idea that parents shouldn't try to be their kids' best buddy? Why shouldn't they?

5) According to Jim, what is one good way to show someone else (even your child) that you respect them? What are some other ways?

6) If you love and respect your parent(s), or have adult children who love and respect you, how did that mutual respect come about? What were the elements in your parent-child relationship that brought you to this place of friendship?

7) Discuss the difference between unconditional love and approval. Does your child's behavior affect how much you *love* them? Does it affect how much you *like* them? (Is there a difference between liking and loving your children?)

CHAPTER 28

Expressing Affection to the Older Child

§

Just as we had done with Jeff a year ago, we had taken Rob to freshman orientation week at his college, several hundred miles away. It was the farthest any of our kids had lived from home and I wondered how he would do there. He was sure this was the college for him though, as it offered the agriculture major he wanted. It was a large state university in contrast to the small, Christian college Jeff had chosen.

Craig and I had decided that if he wanted to change after the first year we'd let him, but we'd encourage him to stick it out through his freshman year even if the going was tough.

By late fall, Jeff had developed a close group of friends who supported each other with prayer, fun and fellowship, but Rob hadn't yet clicked with anybody. Some days I ached, hearing the loneliness in his normally brash and cheerful voice.

One Saturday evening in early November, we called him to see how he was doing. After we got off the phone—everybody had to speak with him—Molly said, "He sounds homesick to me!"

Suddenly I realized I was homesick for him as well.

God, if I could just put my arms around him for a minute...

"Daddy, if we leave now and drive all night, we could be there first thing in the morning and we could visit with him for a while and drive back tomorrow afternoon. We'd still be home in time for school-night bedtime. Please, Daddy, ple-e-e-ase?" Jossie bounced on her toes, looking at her dad with hopeful puppy eyes.

"Hmmm, let me think, girlie." He hugged her close to him.

Craig glanced at me, telegraphing the question, "Whaddya think, babe?" I nodded; I could go for this. I ached to see my boy.

"Okay, Joss, we'll do it! Let the others know that the bus'll leave in half an hour." Squealing for joy, Jossie ran off to collect her quilt and pillow. Jason jumped over the chair in front of him and dashed upstairs, passing her on the way.

Forty-five minutes later, we were barreling down the highway in the van—Molly and Liz in the way back and Jason and Jossie on the middle seat—all settled in with quilts, iPods, books, and snacks. Jason turned on the light over his seat and read while the girls listened to music. I tilted my seat back and tried to grab a couple of winks since I knew I'd have to drive later on.

We drove until three in the morning, when neither Craig nor I could keep our eyes open any longer, and stopped to sleep at a rest area for a few hours. The four kids snored in the back seats, flopped all over each other like a pack of puppies. As we tilted our seats back and let our heavy eyelids finally drop, I murmured to my exhausted husband, "Aren't we a little old for this kind of thing?"

My only response was a gentle snore.

At eight o'clock Sunday morning, we pulled onto the campus, piled out like a bunch of rumpled clowns from the proverbial Volkswagen, and headed for Rob's dorm. The front door was unlocked so we slipped in quietly, seeing no signs of life. Jason volunteered to go up to Rob's room with Craig, whispering, "I'm gonna pounce on him, Mom. He'll never know what hit him!"

We ladies quietly walked down the hall to the restroom where we washed the sleep from our faces and ran our fingers through our hair— none of us having a comb, naturally—and then wandered around the deserted lobby, trying to be inconspicuous. We still weren't sure if we were allowed to be in the dorm this early on a Sunday morning.

What seemed like an hour later, Rob—with his hair sticking up on one side and flat on the other—stepped out of the elevator with his dad, carrying Jason on his back and grinning sheepishly. He dumped his brother on the floor in order to give each of us a hug.

"We didn't want you to be lonely, Robbie," Jossie explained, hanging onto his hand.

"Wow, guys, I can't believe you drove all the way up here last night. And I just talked to you yesterday! Whose idea was this, anyway? Let me guess. Uh. . .I bet it was your idea, Joss."

He twirled her around and gave her another quick squeeze. "Gotta admit, it's good to see the fam. I've kinda been missin' you guys, just a little. Even you, ya dork," and he punched Jason in the stomach. Momentarily doubling over, Jason retaliated by leaping onto his brother's back. Rob staggered and fell, the two of them rolling on the hard tile floor, Jason squealing with twelve-year old laughter.

Afterwards, Rob led us up to his room. "Dave should be decent by now," he whispered in the Sunday morning quiet of the hallway. "I woke him up before we came down."

Dave leaned his head over the edge of his bunk with eyes half closed and croaked, "Hey, dudes, wassup?" I could smell him from where I stood.

Note to self: make sure our children don't address adults like that.

After receiving a tour of Rob's side of the room, admiring how he'd lofted his bed and tucked not only his desk and chair under it but also an ancient recliner and coffee maker, we took him out to brunch off campus.

"You get along with your roommate okay?" I wanted to know.

"Oh, not the best. He spends a lot of time on his computer. I think he looks at porn; it's kind of gross. Makes me not want to spend too much time in my own room. Fortunately, he goes home almost every weekend. He's just here today because of the homecoming game last night."

We went to the local pancake house for brunch and laughed and talked for an hour and a half while the place slowly filled up. We even called Jeff on Craig's cell phone so he could be part of the family circle. Of course, everybody had to talk to him.

Finally, we trooped out, needing a walk before we piled in the van for the long drive home. Rob showed us his favorite places around the town square: the pizza joint, a coffee house, a sports store.

We made quite a procession. Rob was in the lead with his younger siblings hanging onto each hand, Jason doing his best to pull Rob's arm off and Jossie regaling him with the latest school gossip. Craig and I strolled along hand in hand behind them and Molly and Lizzie trailed along after us, giggling and checking out the guys and rating each one with a complicated system known only to them.

After an hour, it was time to start the seven-hour drive home. Rob hugged me hard before we left. "Love you, Mom. Thanks so much for coming. Come back anytime."

"I love you too, bud, so much. Take care of yourself. Be sure to eat well and get enough rest. Take those vitamins I brought you. Call us if you need anything. Promise?"

"I promise."

"So long, son. We'll see you at Thanksgiving."

"Looking forward to it."

"Keep an eye out for cool guys for me!"

"Will do!"

"Save the coolest ones for me. You can give them my phone number!"

"Not on your life!"

"I love your room, Jeff! I left you a note on your windowsill. Don't open it until after we leave!"

"I won't."

"Hate you, snort-head!"

"Hate you too, ya dork!"

We drove away, waving with our hands out the windows until we turned the corner and could no longer see Rob standing there, waving with both hands.

*   *   *   *   *   *

We were still catching up on sleep by the time Thursday evening arrived.

"We on with Jim and Theresa tonight?" Craig asked me as he came in the door from work that evening, sounding as though he hoped the answer was no.

"Yup. And remember, it's not their fault we drove fourteen hours to see our son this weekend. They can't help that we're half asleep."

"I know. I led last week; how about you lead today? I'll catch a few winks and if you need my input, just waft pizza under my nose and I'll perk up, I promise."

"Hmmm. I'm so sure. I can see it now: Craig starts to snore, his head falls forward and his face lands in the pizza. Nope, I think you'd better stay awake tonight."

Thirty minutes later, we slid into the booth with our eyes half shut. Jim and Theresa had already ordered.

"Hi, guys!" Theresa chirped. "It's good to see you! But, whoa. . .this time you *both* look like something the cat dragged in. Guess it's your turn. What's up with you two tonight?"

We exchanged guilty glances.

"We drove all night Saturday to visit Rob at college. And drove back the next day."

"Is he okay? Whatever made you do that? Isn't he, like, two states away?"

"Oh, we just wanted to see him. He seemed glad to see us, too."

Theresa looked at Jim, "Am I the only one here who thinks that's crazy?"

He just shrugged and shook his head. "Don't look at me, girl. I've never done anything like that; believe me!"

"Sometimes you want to say to your kid, loud and clear: 'You are so important to me that if I think you're lonesome, I'll drive all through the night just to see you for a few hours.' And then. . .you crash." Craig let his head drop onto his chest and pretended to snore.

"Just ignore him; he can doze. Tonight we're talking about showing affection to your older child." I tried unsuccessfully to hide a yawn behind my hand as we started in on our salads. Theresa snickered. "This should be a lively evening!"

Craig leaned his head back into the corner of the booth and in thirty seconds he was snoring gently, for real this time. I just rolled my eyes.

"So," I said, taking a bite of pizza, "tonight we're discussing how to build bonds of loyalty and affection with your older child. Right?"

They both nodded.

Theresa wore a pink boat-neck sweater with a string of pearls and had pulled her hair into a high ponytail tied with a pink ribbon. Wispy curls framed her face, and her birthmark was scarcely visible under her make-up. She snuggled against Jim, who wore blue jeans and a flannel shirt instead of his usual chino work clothes.

She sure is a changed woman. Thank You, Lord.

"When kids gauge your love for them, they watch your actions more than your words. How can you let Travis know you love him? Jim?"

"We've talked about listening and explaining rules. . ."

"That's a good way to show him respect. But what about *affection*? And is it any different from respect? What do you think, Theresa?"

She flipped back through her notebook, "You mentioned showing affection through the five *t*'s."

"Go over them, will you?" I asked, wondering how much she remembered.

"Touch, time together, teasing, talk and tradition. We discussed knitting a child's heart to yours with these but what about a pre-teen? I see teenagers all the time who look like they'd rather *die* than be touched or teased by their parents."

"A lot of teenagers give that impression," I hid another yawn, "but if you look below the surface, they just want their parents' love and approval. Trouble is, many parents regard their kids as dumb, rebellious or just plain *weird*. So, the kids don't let their parents into their hearts. They don't want to be hurt, so they keep their parents at a distance."

"Hmmm. Sounds familiar. My dad treated me like dirt, so I just closed myself off from him." Jim chewed his pizza slowly, remembering. It was clear he was holding in barely concealed anger from the way the muscles in his jaw bunched in and out as he chewed.

"We each hold the key to our own heart," I continued, pressing my upper lip to stifle yet another yawn, "and we only open up to people we trust. That's why it's so important to build these bonds of love and loyalty between parent and child. It starts with the things we were talking about last time: being consistent, showing respect, listening to your child, being fair and clear about limits and rules, and punishing when necessary.

"Either of you remember why we punish our children for wrongdoing?" I looked from Theresa to Jim and back while I took a drink of water. Maybe that would help me stay awake.

How much of this was sticking?

"Uh, to make him do the right thing?" Jim glanced at Theresa for confirmation.

"Yeah, but why? What's the ultimate goal?"

"Oh, wait, isn't it something about bringing him back to the place where he can feel your love and approval?" Theresa looked at me triumphantly.

"Why is that so important?"

"Because we all need to feel loved and approved of," Jim waved his pizza for emphasis. A stray piece of pepperoni flew off, landing on Craig's chest. I snickered and picked it off. Craig mumbled in his sleep and groaned. Jim turned beet red.

"Just ignore him, Jim. He'll never know the difference." I shook my head in pity at my unconscious husband and continued, "you're so right, Jim. A kid who feels the love and approval of his parents isn't as likely to act out as a kid who craves that attention. So how do we help our kids feel accepted and loved so they don't have to act out?"

"Tell us how, Katie. We're total novices at this. I'm sure it will have something to do with the five *t*'s, right?" Theresa asked, ready to write.

"Right. Let's start with time together. One of the clearest ways I show love to my kids is spending time with them. Kids know our time is valuable and they also know that when we give our time to them we're giving ourselves to them."

"Ouch, Katie, you're digging down where it hurts. Do we have to do this? Isn't there some easier way?" Theresa held her head in her hands.

"No. Not if you're going to do a better job with your kids than your parents did with you. It hurts because you didn't get your mother's time and attention, right?"

"Maybe." She stared up at me defiantly.

Jim didn't say anything but he glanced toward the door looking like he wanted to leave.

Craig slept on.

God, this is where these guys hurt so bad. Please heal their hearts and help them give the love they never received.

"So, for an older child, one of the best ways to show them you love them is to spend your most valuable currency on them: your time."

Craig muttered, "Preach it, girl," settling his head back into the corner of the booth and groaning slightly. Theresa's face softened and she snickered. I just rolled my eyes and went on.

"You can show your love by spending time with them in different ways. For instance, when I was little, my dad sometimes woke me before sunrise and we walked around a nearby pond, looking for rabbits and watching the sun come up. I loved knowing my daddy wanted to spend time with just me.

"And now that our kids are older, I frequently hear them say, 'Come hang out with us, Mom! Just *be with us* for a little while!'

"I used to say I was too busy—laundry to fold, vacuuming to do, dishes to wash, whatever—until I realized their invitation wouldn't last forever. They'd soon have more important things to do than hang out with their mom, and they wouldn't invite me any more. And I would have lost my chance."

"Yeah, but you *do* have housework. You can't just hang out with your kids every time they call, can you? I'd never get anything done if that were me!"

"Remember that poem by Ruth Hulbert Hamilton I told you about a long time ago?

'So quiet down, cobwebs.
Dust, go to sleep.
I'm rocking my baby
and babies don't keep.'

"Well, I looked it up recently and the previous verse says:

'The cleaning and scrubbing will wait till tomorrow,
For children grow up, as I've learned to my sorrow.'

"Some of the truest words ever spoken. Like babies, teenagers don't keep either. Before you know it, they're out of the house and you won't get to spend much time with them any more. In these years while they're still home, you're laying a foundation for your kids to build the rest of their lives on. Building that foundation is important work. You'll have all the years after the kids leave to do housework. That's not to say, of course, that no housework gets done in these years. Just don't obsess over it so much that you're always too busy to spend time with those you love the most.

"As they move into the teenage years," I yawned hugely—not even trying to hide it this time, "you may be the one that they gravitate toward the most, Jim. As we talked about a while ago, a teenage boy craves his dad's love and respect and the best way to give him that is to spend time with him, teaching him how to be a man by your example.

"In the same way, a teenage girl needs love and attention from you to help her see herself as lovely and feminine. Since she has an inborn need for masculine affection and approval, if she doesn't get them from you she'll get them from other men and boys, guaranteed. And *that* is a scenario you don't want; believe me! Been there, done that and it's not fun.

"So as she gets older, spend time with AdaLayne. Take her out on daddy-daughter dates. The more you reinforce in her the idea that she is precious in your sight, the more she'll begin to see herself that way and the more she'll be able to resist unwanted advances of hormonal teenage boys."

"This is a whole new idea for me, to show respect to my son by spending time with him. My dad sure never did these things, so they just never occurred to me. And daddy-daughter dates. . . wow. I have a lot to learn!"

As if on cue, Craig groaned, shook his head and opened his eyes. "She's right, guys. Hang out with your kids and have fun together. It's worth it; I promise."

"Well, hello, sleepy-head! Have a nice nap?" I reached over to wipe some drool off his cheek.

"You guys just thought I was sleeping. Hah! I heard every word."

"Yeah, right," I snickered.

"So those snores were just for effect, huh?" Theresa looked at him gently, shaking her head in pity.

CHAPTER 28

Expressing Affection to the Older Child

Questions for Discussion

§

1) What was the reason for including the story about going to see Rob? What do you think Rob got out of that visit?

2) Do you have any memories of doing special things with a parent or grandparent that let you know you were important to them?

3) What do you think about time being our most valuable personal currency and that how we spend it tells the people around us a great deal about how important they are to us? Do you agree?

4) God gives each one of us exactly the same amount of time in each day. Some of us have more demands on our time than others but we all have a certain amount of discretionary time available. What do you do with yours? (And no, if you are a parent, you do not have to spend every single minute of it with your kids!)

5) If you have teenagers, have you ever found yourself responding the same way Katie did at first when her kids begged her to hang out with them and just be with them for a little while by saying you were too busy?

6) Discuss ways in which your parents showed you love (or not) by spending time with you.

CHAPTER 29

Touch, Teasing, Talk and Traditions

§

"Leave the poor man alone, Theresa; he needs his sleep. What's next?" Jim chided, looking over at her notebook. "Tell us about touch, Katie. What's that all about? How do you touch an older child in a way that doesn't creep him out?"

"Try an arm around the shoulders or a slap on the back. Give him a high five to celebrate. Males have all kinds of ways to touch without being creepy—you know, the male bonding thing. It can be a special handshake that only you two know about, jockeying for position, even a man-to-man hug once in a while. Just hanging out together in the same vicinity, in the garage or side by side on the couch watching TV can be a way of touching and being physically close.

"Before Rob left for college, he'd often come to our bedroom in the evening—especially if Craig was already there but I was still downstairs—and just lie on the bed and talk. It didn't have to be a major event; he just liked being next to his dad. Likewise, I'll still lie with the girls at night sometimes if they need to talk. Sometimes I'll give them back rubs, or I'll write notes on their backs with my fingers and have them guess what I'm writing. Of course, it's always some version of 'I love you'.

"Don't overdo it—teenagers can be very picky about letting people touch them—but do whatever you can to send him the message—"

"Let me guess," Theresa broke in, "'I love you; you're special to me; there's no one who can replace you in my heart, and I enjoy spending time with you.' Am I right?" She looked at me triumphantly.

"As usual, girl, right on the button." I grinned, settling back. This had been worth coming for, after all. Too bad Craig missed out on this session.

"I think teasing's next," Jim urged us on, "if I can read Theresa's chicken tracks correctly. How in the world can teasing draw us closer? Any teasing I've experienced has only been the cruel kind. Katie, tell us how that works, will you?" he finished his last bite of pizza, pushed his empty plate away and leaned his elbows on the table. "Take notes, Theresa, we might need this information." He looked at me expectantly.

"Here's an example of what I mean by teasing: I took an art class a while ago at the community center and the college-age daughter of one of the moms joined us for the second hour after her classes were over. The class is informal — mostly just us middle-aged women — and some days the mom greeted her daughter by saying, 'Hello, Precious Princess, pretty as a petunia, most beautiful girl in the whole wide world; all that and a brain too!' The daughter, a stoic type with a dry wit, usually pretended not to hear her mother but occasionally you'd see her smothering a faint grin. The mother was really saying, 'Hey, wonderful daughter, I'm glad to see you; you're precious to me', but saying that might have been just *too* mushy for her daughter.

"Of course, it's different for each kid; some teenagers would be mortified to be called Precious Princess, but the message is still important: you and I belong together, and we have a bond that no one else shares. Some parents have nicknames for their children that nobody but the family uses; just another way to reinforce that bond that connects them to us."

"What about someone like me and Travis who are just starting out? I don't know what he likes or doesn't like." Jim massaged the wrinkles in his forehead as he looked at me.

"Relax, Jim. If there's love in your heart, it'll come out. So maybe you give him a nickname, one that only you use. Craig still has nicknames for all our kids, old as they are, and I think they still enjoy them. Just make sure whenever you tease, or whatever kind of nickname you give him, that it doesn't hurt or tear Travis down in any way. I've heard a lot of fathers do that and it's just plain mean.

"If you're genuinely glad to be with your boy, it'll show. Teenage boys generally don't like mushy stuff, which is why teasing can be a back-door way of telling him you love him. But no matter how you express it, you still want to get the same message across: 'You are important to me. We belong together. We have a connection no one else has, and I'm glad.'"

Theresa nodded her approval. Jim just stared at me intently.

"Okay, onto talk." Another yawn threatened to split my face in two. "Talk with your kids. Talk at dinner—another good reason to have dinner together as often as possible. Talk to them when they go to bed. Talk to them when *they* want to talk which, by the way, won't always be the most convenient time for you! Remember, you don't always get a second chance."

I paused for a moment to let Theresa catch up as she wrote. Craig snored on softly.

"Try to dig below the surface without prying; give them a chance to express how they're feeling without judging them. If they need to say they hate someone or if they're frustrated or hurt, let them get it out. Ask them why and listen to the whole story before making any judgments.

"Make talking to you a safe thing for them which means that you guard their privacy. They have to know that what they tell you stays with you. No child wants to hear her private secrets spread all over school because she told them to her mom, who told her best friend, who told her daughter, who told *her* best friend, who texted the news to the whole school the next day. Despite the facades they put on kids are easily embarrassed and hurt and if they think their parents have betrayed their confidence, they'll clam up tight and never trust you again."

"Don't need to tell me," Jim muttered into his fist, massaging his jaw.

"Let them know, by being there for them when they need to talk, that they can come to you with any kind of problem and you'll listen. Kids who have angry, critical, judgmental, too busy or just plain indifferent parents won't come to them when they have a problem; they'll find someone else who will take the time to listen. Kids need someone to open their hearts to, someone who will really listen and not always correct or criticize them. And sadly enough, predators lurk all over the place: on the internet, at school, at church or in the neighborhood. If kids' parents won't listen to them, they're especially vulnerable to predators who will. That's how these evil people gain children's trust.

305

And once they've gained it, they can lure children to do almost anything, often with horrific results. We can't risk losing our kids to evil people like them."

"Not *everybody* who listens to other peoples' kids is a molester! I mean, look at you; my mom sure never listened to me, but you do," Theresa protested, looking up from her notebook.

"I know what you mean, girl. I'm just painting the worst case scenario since it *does* sometimes happen that way. But not all the time; you're right."

"The best way to prevent that kind of disaster is to keep communication open between us and our kids. We have to know what they're up against. The world they're growing up in is light years away from the world we grew up in and it's too easy to assume they face the same issues that we faced. Just look at some of the differences between my high school experience and that of my kids. Computers were first introduced in my senior year and our teachers tried to teach us computer language. And drugs? One day, the principal discovered some kids smoking marijuana— the first time anything like that had ever happened—and the whole school nearly shut down. Classes emptied, kids sat on the stairs talking about the scandal, parents were called. That's nowhere *near* the way it is now."

"Huh! I'll say. Those were like the dark ages, Katie. Nobody even *remembers* those times." Theresa snorted, tossing her ponytail.

"Well, I guess that dates me. But that's exactly my point. We have to stay in touch with our kids and learn about the world they live in, not the world we grew up in. We can't assume everything's okay with them just because it looks that way on the surface. We have to take the time and effort to talk with them, to ask how they're doing, to know what they're involved in, who their friends are and what's going on at school. It's hard work and it takes time and perseverance, but if we don't do it we risk losing our kids."

"This is starting to sound like a full-time job to me," Jim observed, munching on the last of his salad.

I could feel my eyelids drooping. I gave my temples a brisk rub and continued.

"Yeah, it kinda is. At least it needs a lot of your time and attention. So, when your child comes to you with a complaint, especially about school, make sure to hear him out. Sometimes he may just need to blow off steam and the best thing you can do is just listen. Travis and AdaLayne will need to know that you're on their side. Even though they may seem disinterested or hard on the outside, they're still vulnerable on the inside and need your love and support. So listen, be supportive, and hear them out before you make any judgments."

Jim rested his chin on his fist, eyes moist. "Wonder what that would have felt like. . ." he mumbled under his breath.

"But," I continued, "they also need to know that you'll find out the other side of the story too. I tell our kids that if they're having a problem I'll hear them out and then I'll go hear the other side of the story and after that we'll work it out. Sometimes that's meant my child's had to apologize or sometimes the other person's had to.

"I don't want my kids to think that I'll always bail them out of trouble, 'cause if they're at fault I won't. But I do want them to know that I am always their mom and their advocate. Even if they're at fault, they need to know I'm still *for* them, 100 percent."

"Fortunately, you have a wonderful example of how to be a wise and just advocate in Craig here. He can give you all the pointers you need." I gazed at my sleeping husband: head back, gentle snores emanating from his open mouth, the picture of wisdom and all things fatherly.

Theresa snickered again.

Jim nodded sagely, hiding a smile.

"Now what about tradition for an older kid?" Theresa, still giggling, consulted her notes and looked up at me expectantly, just as I covered my face with my hands to hide still another face-splitting yawn.

"Sorry, guys, it's not the company, really. I just haven't caught up on my sleep yet. Let me think a sec." I rubbed my eyes and stretched my neck.

"Even as they get bigger, our children still like traditions. Traditions bind a family together, giving each person a sense of belonging. Especially during the school years when students face so much risk and challenge, knowing that some things never change is comforting. Traditions don't have to be big and they don't have to last forever, but especially during the teenage years, family traditions help create stability. I can still hear one of our kids wailing as I proposed a change in our Thanksgiving celebrations, 'But Mom, we *always* do it this way!'

"Make sure the traditions are positive. Negative traditions (like the younger generation *always* getting stuck with the dishes after our Christmas feast), don't help much. Remember, you're adding to your kids' stores of happy family memories that will influence them for the rest of their lives."

"So what are your family's traditions, Katie? Give us some ideas here." Jim pressed me for details.

"Theresa knows this one; she saw us doing it when she lived with us. Whenever someone has a birthday, I always decorate the table and hang streamers and balloons in the dining room. But the most important tradition we have, the one the kids never let us miss, is our habit of going around the table and giving all the family members a chance to tell the birthday person something they especially love about him or her. It's a tradition we started when the kids were tiny and we do it still, even with Jeff and Rob being college-aged.

"Another tradition we have is to have a Christmas feast on Christmas Eve where each person gets to ask for his favorite food, no matter how awful or outlandish it might be. (I always ask for pickled herring in sour cream, which I get to eat all by myself.) We set the table with candles and china and my best silver, really making a big deal of it.

"Jeff was born on Christmas day, so we save that day to celebrate his birthday. We had to start this tradition after I forgot his birthday a couple of years, in the midst of everything that goes on at Christmas time. He was *not* thrilled, so we had to do something.

"This is a small one, and one many people do, but it's still important to us. Just about every time any one of us ends a conversation on the phone or walks out the door we always say, 'I love you.' I always want that to be the last thing any family member hears from me each time we part.

"Aside from those. . .I guess you could say that eating dinner together each night is sort of a family tradition. I know lots of families don't do it, I know it's hard to do in today's society, we sure aren't perfect at doing it but it's important enough to us to keep striving for."

"Wow..." Jim said thougtfully. "I can see I have a lot of changes to make."

"Not to put a heavy on you or anything. . ." Craig mumbled, shaking himself awake and wiping his mouth on his sleeve. "But she's right, folks. I heard every word and she's absolutely right. Make traditions with your kids, create memories, and have fun with them while they're still under your roof."

I turned to him in amazement. "You'd better not tell me you've been faking it all this time, you big lug! Have you been lounging over there, taking your rest, listening to every word we've been saying?"

"No, honest, I haven't! I'm innocent as the new-driven snow. I just heard the last few comments. Since they were such pearls of wisdom, I had to repeat them."

"Oh, you are *such* a faker! Flattery will get you nowhere. Next time *you* teach and *I'll* sleep!" I punched him in the arm.

"So, there you have it, guys. Pearls of wisdom from the horse's mouth. Come back in a few weeks and we'll see what the *other* horse has to share." Nudging Craig in the ribs with my elbow, I looked over at the two across the table from us. Jim watched us, wide-eyed, while Theresa shook with laughter.

"Katie, thanks for another evening of great information. I have pages of notes; it'll take us a while to digest it all. Come on, Jim, let's let these guys get their beauty sleep. Not that it'll help *some people* very much!" Patting Craig's arm, Theresa slid out of the booth and kissed me on the top of the head. Jim followed.

"Okay, mister, you get to drive home, since apparently you've had your beauty sleep already."

"That's a little harsh. I was just resting my head," he protested as we slid out of the booth.

"Mmmm, right. Well, now it's my turn."

I was asleep before we left the parking lot.

CHAPTER 29

Touch, Teasing, Talk and Traditions

Questions for Discussion

§

1) What do you think about showing you love your kids by touching them? Did your parents touch you lovingly (and appropriately) when you were a child and a teenager? What are the limits for touch between parents and their children of the opposite sex?

2) Some families are the "huggy" type and are always touching and hugging; others are more stand-offish and rarely touch. Which kind of family did you grow up in? Which kind of family do you live in now? Do you wish it were different and, if so, how would you change it?

3) Is teasing a part of the family you currently live in? Was it a part of the family you grew up in? If so, was it kind teasing or hurtful? Have you ever experienced the kind of teasing that makes you feel like you belong, like you're special, the way Katie describes in this chapter?

4) As a child or teenager, were you able to talk honestly with your parents about anything that might have been bothering you? Do you now have the kind of relationship with your children, if you have any, in which you can discuss anything they need to talk about? If not, how do you think you might be able to change that?

5) Katie described some of the most glaring differences between her school experience and that of her kids. What are some of the main differences between your school experience and the one your kids are (or will be) experiencing? How can you keep in touch with what's going on in their lives?

6) Are there any special traditions that you remember from growing up? Have you carried any with you into your current family? Traditions can be both a positive thing, creating warm memories and family togetherness, or they can bind and constrain us into always having to do certain things in a certain way. Discuss some traditions you might want to start or ones you might want to discard.

CHAPTER 30

Bringing Order into Our Lives

§

I was hanging out our bedroom windows one warm early March afternoon, washing windows and straining to reach the tops of the outside panes, when my cell phone rang. Sighing with exasperation, I wriggled back into the house, accidentally dropping the roll of paper towels in the garden below as I went.

Drat it all!

I fished the phone out of my jeans back pocket and poked at the answer button with a grimy finger. "Yes?" My voice sounded more impatient than I meant it to.

"Katie? It's Theresa, what're you up to? You sound out of breath."

"I'm hanging out our bedroom windows, trying to get a whole winter's worth of filth off the outside. Why, what're you up to?"

"Just need some advice is all. I can call back later."

"No, hang on, that's okay. I can stop for a minute. What's up?"

"It's just been a rough couple of days. Do you have a minute to talk, or do you want to get together later?"

"I can talk for a minute now. What's been going on?"

"Well, Travis is here for his spring break. I'm glad he wants to visit us, and he's a nice kid and all. . ."

Sniff. Gulp.

"But what?"

"But I haven't the faintest idea of what to do with him all day long! He's driving me crazy! Any suggestions before I go completely bonkers or run away? Between him and AdaLayne. . .I don't know, Katie, how did you do it with six children? All that noise and commotion and mess, all that laundry, all those dishes. Yuck! I'm hardly even happy to be here any more. Jim tries to help out, but he's got to work, so I've got the two of them all day long, and I think I'm going to go crazy! Can you help. . .please?" Her voice sounded more than a little desperate.

"Give me some idea of what your days are like."

"Well, Jim gets up early and is out of the house by 6:30, so I have the two terrors from then until he gets home at 5:30."

"Tell me what you do all day long."

"I sleep as late as I can, usually until I hear AdaLayne starting to whine for breakfast and Trav turning the on TV to watch cartoons. Once I get up, I already feel like I'm behind schedule and never catch up. Trav eats his breakfast cereal in the living room and of course that means Addie wants to eat hers there too but I can't let her; she'll spill everywhere. So she screams since she wants to do everything he does.

"Then I have work to do—the laundry and dishes don't just do themselves—and meanwhile the kids are starting to bug each other. Then they start to bug me about being bored, which drives me crazy! About that time I'm wondering if I'll make it through to lunch, much less the whole day. I hate it, Katie. And I'm starting to hate the kids, too. I mean, not really hating them, but resenting them. Did you ever feel this way? Please tell me you did, or I'm going to hang up right now and go dig a hole and crawl in forever."

"Oh, girl, of course there were days when I felt like I would go bonkers before lunch, but it was usually when I let things get out of control." I reached back out the window to try to wash while I talked, but the cell phone kept slipping away from my ear so I folded myself back in and slid down against the wall. I decided I might as well take a break while we talked.

"Let me tell you about order, Theresa."

"Hang on while I run and get my notebook."

Pause.

I collected my thoughts.

God, please give me Your wisdom!

"Okay, I'm back. Give me all you've got. I mean, do you have time now? We could set something up for later, but I'm afraid I'll commit hari-kari if we wait too much longer."

"No, I'm fine, girl. I'll finish the windows later."

"Okay, order. Fill me in. I haven't had much order in my life. Until I met you, that is."

"Think about order for a minute, Theresa. It's everywhere you look and the universe couldn't exist without it. Think of the planets in their orbits; the seasons cycling around; day following night and night following day. Seed time and harvest; cold winters and hot summers; everything in the natural world has an order. Even the seemingly random things like wind blowing and streams gurgling have laws that govern them.

"Or look at language. It has an order to it which is necessary if we're going to understand one another when we speak or write. That's all grammar is—just an order to the formation of words and sentences so we don't all have to make it up from scratch each time we speak or write.

"God's laws reflect His order for our world; He has an order for our lives and relationships, and for the natural world around us. So, clearly, in order to reflect His life, our lives need a certain amount of order as well. In that, we're no different from the rest of the created world. If we don't eat at reasonably the same time each day or get about the same amount of sleep per night, our systems begin to rebel and break down.

"Yeah, I guess I can see that. I'm learning that studying all night really isn't very efficient."

"And once we establish order in our lives we can set realistic goals and actually attain them. If we don't have a goal to work toward, we're not going to get anywhere. The Bible says in **Proverbs 29:18,** *'Where there is no revelation, [or vision] the people cast off restraint; but happy is he who keeps the law.'* In other words, where there's no plan or goal, no vision for what your day should look like, everyone does their own thing. Sounds like that's what's happening in your house."

"You got it. It's awful. So show me how to fix it."

"Hold on, I'm getting there. So, you need to think about order and goals in a couple of different ways. One is physically: where do things belong? Another is chronologically: what do we do at this hour of the day?"

"Keep going, I'm following you but I don't have a clue as to how to do all this yet."

314

"Let's take stuff, for example. Mess. Clutter. It can drive us crazy. So, look at each room, and see if there's a place for everything in that room. If there's not, either there's too much stuff or not enough storage space.

"Look around the kids' rooms; do they have a place to put all their things? If so, cleaning up should be a snap. If not, you can buy, find or make large boxes to hold their toys, books and stuffed animals. If you don't have a book shelf, set a box up on its side and slide the books in. Keep it simple. Get rid of stuff if you have to. Kids don't need a jillion toys—it's just that much more stuff to take care of. Let them have a few toys they really like to play with and put the rest in the basement, or better yet, give them away.

" Make sure they understand where their clothes go in the dresser—underwear and socks in one drawer, pj's in the next, pants and shirts in the next, for example—and in the closet. AdaLayne may be a little young to do this by herself yet, but the point is that you're training them. At first, or when they're still little like Addie, you work along-side of them, reminding them where things go and helping them put their stuff away if need be.

"It's important to instill in them the concept of cleaning up after themselves. Some adults I know *still* don't have this down pat!"

"Tell me about it," she groaned.

"They need to put things away after they're done using them. Teach them that they can't start another activity until they've put away everything from the previous activity and that a job is not completed until you've put away everything you got out to do it. Then you can have a general clean-up time at least once a day before bed, so you start the next day with a neat house."

"Wow. I can see this is going to be good for me too! I wish someone had taught me these ideas when I was a kid. Whenever both kids are here, the apartment is always a mess!"

"I know. Motherhood can either drive you crazy or help you get organized. Hopefully the latter. You suddenly realize you have to be a good example of the order you're teaching your children, and you can't just let your own room stay in a slovenly mess.

"The kitchen is where this applies to the mom especially. Many women I know let the dishes pile up day after day until they have a huge mess on their hands that takes several hours to clean up. (And who has several hours to devote to a task like that?) Good grief, Theresa, I even heard of a lady once who simply never did her dishes. She'd let them pile up and pile up until there wasn't a clean dish in the house, and then she'd throw them all out and *go buy new ones!* Can you believe it?"

"Now that's truly disgusting! Even I'm not *that* bad."

"I grant you; that's a little extreme. But the principle still holds. If you do them at the end of each meal, they won't pile up and become a daunting task that nobody wants to do.

"Housework is like that, too. I once heard one of these housework gurus explain that she kept up with her housework by doing her MMM: Minimum Morning Maintenance. Every morning before she left the house or got started on the activities of the day she'd make sure her dishes were washed, the beds made, the floor swept (at least the kitchen floor), and the clutter from the previous evening put away. That way, she had a fresh start to the day and wasn't staring a huge mess in the face by lunch time. I try to follow her example and it really helps."

"Hmmm, I'll have to think about all this. *Maybe* I'll try to put it into practice, but no guarantees."

"Here's another little tip. Look in each room, and see where clutter usually collects. For me, it's the corner of the kitchen counter where all the day's papers start to pile up. After a few days, we have a heap of bills, school permission slips, junk mail, weekly magazine—you name it—over in that corner, and it's a mess. Plus, it takes me quite a while to sort through all that junk and put it all where it belongs. If I'd just sort each thing as it came in, we wouldn't have this problem.

"Or what about the bathroom? Is there an area in there that's chronically a mess? Do dirty clothes and damp towels pile up on the floor? Make sure there's a place to put dirty laundry and show everybody, even AdaLayne, where it is. She can put her dirty clothes there at the end of the day. You may have to tell her to do it repeatedly but eventually she'll get it.

"What about the living room? Do you have places to put things like magazines and newspapers? Do the kids know that their toys don't belong in the living room in the evening when other people want to use that room too?"

"Jeesh, Katie, this is a lot to remember, even for me! How am I going to get the kids to remember it all?"

"That's where order comes in. Have a general schedule for each day and eventually it becomes habitual. At first, make a job chart for you and the kids. Yours might have things on it like MMM, whereas the kids might have FHT on theirs."

"And pray tell, what is FHT? You sound like a government agency!"

"Face, Hair, Teeth. When our children were little, before they left the house in the mornings we'd ask them if they'd washed their faces, combed their hair and brushed their teeth. It's easy even for moms to forget to do this, especially if they're going to be home with the kids all day. They may think, what's the point?"

"Been there, done that, most days. What *is* the point?"

"The point is, you're setting an example for your kids. Plus, I know I feel better if I have my hair brushed and my face washed. Otherwise, I feel like I've just rolled out of bed and when I still feel like that at four in the afternoon, I'm in trouble!"

"That used to be my everyday look, remember?"

"Look *and* smell; yes, I remember." I chuckled.

"Katie! I heard that!"

"Girl, you did smell, just as I or anyone else would have if she hadn't showered in several days. You smell great now, I promise!"

"How to make a person feel bad. . ."

"Theresa, you've changed so much over the last two years that I don't think you or I would even recognize the old you any more."

"Thank goodness!"

"It was the same for me, I assure you. You just didn't know me back when I was a mess. . .

"Your goal is to have a clean, workable house. It's important to keep your goal in your mind, and make sure it's an attainable one, otherwise all of you will be frustrated. Remember I told you that when the kids were younger, I told them they had to be either adult or quiet to be in the formal living room? That's because one of my goals was to have at least one room in the house where order and quiet prevailed. That also meant that I didn't care quite so much about the other areas of the house; they could look a little more lived in and I wouldn't gripe.

"Now, on to schedules. If I were you, I'd have a set time for you and the kids to get up in the morning. And get up before they do so you can have a little quiet time for yourself to pray and read the Bible, do a workout routine or just sit with a cup of coffee and think about the day. I was talking last Sunday to a mother of three young children about exercise and she told me that the only way she gets it is to get up and go running before the rest of the household wakes up."

"Huh! You'll never catch *me* doing that!"

"Well, maybe you don't like running, but having a little time to yourself before the onslaught of the day is a good idea. After all, you may not get it again until you go to bed."

"Yeah, and even there I don't always get it!"

"I know what you mean, girlfriend." I chuckled and stretched my legs as I glanced at the clock. My schedule was certainly going out the window. Oh, well.

"You're not the only one who needs a schedule; the kids do too. For example, you might tell them that no matter what time they wake up, they have to stay in their rooms until 7:00. Tell them they can play quietly or read, but they cannot go out of their rooms or make noise until 7:00. For AdaLayne, you could draw what the numbers look like if there's a digital clock in her room.

"Yeah, I could do that."

"Then teach them what comes next. And here's where *you* have to be disciplined as well. Whatever order you choose, the following have to be done: getting dressed and doing FHT; making their beds (it's hard for a little person, so maybe all AdaLayne needs to do is to put her pj's away) and making, eating and cleaning up from breakfast. It doesn't have to be written in stone, but the more you can do things the same way each day, the more they'll be able to remember what they have to do, and the more order you're going to sense in your own life."

"I can see this is going to help me more than them."

"Maybe you'll want to do some exercises after that. Remember the idea of setting a good example for your kids to follow? So involve them as much as possible. Set up a progress chart and set you and your children some goals and get a little competition going to reach those goals.

"When the twins were little, and it was hard for me to get out to exercise, I'd do my stretches on the floor with them."

I smiled ruefully, remembering those days when the twins were so little and I felt so overwhelmed.

"We'd sit on the floor with our feet touching to make a circle. Holding hands, one of us at a time would lean back as far as we could go, pulling the other two forward. You can get a decent stretch when your little partner is lying back flat on the floor, pulling you forward!

"Then we'd do push-ups and sit-ups. Obviously, they didn't do many, but I could do them. Probably letting them know by my example that exercise is an important part of daily living was just as important as strengthening my own body. You can preach that kind of stuff all you want, but if you don't do it yourself, your kids will follow what you *do* a lot more than what you *say*!"

"I'm writing all this down. Keep going."

"I'm a big fresh air fanatic, so I always took the kids outdoors for a while no matter what the weather looked like. Let them run around in the sunshine and wear off some energy; it's good for them and for you, too. If you're feeling energetic, run around and climb with them. Often that bored, restless feeling we get when we're inside all day comes from not having had a chance to burn off some energy. Plus, you'll feel great with all those endorphins racing around in your system."

"What the heck are endorphins?"

"Feel-good hormones that you get from exercise. Hey, they're free and make you feel good. What could be better?"

"Okay, got that: feel-good hormones. What next?"

"Have lunch at a reasonable hour, close to noon. That was always hard for me because I could easily go to two or three o'clock before I got hungry, but by that time, even the older kids were whining. Eat in time to keep everyone's blood sugar at an even level."

"Blood sugar?! How am I supposed to know about that? This is getting way too hard!"

"It's not really that big a deal, Theresa. All you need to remember is to feed yourself and your family at regular times. The blood sugar will take care of itself if you do that. Just remember that your blood sugar has a lot to do with your moods, so if you're all getting a little grouchy, maybe it's time for some food.

"After lunch is a good time to rest: naptime for AdaLayne, quiet time for Travis, and break time for you. That's when you can have a little *you* time. Read a book, take a bath, take a nap or do whatever refreshes you. It's nice to have that to look forward to each day."

"I can hardly wait already!"

I laughed.

"I know what you mean, girl! Boy, do I remember those days!

"After naptime (and I'd make it an hour if you can), let the kids have some free play time. This is when you might want to get a head start on dinner or fold a load of laundry, or pay some bills. Give them a snack in the middle of the afternoon to ward off the before-supper whiney blues. After snack, you might read to them for a half an hour or so and then get supper going.

"If they want to help you with supper, all the better. Give them a job they can do. Maybe AdaLayne will just watch at this point (put her in her high chair so she can watch without getting in the way), but Travis can help by setting the table or chopping lettuce or doing some other helpful task. If you're too tired and don't want to mess with it and they don't want to watch or help, let them go somewhere else. This might be a good time to save for that half hour of TV, if you're going to do that."

"That sounds like a great idea."

"Then the last step is bedtime. The more you make this a peaceful, fun time, the easier it will be. Play a short game or read to the kids or sing and pray for them. Spend some time winding down and cuddling. Of course, in your situation, Travis will go to bed later than AdaLayne, but maybe that would be a good time for him and his dad to do something together. That'll also give you a break for a little while in the evening. And remember, mom and dad need time together too, so send Trav off to bed by eight-thirty or nine so you and Jim can have a little time to be together. Travis can play quietly in his room or read in bed if that's too early for him to go to sleep."

"Wow. I think I've got it all down. Did you honestly do all this with your kids, Katie?"

"I wish I could say I did. I tried, but wasn't as disciplined as I'd have liked to have been. I got in most of the elements I told you about, but not always as smoothly as it sounds here. These are just goals for you to think about—suggestions to help make your life easier. They're not hard and fast rules."

"Wow, I'm glad to know that! I was beginning to wonder where to buy my supermom cape."

"You goose!" I chuckled, standing up and stretching my legs. My window washing would have to wait until another day.

"Theresa, I've got to go. The twins'll be home any minute and I need to start supper. We can talk some more on this topic if you like. I have some more thoughts to share on this subject."

"Give me a call whenever you can; I need all the help I can get."

CHAPTER 30

Bringing Order into Our Lives

Questions for Discussion

§

1. Have you ever thought about the order in the world around you? Does your life reflect that order, or does it seem chaotic and crazy with no order in it at all?

2. Does God seem to favor order in his creation? Give some examples.

3. How do you feel when your house or room is a chaotic, disorderly mess? (If it ever is?)

4. Do you think it makes a difference to people, children especially, if they can count on meals and bedtimes being at roughly the same time each day?

5. How does order tie in with consistency? Do kids grow better in a home where there is order and consistency, or does it make any difference?

6. In some families, both parents work outside the home all day yet they still manage to retain a sense of order in the midst of seemingly crazy schedules. Discuss ways in which parents can make that happen—no matter how full the day is.

CHAPTER 31

The Use of Leisure Time

§

A few mornings later as I was cleaning up the kitchen I called Theresa back.

"Hey, girl, you have a minute to talk? I have some more thoughts about what to do with kids when they're home from school all day. You interested?"

"Oh, my gosh, Katie, of course I'm interested! I'm still going a little stir-crazy here. Whatever words of wisdom you have, pile it on. Hang on a sec, let me get my notebook."

I gazed out the kitchen window at the blustery March day, collecting my thoughts. The wind whipped the early red tulips back and forth.

"Okay, I'm back."

"I've been thinking about how to move kids from being whiney and bored to something more productive. We parents need to know how to get our kids to entertain themselves."

"Fire away, Mama. All of us in this family need to learn how to do this, that's for sure. Jim and I both grew up in front of the TV. I think Trav's mom uses it as a babysitter too."

"Let me start with something I call 'diddle time' then."

"And what's that?"

Leaning against the counter, I pulled a pad out from the drawer in front of me and began idly doodling as I talked.

"'Diddle time' is when people don't have anything particular they have to do so they have to entertain themselves for a while. It's that time when kids can begin to make up things and use their imagination. It's when a child can experiment without the pressure of competition or fear of criticism. If every minute is filled with watching TV, playing computer or video games, or participating in too many structured activities, we deprive our children of having to use their own imagination."

"Oh great, so now I have to teach these two how to use their imaginations on top of everything else? What do you take me for, Katie? Mary Poppins?" Theresa wailed.

"Theresa, kids are born with an imagination and often they just need the time and space and encouragement to use it. Many kids never have to use it since all their waking hours are filled with ready-made entertainments. Your job is to provide some basic materials and a little time and see what they'll come up with."

"Be specific here, please, Katie. This is all new territory for me. You know that."

"Let's think about their toys for a minute. Do their toys encourage them to create things and use their imaginations? Do they have things like dolls, Legos, building blocks, dress-ups, paper and crayons, or play-dough? These are all things they can build with, pretend with, or make stuff with."

"Yeah, I think they have some of those things, but they hardly ever use them. They mostly want to watch videos or bug me."

"Then you have to do a little encouraging. Get out the play-dough and make stuff with them. Let them use cookie cutters—use the top of a drinking glass if you don't have any real cookie cutters—and dull knives to cut the play dough with. Make pretend pizza or cookies. Roll the play-dough into balls and make little snowmen. Make cups and saucers and pretend to have a tea party. All it takes is about half an hour and a little imagination. Watch out though, your kids will probably want you to do it again tomorrow!"

"Oh, great, just one more activity I have to squeeze into my day!"

"Theresa, you're teaching them how to entertain themselves. That's one of your jobs as a mom. It may take a little while, but you're training them to find fun in things they can do on their own instead of always relying on man-made entertainment. In the process, you're encouraging their creativity and teaching them to think for themselves."

"I had no idea that keeping kids busy could foster all those great attitudes!"

I smiled and sat down on a stool at the counter, still doodling while I talked. It seemed to help me think.

"One of the best ways you can do this, aside from showing them, is to give them both a little 'alone time' during the day when they have to play in their rooms away from you. Make sure they have some toys they enjoy playing with in there. Then tell them they can come out in half an hour, close the door and walk away. Obviously, AdaLayne might be a little young to understand the concept of time, but just tell her that you'll come get her in a little while."

"So what's the point of all this, Katie? It's a whole lot easier to park them in front of the TV or let them watch a video when they—or I—can't think of anything for them to do!" There was a hint of desperation in her voice.

"Yeah, and what's that teaching them? As soon as you're bored, plop down in front of the boob tube?

"You know, Theresa, we live in a leisure-based society. We don't have to work every minute of every day just to survive. Even though we all say we're so busy, in general, people have more free time now than they did in previous generations. I believe we need to teach our children how to fill that free time in ways that develop the talents, minds, and hands that God gave them instead of letting them be passively entertained all the time. What are we teaching our children about how to occupy themselves with their own minds and imaginations if we just let them sit in front of the TV for hours? Do we want them to know how to fill their free time in interesting and creative ways or do we want them to be forever dependent upon the entertainment industry to fill their free time and their minds?"

"Yeah, I have noticed that even kids' programs seem to have an agenda. Save the rainforests, save the whales, save the panda bears. . ."

"You noticed, huh? And while there's nothing wrong with those things, many kids' TV programs have agendas that I don't want my children exposed to, especially at an early age. Young kids don't have the ability to discern for themselves what is right or wrong. They'll swallow pretty much anything anyone teaches them, including the characters on TV."

"So what are you saying? That we can't watch TV at all?"

325

"No. It's certainly okay for adults to watch TV for relaxation at the end of the day, or for our kids to watch a few select shows each week, but not as a steady diet. We need to know what they're watching—watch the shows with them a time or two so you know what's going into their impressionable minds. Make sure it's not a lot of junk. There are enough good videos for kids out there, like the Veggie Tales series for example, that you'll be able to find something good for them to watch."

"Okay, if they're not going to watch TV, tell me what they are going to do. I need help here, Katie. I'm not the most creative person in the world, you know. And I sure didn't have any of this 'creativity training' when I was a kid!"

I had to smile. This was one of my favorite topics. We'd moved to a rural area on purpose so our kids could have plenty of space to play outdoors and would have to learn to entertain themselves. Craig had built them a sandbox when they were small and later we bought a trampoline on which the kids, sometimes all six at once, entertained themselves for hours, making up games and laughing. They built forts in the cluster of trees behind the house or waded in the creek catching crawdads. They knew if they whined to me about being bored I'd find them some exciting job—like scrubbing toilets, maybe—to occupy their time, so they avoided even the appearance of boredom.

"You know, Theresa, I'm reminded of my younger brother each time I bring this subject up. He was never terribly good at school, but as a kid he loved to fool around in my dad's woodworking shop in our basement. He had a little work bench down there where he built wood-and-glue creations halfway up to the ceiling; pieces of wood nailed on every whichaway and glue dripping in great globs on the bench. Nobody told him what to do or how to do it; he just experimented. When he felt like it, he tore the whole thing down and started over. He's now a very successful cabinet maker, and when people ask him where he got his training, he just grins and says, 'As a kid in my dad's shop.'"

I doodled a little stick figure with a hammer in one hand and a bottle of glue in the other and added huge glasses and a hat on backwards. I shook my head, smiling at myself; my artwork was hopeless.

"May I remind you that not all of us have dads with workshops in the basement?"

"Yes, you may remind me, girl. But we don't have to have a whole workshop to do what I'm talking about. Have a box of craft stuff: paper, pencils, crayons, glue, glitter, scissors and a paint box and sit down and use it with your children once in while. When my kids were little, I used to cut out different shapes of construction paper and have them glue the shapes onto different colored construction paper for an art project.

"Some kids love this kind of crafty stuff; others are bent toward sports and athletic pursuits. But the point is to let each kid have some time to do just what he wants for a while."

"Yeah, I noticed that about your twins. Jason was always rushing out the door to play basketball with his buddies, while Jocelyn still liked playing games with her Barbies."

"Exactly. Each kid is different and we need to encourage them in their interests. Part of this process is allowing our children the time to get to know themselves."

"Huh? Tell me what you mean."

"Do we want our children to be so in the habit of rushing from one structured activity to another that they don't get the chance to learn who *they* are, what *they* like to do and how *they* function? Not everyone functions at the same speed or likes the same level of activity. Some kids thrive on competition; others hate it and just feel like they're never measure up."

"Count me in on that last group!"

"Yeah, me too. I was terrible at organized sports, but I loved making things with my hands. So, for some kids, it's in the unstructured, unpressured moments that their creativity can blossom. They can try things—like my brother in the workshop—without pressure to perform or compete. They can make up games, create whole worlds for themselves, and pretend to be anything they want. It's difficult to foster this kind of creativity when your soccer coach is yelling at you or you've just missed another basket or you're flopped on the couch watching some TV show.

"If you think about it, a kid sitting and watching characters act on a screen is just being passively entertained. He's not using his mind much, or his hands or his body. He's just sitting, being amused. No wonder we have an obesity epidemic in this country!"

"Yeah, I have kind of noticed that."

"Did you know that the word *amusement* really means anti-thinking?"

"No, I didn't, but I have a feeling I'm about to know."

"You're right; you are. *Muse* comes from the Latin word for *mind* and the prefix *a* indicates negation. In other words, a negation of the mind."

"I'll remember that next time I watch TV, I promise."

"Now, girl, I'm not saying you or your kids can never watch TV or play computer games! Just don't let that be their steady diet. Let them exercise their bodies and their imaginations too. Encourage their creativity. Put their pictures up on your fridge, admire their play dough creations, and enter into their imaginary games."

"I can see we may have to make some changes around here. . ."

"And here's one more thing for you to think about while we're on the topic: reading out loud to the kids. Addie's what, two? And Trav is twelve? It might be hard to find books they both enjoy, but I guarantee that they'll both enjoy the time you spend reading out loud to them. For one thing, it gives them undivided time with you. Sitting down next to them, reading, talking and cuddling with them is priceless. I don't know about you, but in our house for me just to sit and spend time with my kids like that is a rarity. My default setting always seems to be on *busy*. It takes a conscious effort for me to stop my rushing about and sit down and just spend time with my kids."

"Tell me about it! And when I do sit down, a lot of times I really don't know what to do with the two of them, or just Addie by herself when Trav's not here."

"I know. It takes a while to get in the hang of thinking of things the kids like to do. But especially for small children, usually the thing they want the most is unhurried, undistracted time with Mom when they're the center of her attention for a while. Particularly in our society, where being busy all the time seems to be almost a status symbol for us grown ups, taking the time to just *be* with our kids is a rare gift to them. And believe me, they'll notice."

"I sure can't ever remember my mother taking the time to read to me or just sit with me. It would've been weird if she had."

I tried to draw a stick figure sitting on a couch reading a book, but I couldn't get the perspective right, so I turned it into a cat.

Switching the phone to the other ear, I continued. "I'm always surprised at how many parents don't take the time to sit down and read to their little ones, since it's such a great way to spend one-on-one time with them.

"Having someone read aloud to you is completely different from sitting and watching television. As you read to AdaLayne, her imagination is engaged as the story progresses. She can see in her mind's eye the little princess or the three bears or whatever the story is about, especially if you stop every once in a while and talk about it. This is an excellent exercise for her mind, and one that's far healthier—in my humble opinion—than sitting and passively watching characters cavort around on a screen. Nothing's left to the imagination there; it's all done for them."

"And I thought that all that reading stuff was just for school. Like we're supposed to let the teachers take care of all that." Theresa sounded thoughtful. I could hear her tapping her pencil on the other end of the line.

"Nope. Reading aloud is for parents; *especially* for parents. A side benefit of reading aloud to your children is that you can control what they are being exposed to. When my children were little, I had a goal of reading them stories from as many different countries and cultures as I could. I wanted them to learn that the United States is not the only country on the earth and that the lifestyle we live here is different from lifestyles in other countries. I wanted them to see how other people lived and thought and acted."

"Kind of like Katie's home travel agency, huh?"

"I know. Laugh all you want. But it is a good way to expose our children to other people and cultures. And you can also expose them to good role models through the books you select. Choose books about people with character qualities you admire: honesty, loyalty, hard work, courage, or self-sacrifice. Read to them about whatever *you* think is important. Choose books that are funny or goofy—Addie will love those, at her age. Choose books with interesting illustrations or unusual stories. Choose books about real people and their real-life adventures. Or pick books of fantasy like C.S. Lewis' books about the imaginary land of Narnia. Read to Travis about the Old West, missionary doctors in Africa, mystery or adventure stories. There's practically no limit, once you get started, to the things you can read to your kids about."

"I'll never have time to do all this before Travis goes back to school in a few days, but maybe if he comes to see us this summer I can do some of these things. And Katie, I have just one other teensy weensy little problem. Just where am I to get all these wonderful books?"

"Well, you could start by borrowing them from us. We have gobs of books from when the kids were little. And then there's always the public library. If you'll use it, I'll buy you a library card as an early mother's day gift. The librarians there can show you what books are good for what ages. Or, if you'd like, I'll go with you and help you to pick out a selection of books that both kids might enjoy."

"And to think I never knew about this treasure trove. . ."

"There are a lot of things you don't know, girl, and I'm making it my personal mission in life to pass on as much as I can of what I know!" I drew a big smiley face on my now full page of doodles.

"I know, I know, Katie, and I love it. Please keep going."

"Okay, one more thought and I'll get off my high horse."

"I really am listening—and writing all this down—I promise. I'm even going to talk about all this with Jim. Go ahead."

"Okay. Kids believe everything we parents tell them up until about the age of ten. At his age, Travis may be starting to question your wisdom a bit, but AdaLayne will look to you as the source of all truth for a few more years yet, so use every chance you get to fill her heart and mind with the beliefs and values *you* think are important. There's so much trash that comes at our kids from the outside world; we have to counteract it at every opportunity with what we think is right and good.

"I began talking to my children about God and His amazing creation before they were weaned. I started talking to them about the dangers of smoking, drugs, and drinking before they were out of diapers. From the earliest ages on they knew that we believe that marriage comes before sex. We read them Bible stories when they were little. What you put into their hearts and minds now is what will help to form the foundation for the rest of their lives. This opportunity does not come around twice, so use it while you can."

"Instill. . . good. . . values. . .early. Okay, got it."

330

"And one last thing: another benefit of reading aloud to your kids is that it can give them a lifelong love for books. Chances are, they'll associate cozy memories and happy feelings with reading and hopefully use that to their advantage as the school years go by."

"Wow, Katie, as usual, you've given me a lot to think about. I don't think I ever gave reading aloud a single thought before. I'll have to give it a try. And by the way, if you're serious about that library card, I'll take you up on it."

"It's a deal, girlfriend."

CHAPTER 31

The Use of Leisure Time

Questions for Discussion

§

1. Have you ever thought about how you use your free time? Do you see time as a gift or just as something to "kill"?

2. Do you think that some people are just born creative or do you think a person can learn to be creative, given the right resources?

3. Did you have the kind of childhood where you were encouraged to play, make up games, go outside, and read books, or was your time spent watching TV, movies, and playing computer games?

4. In the book To Kill A Mockingbird by Harper Lee, the main characters Scout and Jem, two kids ages six and ten, play endlessly with the boy next door, creating a whole world for themselves in the neighborhood in which they live. Together, they lived through many adventures, sometimes amusing and sometimes frightening but always imaginative. As a child, did you have a sibling or close friend you played with like that? Or did you wish you did?

5. Have you ever looked at toys with a critical eye? Some of them are designed for imaginative play—dolls, blocks, trucks, Legos, books—while some toys seem to do everything for the child. What kind of toys does your child have, if you have a child?

6. Was there anyone in your childhood who read to you or told you stories just to spend time with you, maybe cuddling together?

7. Discuss how you want your family to be in this area. Are there changes you'll want to make from the way you were raised?

CHAPTER 32

Service and Self-esteem

§

The next few months flew by in a blur. After spring break, I always felt like we raced faster and faster toward the end of school. April tantalized us with balmy days, making it hard to stay inside and work, and May crescendoed towards the grand finale: high school graduation! Final exams, senior prom, graduation pictures and graduation parties filled our days. Again.

This year Lizzie was the graduate; what a difference from her brothers! They'd had little or no interest in clothes, graduation parties or senior pictures, while Liz agonized over every event as if it were her last. In fact, she kept reminding me that this was her last spirit week, her last prom, her last track meet, or her last exam as these events ticked off her schedule, one by one.

Needless to say, I didn't think about our talks with Jim and Theresa until sometime in June when the summer rolled in on us with its heat and slightly slower pace.

Each summer after school was out, I cleaned the house from top to bottom. We never had the time to do it during the school year, and by June, it needed it. It was a huge job. So, this fine June day, I corralled Jason and Jossie to help me. As I did, I got to thinking about the benefits of teaching kids how to work and serve others.

I really should teach them how to serve others better. Including me.

But, God, it's so much easier to do it myself!

But what are you teaching them?

Jossie decided to work alongside of me, but Jason wanted a list so he could do his chores at his own speed and go play basketball with his buddies. I wrote out a list for him:

1. Wipe down <u>all</u> baseboards on the first floor, using a bucket of water and a damp rag that you rinse out <u>often</u>. Wipe up <u>all</u> spills.
2. Wipe down <u>all</u> the dining room chairs with furniture wax. Use wax <u>sparingly</u>! Do <u>not</u> get the wax on the fabric of the seats.
3. Using the Magic Eraser, dampened, wipe around all doorknobs and surrounding areas on <u>all</u> doors on the first floor.
4. Still using the damp Magic Eraser, rinsed and squeezed out, wipe down all the hand railings on the front and back stairs, <u>all the way</u> to the second floor.

I figured that would keep him occupied for a few hours.

I figured wrong.

In half an hour, he made a break for his freedom, yelling as he burst out the back screen door, "I'm finished, Mom! Going to play basketball with the guys, be back la—"

"Oh, no you don't," I hollered from the family room. "I've got to inspect your work, Jason. Get yourself back in that door!"

"Aw, Mom," he pressed his face against the outside of the screen, "it's a beautiful day out here and—"

"Yeah, well guess what? It's a beautiful day for me too, but these jobs have to be done before you go anywhere. Let's check the baseboards first. Come back in that door!"

The screen door slammed and I heard reluctant footsteps slapping toward me.

I knelt down and swiped my hand along the top of the nearest baseboard. It was bone dry. Even a little dusty.

"Jason, you little skunk. You didn't even do these baseboards."

"I did so, Mom. I swiped 'em all!"

"Show me the rag."

"Uh, I threw it out. It was a paper towel."

"Then it must be in the trash. Go get it."

"Okay. I didn't do them. They look clean to me, so I figured I didn't have to do them if they were clean."

"Did I ask you to figure out whether or not they were clean or to wipe them? Hmmm? How about a little obedience here, fellow?"

"Al*right*, I'll *do* them. Even though the guys can't *play* until I *get* there. . ." he muttered, "and I'm just *wasting* a beautiful day. . .I'll do these stupid *baseboards* for you. Who *cares*, anyway?" He picked up the bucket, knocking it against a chair.

"Jason, doing what I ask you to do with a snotty attitude does not make me happy, nor is it work well done. You go to your room until you can get your attitude right and do this job pleasantly!" I reached out to swat him on the bottom with my rag, but he hopped out of the way.

"I'll change my attitude—look, I'm good now, Mom, I swear. I'll be the happiest little cleaner you ever saw. See, here I go." And humming loudly, he flicked his rag over the baseboards, barely bending from the waist.

"Jason, buddy, you are really pushing it. If you want to go out and play at all today, you'd better straighten up and fly right. Get down on your hands and knees, dip that rag into the water that I don't see in the bucket that you haven't even filled yet, and wipe each baseboard thoroughly. I will inspect and I want to feel each one of them *damp*. Not *wet;* not *drippy*, but *damp*. And I do *not* want to see *any* water on the floor. Am I making myself abundantly clear?"

"You don't have to *shout*. I'm right *here*."

"I absolutely am not shouting. I'm just emphasizing so I'm sure you'll understand. Got it?"

"Yes, Mom. I've got it."

Jossie, busily dusting a few feet away, gave Jason an angelic smile and said, in a clear voice, "I'll be happy to do the vacuuming, Mom. And the sweeping. And anything else you want done. In fact, I'll sweep right here in the dining room. I'll keep an eye on Jason for you, Mom."

Oh gag!

Who had the worse attitude here?

And what was it I said about it being easier to do it myself?

It took Jason the rest of the morning and all of my patience before he finished, to my standards, the jobs I'd given him. I probably checked each task four times before it passed muster, but pass it finally did. As he ran outside, free at last, I heard him yell back to his sister, "And don't you go running your hand down those railings! Those things are *clean,* man!"

At supper, I noticed him bending down to brush a speck of dirt off the newly washed baseboards.

As Craig and I were getting ready for bed that night, Jason popped his head in our door. "Any time you want something really *clean,* Mom, you know, the way the pros do it, I'm your man. Just call on me. Nobody else around here does as good a job as I do." I nodded soberly, as if the idea had never occurred to me.

"Great idea, son. I'll keep it in mind. Thank you."

"Maybe we ought to get together with Theresa and Jim soon again," I murmured as he left, "and talk about how to train kids to work."

"Give her a call."

*   *   *   *   *   *

We met a week later at their apartment.

Theresa met us at the door wearing a hot pink hip-length tunic and a pair of black capris. "Wow, cute outfit!" I crowed as I gave her a hug. She just grinned.

"So," Craig said as we settled onto the red couch in their tiny living room, folding our knees behind the packing box coffee table, "how are things going in the parenting department?"

"Or the husband-wife department, for that matter," I chimed in, looking eagerly from one to the other.

Jim and Theresa looked at each other guiltily.

I elbowed Craig, grinning.

"I knew it. I just knew it! Oh you two, I'm so happy for you!"

"Happy? What? We haven't said a word! What are you talking about?"

"You're going to have a baby, aren't you? 'Fess up now, I'm right, aren't I?"

"Katie, how can you tell? We just found out for sure yesterday."

"It's written all over your faces, plain as day."

"Well, even if it is, Katie girl, they might have wanted to tell us in their own time and way, you know." Craig nudged me with his elbow.

336

"Okay, so tell us." I looked eagerly from one to the other, ignoring him. "Tell us! In your own time and way, of course. . .but *now*. Immediately. Please!"

"Well. . .we're going to have– " Jim began.

"Twins!" Theresa finished, laughing and shaking her head and holding her tiny belly all at the same time.

"Oh, my gosh!"

Was that Craig or me saying that?

After congratulations all round and inquiries about Theresa's state of queasiness and Jim's mental preparedness for two more babies in the house, we got down to business.

"So, where did we leave off last time?"

Theresa checked her notebook. "Katie, you and I covered order and the use of free time on the phone back in March, so I think we're up to service and self-esteem. Right?"

"I think that's about right." I nodded at her. "So Craig, where do we start?"

"How about with service, as in teaching kids to work?" He turned to the two of them. "Once the twins come, you're going to need all the help you can get for about the next five years or so!"

"Five years, nothing. That's just the beginning." I groaned. Not to be too encouraging or anything.

"From the very beginning, guys, it's a good idea to give your kids jobs around the house. For one thing, it helps you out, and believe me, you'll be needing all the help you can get."

"Don't scare them off, Craig. We lived through twins; they will too."

"Let's put that in the present tense, lovie. We are *still* living through twins, if I remember correctly. But back to the topic at hand. Giving your kids jobs around the house that they're responsible for each week produces a number of benefits."

"Such as?" Theresa had her pencil poised.

"Helping them to acquire a sense of responsibility, for one. When a kid is born, he thinks the world revolves around him and actually, for a while it seems to. But he's got to move beyond that thinking pretty quickly or he turns into a spoiled brat. Nobody likes a spoiled brat, whether they're three or thirty-three. I know plenty of spoiled brats at work, and believe me, they are a pain in the you-know-where!"

"How-*ie*," I remonstrated, elbowing him.

"It's true, Katie, and you know it. These guys know what I'm talking about.

"Having a job in the household, even if it's a small one like something AdaLayne might do lets them know that they're part of a larger group and that they're needed in that group. It's all part of that knitting together as a family that Katie's always talking about."

"I seem to remember something about that. . ." Theresa glanced my way. I raised an eyebrow at her.

Remember?

Maybe this was sinking in, after all.

"Part of what knits us together as a family is taking care of one another and watching out for each other. As I said, this doesn't come naturally so we have to train our children to do it. And part of that training is to give them jobs they are responsible for."

"Like? Be specific, Craig, so I can write it down to remember it. I'm a little distracted these days, as you might imagine."

"Okay. Let's see, Travis can load and unload the dishwasher each night. AdaLayne can put the silverware in. They can each pick up their own clothes and put them away or in the laundry hamper. On Saturdays, they can each do a general household job. Travis could empty the trash or even do the vacuuming and AdaLayne could help you pick up. Of course, the hitch to all this is that you have to supervise."

"And believe me, that can be more of a pain than doing it yourself," I added helpfully.

"But the point is not to have the housework done in the most stellar manner possible; it's to train your kids to work, to think of someone other than themselves, to teach them responsibility and to begin instilling in them a work ethic."

"Yeah, I wish a few more parents would care about this kind of stuff," Jim said. "We can't keep good help in the shop for more than a few months. Invariably, the younger guys come to us, saying the work's too hard, the hours are too long, their hands are all banged up, or they can't come in as early as we need them. It makes me sick, to tell the truth."

"Plus, there's always the idea of helping others," I added. "We live in such a 'me-centered' society—it's all about me and what I want and what I need, or think I need—that we need to consciously counteract that trend. Jesus tells us in **Matthew 10:39** that he who finds his life will lose it, and he who loses his life for Jesus' sake will find it."

"Okay, Katie, please translate. That just sounds like gibberish to me. I'm not a real Bible scholar, if you remember." Jim looked at me plaintively.

"Craig?" I looked at him. He could usually interpret scriptures in a way that made sense to Jim.

"Well, let's look at it." He picked up his Bible off the coffee table and thumbed through it. "Here it is. *'He who finds his life—'* This is the person whose sole focus in life is the search for his own personal happiness. Making that his focus causes him to miss the deeper meaning to life where true contentment lies, because we are put here on this earth to serve one another, not simply to fulfill our own needs. Doing that leads back to yourself alone, a lonely place to end up in." He looked back at the Bible.

"*'Will lose it,'* Ultimately, a person in this situation begins to wonder, 'What am I doing all this for? What's the point? Have I lost everything that really matters?'"

"You don't have to tell me," Jim commented. "Before I met Theresa and AdaLayne, my life was just one long cycle of making money to feed my own face so I could get up in the morning and make more money to feed my own face again."

"Now," Craig continued, "I'm not talking about people who happen to live alone and work to support themselves. There are plenty of loving and sacrificial people who live and work alone. I'm talking about an attitude—the attitude of 'the world owes me.'

"So, going on, *'and he who loses his life for My sake will find it.'* I take that to mean that we find true happiness in doing whatever Jesus has called us to do, which I'd be willing to bet will involve working with or helping people somehow, being part of a team, or of something greater than yourself."

"So, in these early years," I joined in, tucking my leg under me and turning so I could see both Jim and Theresa, "it's our job to train our children to be part of a team, to think of others, to put their own needs and wants after those of the people around them."

339

"And giving them household jobs to do is going to accomplish all that?" Theresa sounded more than a little skeptical. Flapping her top a little to give herself some air, she loosened a strand of hair from her ponytail and began to twist it around her finger.

"You betcha!" Craig assured her solemnly. "It's the snake-oil remedy of our times. It'll cure dandruff, hives *and* selfishness."

I poked him. "Don't listen to him, guys. It's coming up on the weekend; he always gets this way when he can see light at the end of the tunnel."

"No, seriously, guys, training my kids to work is something I do take seriously. I want them to be able to hold down a job when they are older, but even more importantly, I want them to be compassionate human beings who think of others' needs before their own. That doesn't come naturally, in case you haven't noticed. There's a lot to be said for serving one another and it's sure not something the world around us promotes very highly."

He flipped open the Bible to where he'd been holding the place with his thumb. "Look in the verse before the one we just read. It says, *'And He who does not take his cross and follow Me is not worthy of Me'* (Matt. 10:38). I take that to mean that we are to practice being like Jesus in laying down our lives for others."

"Hang on a second, guys, I need to use the restroom, but I don't want to miss a word of what you're saying, Craig. Hold everything, will you?" He obediently froze.

A minute later, she returned.

"Ah, much better! How two tiny bodies the size of my baby finger can cramp my bladder so much, I don't know, but they do. Now, you were saying?"

"We're talking about teaching our kids to lay down their lives for others. Obviously, we need to model this in our own lives first, because as you know, they learn by watching us far more than by listening to all the pearls of wisdom that fall from our mouths. And the amazing thing is that we get the opportunity to lay down our lives every day, if we'll just keep our eyes open."

"Be specific; what do you mean, Craig?" Jim leaned forward, elbows on knees, eyes on my husband.

"Well, we have the chance to lay down our lives for our wife and children from the time we walk in the door after work until we go to

340

bed at night. Am I going to head straight for my easy chair and sit and relax while Katie carries on with supper and cleaning up and seeing that the kids are taken care of, or am I going to pitch in and help with all those things?

"Laying down our lives for one another rarely takes the form of jumping in front of a moving car for another person. No, it's faithfully doing our job each day, moving our body out of the recliner to help our wife when all we want to do is relax, or being the one to get the phone when we're both sitting down for the first time all night; that sort of thing."

"Being aware of how the other person feels, you mean? And trying to be sensitive to that?" Theresa asked, her pencil hovering over the notebook.

"That's exactly it, Theresa. It's watching how the other guy's doing. Is he—or she in my case—tired out and up to here with the kids? Does she need a break, a hug or an encouraging word?"

"So, getting back to our kids. How does all this relate to teaching them how to work?" Jim asked.

"Talk to them about the value of work, of helping out. Let them know that their contribution to the family is important. Thank them for the work they do. I don't mean you have to compliment every little thing like, '*Wow*-sers! I am *so* impressed that you've set the table, the job we ask you to do *ev*-ery night!'"

Theresa and I both giggled.

"But just let them know that the whole family benefits when they do their part. Help them see themselves as a part of the team and not just a solo character sailing through life, tending only to their own needs."

"And you know," I broke in, leaning forward, "another benefit of teaching our children how to work and do it well is that it strengthens their self-esteem. Learning to do a job well is good for children; it gives them something to be proud of. There's so much talk these days about how kids need self-esteem, but I don't hear much talk about requiring them to earn it. It doesn't grow free on trees, you know," I ended emphatically, rolling my eyes and shaking my head in disgust.

Craig looked at me, bemused. "Gee, Katie, tell us how you really feel, why don't you?"

I kicked him.

"Sorry, babe." He tried to look contrite. "Go on, I'll be quiet. You're onto something here."

"Okay, *if* you're done." I gave him a mock glare and turned back to Jim and Theresa,

"I believe self-esteem has to be earned. Yeah, every child needs a certain amount of 'I love you just because you're you, and you're wonderful just the way you are', but kids also need to earn approval from work well done."

I took the Bible out of Craig's hand. "See, here in *Genesis 4:6*. We've discussed this passage before. God is talking to Cain after he'd brought the wrong kind of offering, remember? Cain's all mad and downcast because God hasn't accepted his offering—which tells me he wanted to do it *his* way and not God's—and God basically says to him, 'Why are you angry, and why such a droopy face, as if you're surprised that I didn't accept your offering? If you do the right thing, don't you think you'll be accepted and feel My favor? And if you don't, well, sin—the temptation to be angry and feel sorry for yourself—is waiting for you at the door and it'll swallow you up if you let it.' To me, that's gotta be the basis for self-esteem: do the right thing and do it well and you will feel approval from others and, incidentally, from yourself as well.

"So," I continued, looking at Theresa, "bringing this back to the present. Here's what we did. I took six household jobs—dusting, vacuuming, ironing, cleaning both bathrooms (that counted as two jobs), and taking out the trash—and divided them up amongst the kids. Each kid was responsible for his job for a month, and then we'd switch. The kids had to do their jobs every Saturday morning before they could do anything else. Sometimes, I'll admit, there was griping and complaining and I had to hound them fairly often to get them done but overall, the system worked."

"Did you pay your kids to do these jobs?" Jim asked.

"You know," Craig answered him, "we went back and forth about that and finally settled on the idea that these jobs were just part of living here. We paid each kid a minimal allowance weekly, and if they needed to earn money for something special, we'd pay them for doing extra work around the place, but doing these weekly jobs was just each kids' contribution to the family, much like me going to work or Katie managing the household.

"Besides, we wanted them to know that you don't get paid for everything. Some things you do just because it's your responsibility, so you do it without expecting to be rewarded."

"One more thing," I said, unfolding my legs and scooting sideways down the couch to get out from behind the coffee table, "and we'll be out of here and let you guys get some sleep." I stood up and stretched.

"Let's take the idea of doing jobs for no pay one step further. We live in such a 'me-centered' society that it's easy for kids to think the world revolves around them. Look at school for a moment; it's all about competing against other students for the highest position in class, the last spot on the soccer team, or the most-favored-student status. For many students, it's all about them. So look for opportunities to encourage your kids to help others. Maybe they can help you prepare a meal for a new mom."

I bent over and kissed Theresa on the head,

"Or maybe it's raking leaves for an elderly person or saving money to give to charity, but whatever it is, let them know that helping other people is a good thing to do, just for its own sake. Encourage them to develop the mind-set of looking for ways to bless the people around them. They'll be better people for it. As they get older, encourage them to get involved in volunteer work or mission trips, or to just be the one willing to take on extra responsibilities at home, at school, or at church."

Craig stood up. "Hey, guys, it's been a fun evening. Call us when you want to do it again."

"And don't you dare wait until the babies are born to call us again! I don't want to hear any of this, 'Oh and by the way, guess what, Katie? I had the twins two weeks ago' business, you hear?"

"Yes, Mama."

I blew her a kiss, and we were out the door.

CHAPTER 32

Service and Self-esteem

Questions for Discussion

§

1. Have you ever thought about the idea that we find true happiness when we feel that we are part of larger whole than just ourselves? What do you think about this idea?

2. It's written in our Constitution that we all have the right to "life, liberty, and the pursuit of happiness." Just what is the "pursuit of happiness"?

3. How were household jobs handled in the home you grew up in? Did you have to pitch in and help or did the adults do all the work around the home?

4. If you have a family now, (or want one someday), how do you divide up work around the house? At what age do you think children can be asked to start helping out?

5. How does having household jobs and being required to do them by a certain time each week contribute to order in a family?

6. What do you think of Katie's belief that children need to earn self-esteem, not just have it handed to them, regardless of whether or not they do a good job?

7. Mothers in some cultures *force* their children to be the best in their classes, and *force* them to practice long hours at musical lessons or homework, depriving their children of play time with friends, sport and other activities they consider "unprofitable". Discuss what you think of that approach.

CHAPTER 33

Being an Authentic Christian

§

Theresa called again halfway through the summer.

"Hey, girl, how ya doin'? I've been thinking about you guys. It's been a while. What's up?"

"Oh, I don't know. Not much, I guess. The summer's dragging on. I'm hot and tired; the kids are hot and tired, so I thought I'd call you. You always have a way of perking me up."

"Well, thanks, I appreciate the compliment. Want to come over for dinner tomorrow night? I think all the kids will be home, quite a rarity these days. Come on over, and we'll barbecue. The girls can watch Addie afterwards and Travis can play with Jason while we talk."

"I was *hoping* you'd say something like that. I'm so tired of being the *mother* all the time!"

"I know just how you feel, girl. Come on over and I'll mother *you* for a while."

"Can we go through our next topic as well? I want to get all this stuff tucked under my belt—if I could only wear one—before the babies come, 'cause once they're here, I don't think I'll have time to brush my hair, let alone absorb all the info you guys give us."

And you don't know the half of it, dear girl. Some things you just have to live through. . .

*   *   *   *   *

The evening sun reached long, golden fingers across the grass and the air turned balmy. As the heat abated, it left behind a soft dusk, a lovely time to sit outside and talk. Travis, Jason and Jossie—with little AdaLayne toddling along behind as fast as she could go—ran around in the wet grass with mason jars, chasing fireflies. The older two boys had gone inside and Molly and Liz joined us around the glimmering embers of the barbecue pit.

Oh, Lord, I love times like this! Thank You.

I looked around contentedly at the people I loved.

Theresa stirred herself and reached into her bag for her pen and notebook.

"I think we have just two more categories to study before we become genuine, certified, expert parents, equipped to handle any and all situations that might arise in the business of raising children—old, young, newborn and duplicates."

"Wow," Craig said, putting down his soda and looking over at her, "show me where you're getting all this expertise! Maybe we can bottle it and sell it. Whaddya think?"

"I would if I could; believe me. Maybe I'll do the next best thing and put everything you've taught us into a book someday—*after* the kids are raised."

"I wouldn't put it past you for a minute, girl. Just let me know when it's published, so I can be one of your first fans." I grinned at her.

"So what's the topic tonight?" Jim wanted to know, all business as usual.

"I believe it's 'being authentic,'" Theresa answered, looking back in her notes.

"Ah. . ." Craig rubbed his hands, "one of my favorite topics: how to be a real Christian in front of your children, who see you at your best and your worst, but usually your worst. So, how can we be godly adults in front of them when they're fully aware of our flaws? Do we put up a façade and try to be perfect? Or just let it all hang out? What do you think, guys?"

"Daddy, can I say something?" Molly spoke out of the gathering darkness.

"Sure, love-bug. What is it?"

"You want to know one of the things that most impresses me about you as a godly dad?"

"I sure do. Say it nice and loud and clear so all these good folks can hear what a great guy I am."

"Daddy, don't be silly. Do you want to hear me or don't you?"

"I'm listening, sweetheart. I'm sorry. Go on."

"Well, you kind of did it right then."

"Did what?"

"Well, one of the things that I admire most about you is that when you've done something wrong, you're quick to repent. I mean really repent, the way a kid can believe—you know, from the heart, like you really mean it. It's like you think it's the most important thing in the world to have us forgive you. When you humble yourself like that, I always think, 'that's the kind of man I want to marry: a *real* Christian.'"

An uncharacteristic moment of silence followed before Craig said, a bit choked up, "Thanks, sweetheart. I'll always remember that. And no doubt, I'll have a chance to practice it before the evening's over."

"I'm sure you will. You *are* human, you know."

We all burst out laughing.

"So, what can we add to the words of wisdom from the mouths of babes?" Craig asked a minute later, wiping a tear from his eyes as the laughter subsided.

"What *does* it means to be authentic, and what does it have to do with good parenting?" he asked, looking at each one of us.

"Theresa? Got any thoughts?"

"Uh, so that we won't be phonies? I don't know. You tell me, you're the teacher."

"What about you, Jim?"

"All I know is that I hate a fake. I hate it when anybody tries to be something he's not. It makes me want to gag."

"You know, I bet God feels the same way when we try to be something other than what He made us to be.

"So imagine with me: God has a master plan, which we all fit into somewhere. If we try to be something or someone we're not, we mess up His plan. That's not to say He can't fix it—He'll accomplish His will regardless—but it may take *us* a while to get ourselves back in line with Him."

Jim shot a glance at Theresa. "This all sounds strangely familiar."

She pursed her lips, nodding softly. "Yep, been there, done that, for sure."

"So," Craig continued, "in my book, being authentic means just being myself, just plain old Craig. God made me the way He made me, and allowed me to have the life and experiences I have for a reason. If I try to be something I'm not, I could miss the whole reason He put me here on this earth."

I smiled at him. I loved the way he put things in down-to-earth terms.

"That's all well and good, Craig, but what does it have to do with good parenting? I don't get the connection." Theresa frowned, pressing her pen against her lips.

"It has to do with parenting because before all else, our lives are examples to our children of how to live, or not live, as a good Christian."

"Wow, I think I'll just give up right now, thank you. If I have to be an example to AdaLayne of what it means to be a perfect Christian all the time, I might as well quit now!"

"Ahh, girl, I didn't say 'an example of being a *perfect* Christian'; I just said 'a *good* Christian'.

"Explain. Please." Sprawled out on a chaise lounge, she pulled a strand of hair out of her ponytail and flicked it back and forth between her fingers.

"Okay. We're to be an example of how to live a godly life the best way *we* know how, with all our failings and mistakes as part of that. If we put on a façade of being perfect, our kids will know we're fake and they won't want to follow us as Christians or anything else. If, however, we admit our failings, struggles and weaknesses, and if they see us asking God to forgive us, they'll see how a godly adult handles such things. They'll realize that it's not bad to fail, receive God's forgiveness and keep going."

"Okay Craig, I'm going to play devil's advocate here." I jumped in.

"Yes, my love, my little turtle dove?"

I shook my head and rolled my eyes.

"What about where we're told to be perfect, even as God is perfect *(Matt. 5:48)*? How does that fit in?"

"Another translation of the word *perfect* is *holy*. Holy means 'set apart'. We're to be set apart for God's purposes, not the world's."

"So," Jim asked, leaning forward, "give us some specifics here. You know Theresa and me; we're pretty simple people.

"Well, I'd say the first reason to be authentic is so we can fit into God's plan like a puzzle piece fitting into the whole puzzle. This is how we honor Him best. If we're wriggling around, trying to be something He didn't create us to be, we won't fit into that particular spot He's got for us. We need to live our lives as real people with all our faults, repenting when we've blown it, admitting we are selfish, sinful, and imperfect. In other words, we need to be real and humble."

"Yeah," a voice piped up from the darkness, "that's what I meant about Dad. When he repents like that, he's so *humble*. It makes me just love him to pieces. It makes me forget all about why I was mad at him in the first place or what stupid thing he'd done."

"And that's the way our children will know that the life of one who follows Christ is not one of trying to be perfect, but rather of repenting for the sins that we do every day. Come here, girlie." He held out his arm to Molly, who got up and stood next to him, not quite willing to sit in his lap in front of our friends. He put his arm around her.

"Yeah," Jim muttered, "humbleness I can relate to. Being a perfect Christian, on the other hand, is so far above me I might as well forget it."

I leaned forward on my chaise lounge, hugging myself as the evening dew brought a slight chill to the air, and joined the conversation.

"Another thing we need to do to be authentic is to name things for what they are—like you and I talked about a long time ago, Theresa, calling a spade a spade. It's hard for me to admit that I lie, or am selfish, but if I don't admit it, and receive God's forgiveness for it, I start to live a more and more phony life."

"Give us an example, Katie," Craig prompted. I winced, embarrassed.

"Okay, this is what I mean about naming sin as sin. This past Christmas I made cranberry muffins for our extended family and Craig's co-workers at the office. When I took them to the post office, the mail lady asked me if there was anything breakable, liquid or perishable in the packages and I said no thinking that if I said yes, she

349

might not let me mail them. In other words, I lied—not that I admitted it to myself.

"Some time later, my sister-in-law called to thank me for my gift. 'But,' she said, 'I have to tell you, the muffins were green with mold. Just thought you'd want to know.'

"Oh my gosh! Was I ever mortified when I thought of all the people who had received moldy green muffins from me! And all because I had lied and said there were no perishables in the package. God gave me a jab in the side: 'Hmmm, you think you don't lie? Let's get real here, sweetheart.' And I saw that, yes, I do lie. Ouch!"

"So even the holy mother was caught in a lie," Craig murmured, just loud enough for us all to hear.

"Well, if even *you* lie, Katie, and *I* think you're pretty close to holy, then there's hope for the rest of us!" Theresa said loyally.

"Thanks, girl. And there's hope for all of us because we all have the same loving Father Who is *always* ready to forgive us and set us on our way again. Remember, we talked about this as being the definition of grace?"

"Yeah…like the baby just learning to walk? Yeah, I do remember, and now I really know what you mean since I've watched Addie learn to walk. I'll pick her up as many times as she needs to help her get going again."

"And that's exactly what God does with us!"

"So I'd say," Craig continued, standing up and warming his hands by the barbecue, "that the most important thing we can do for our children is to introduce them to the living Lord and encourage them to build a personal, real relationship with Him. After all, if they don't know Him and know how much He loves them, they won't know where to get forgiveness when they blow it. As children feel loved and accepted *as they are, for whom they are* by Jesus, they're more able to live enthusiastically and joyfully. They can be themselves, not putting on facades or trying to be super-spiritual. That's true for us adults as well and that's what I call living authentically."

"I'm intrigued, Craig. Tell me how love and living a full life are connected." Jim asked.

"Well, it's like this," he said, stretching his hands out over the coals, "if I know someone loves me, I'll *want* to do my best for them, but if I think they're watching over my shoulder just waiting for me to mess up I'll be far less eager to do a good job for them. Rules without love just breed rebellion.

"Here's an example. I've already told you that my dad wasn't they most loving guy. He was an over-the-road trucker, and I thought his big rig was the coolest thing in the world. The times he'd let me come with him, I'd do anything to please him: wash the cab, vacuum it out, pack us some sandwiches—whatever I could do to win his favor. Those times, I felt he loved me even a little bit and I responded eagerly. But I hated it on the Saturdays when he was home and angry, demanding that I do this, that and the other for him—and make it snappy, boy! Those days I hated him and didn't want to do anything he asked."

"So connect that to being authentic, will you?"

"It's the same principle. If we really understand God's utter love for us, we'll *want* to follow His commands, out of love for Him, just like I'd do anything to please my dad when I thought he loved me. On the other hand, if we just have to follow a bunch of rules to please a demanding God, we're not going to *want* to follow God with all our hearts. And if *we* don't want to, it's doubtful our kids will."

"Well," Theresa challenged, "aren't there some 'should's' in the Christian life? Like what about the Ten Commandments? They're not just suggestions to do if and when we feel like it, are they?"

"You're right," Craig turned toward her, warming his backside at the low coals in the grill, "they're not optional. Remember when you first came to our house and Katie told you our rules, like we all eat together in the evening? Did you feel like following those rules?"

"To be honest, no. I never told you guys, but when I first came I thought you all were *weird*. The last thing I wanted to do was to follow your rules!"

"So what happened?" I laughed, looking at her through the dusk and loving her. "Something must have changed, or we wouldn't be here tonight!"

"I was blown out of the water the day you followed me over to Jeannyne's house and asked me to forgive you. I'd never experienced that kind of tenderness before, and it cracked open a part of my heart I didn't even know was there. I was intrigued enough to follow you back home and give it another try. And then I began noticing your family and how you'd say things like, 'I'm sorry; please forgive me,' or 'I love you' to each other. That's when I decided I wanted more of whatever you all had."

"So you shocked my socks off by coming upstairs the next morning dressed, showered and ready to help with breakfast! I tell you, I nearly fell on the floor when I saw you."

"And you know why I did that?" Theresa smiled at me through the deepening dusk. "I figured, 'Katie cares enough about me to ask my forgiveness and stay up late talking to me, so the least I can do is follow her rule about showing up for breakfast dressed and clean.'"

"So," Craig stretched his arms over his head, looking up at the stars, "do you see how that translates exactly into what we're talking about with God? Once we can feel how much He loves us—enough to die for us—then we begin to respond the way you did, Theresa. We think, 'At least I can *try* to follow His rules 'cause I know He loves me.' We can even trust that the rules—the Ten Commandments and all the rest—are for our good and not just to make life difficult for us."

"So we respond better to His rules when we first understand His love for us, don't we, Craig?" I interjected.

"Absolutely. Which is why I always obey all the rules you lay down for me: wipe your feet before you come in the house, chew with your mouth shut, eat all your veggies, pick up your clothes and put them away before you even *think* of going to bed. It's 'cause I understand they're all because you love me. Right, sweetie?"

He smiled blandly at me. I made a face at him.

"But," Jim pressed on, ignoring us, "how are we supposed to have a loving relationship with God if we haven't known any love from our own father? And how do we convince our kids of God's love if we're not even sure of it?"

"Good question, Jim. A lot of us, me included, have a hard time believing God loves us because our earthly father never did. Thoughts, Katie?"

"All I know is you've done an amazing job of loving our kids, even though you never received much love from your dad. Because of that, I think they'll have an easier time of understanding God's love than you did."

"Thanks, my love," Craig murmured softly, blowing me a kiss in the dusk.

"So," I continued, "if we take our eyes off the poor examples our earthly fathers left us, and instead focus on God, we'll become more like *Him* instead of like our human fathers. And, like Him, we'll be loving."

"So you're saying," Jim hunched forward, clasping his hands loosely between his knees, "that even though I never experienced love from my father, I can ask God to fill my angry, closed heart with *His* love so that I can love my son just as if I had a dad who loved me? And God'll also help me to be more like Him so I *can* be a good dad? Is that what you're saying? Because if it is, that's pretty incredible." Jim's eyes bored holes in me searing me with his hope.

Yes!

I softly pumped my fist in the dark.

He's getting the idea.

"That's exactly what I'm saying, Jim. The God of the universe loves us enough, and loves our kids enough, that He'll fill us with His love so we can love our children. You're right, it *is* incredible. Our part is to be paying attention to Him."

"So," Theresa said, busily writing by the light of the fading coals, "the first thing we need to do as parents is cultivate our own relationship with Jesus. Right?"

"Right. We can't pass on what we don't have. Developing our own life of devotion—spending time talking to Jesus, confessing where we've messed up, reading the Bible—has got to be the first step in living an authentic life."

"He *wants* to lead and guide you with his eye upon you, as it says in **Psalm 32:8.** *'I will instruct you and teach you in the way you should go; I will guide you with My eye.'* In other words, God wants to lead you gently through your spirit, so be responsive to Him and He won't have to knock you in the head with a two-by-four to get your attention the way He's had to with some of us.

My legs were starting to twitch; a sure sign that it was time to call it a night. Setting my feet down on either side of the lounge chair and sitting up, I began to wrap our conversation up. "So, let me summarize. If we love God and know beyond all doubt that He loves us, we'll *want* to serve Him with all the personality, talent *and* weaknesses we possess. If we spend time with Him and read His word, we'll find out how He wants us to live.

"If we ask Him to use us—*our* arms, *our* hearts, *our* words—to love our children, He will, and as they grow up, they'll feel His love. If we're humble and real, admitting our mistakes and asking our children's forgiveness when we've hurt them, they'll learn that the life of one who follows Christ consists more of grace and forgiveness than rules and regulations.

"And if they learn that, I believe our children will want to follow in our footsteps."

"You make it sound so simple, Katie." Theresa said, putting down her pen and massaging her temples.

"Ah, there's the rub: actually walking all that out, day by day! I constantly have to struggle with myself, wanting to do things *my* way, and I continually have to let God gently but firmly lead me back into *His* way. It's a lifelong battle, but I think that's what keeps us focused on Him."

"Yeah, if yielding to Him to do things His way weren't a struggle that we needed His help with every day of our lives, we might just start to think that we were pretty good and didn't need Him any more. Then what a mess we'd be in!" Craig remarked, walking over and offering me a hand up out of my chaise lounge. I gratefully took it, that strong hand I knew so well, and stood up and stretched.

"Ahhh, what a lovely evening. And the kids have been *so* good! I can't believe Addie's still up."

A voice came out of the darkness. "She's asleep on my lap, Mom."

"Carry her inside for Theresa, will you, honey? That way Jim can get Travis."

"Actually, Jim needs to get Theresa. Come haul me out of this chair, will you, babe? I can hardly move."

"Ready? One, two, three, heave!" he grunted, pulling her up.

"Can we get together again before the babies come, Katie? I want to get all this down before I drown in baby care."

"I'll give you a call, girl. We won't leave you hanging, I promise."

I put my arm around her thickening waist and helped her walk through the dark and the wet grass back to the house.

CHAPTER 33

Being an Authentic Christian

Questions for Discussion

§

1. Truly *feeling* the love of God is something that many people seem to struggle with. What is it like in your life? Do you know—and *feel*—God's love for you, or not? If not, why not?

2. Do you know anybody who is just a little *too* spiritual, like they're a little holier than you (in their own opinion, perhaps)? How does that attitude make you feel?

3. My son, an ex-cop and a Christian who doesn't go for all the "gushy stuff", has a job as a security agent for a large, Christian ministry. As he was driving one pastor to his hotel, he told him, "Just so you know, I don't like pastors. But you're okay." What do you think he meant by that remark? What about the pastor might have attracted him?

4. Have you ever found yourself in a position where you had to repent to someone of something you'd done wrong and it was embarrassing and hard but you did it anyway? How do you think that apology made the other person feel, especially if they were not a follower of Jesus?

5. If you are a follower of Jesus, how can you be real to those around you so that they will be interested in what you believe?

6. How can we be our real selves without looking like the rest of the world?

7. Discuss the things that have attracted you the most to some Christian you know. Is there anything about that person's life that draws you to him and makes you want to know more about the Jesus he loves and serves?

CHAPTER 34

Garbage In, Garbage Out

§

School started unusually early that year; it seemed like it was only half way through the summer. But August 18 was August 18 and there was no getting around it, summer was over. We were down to a skeleton crew now with three away at college. Lizzie, true to form, had selected yet a third college, in the opposite direction of her brothers.

Remembering what had happened last year when I'd told Theresa I'd call her as soon as school started and then forgot until October, I resolved to call her before I got caught on the merry-go-round of fall school activities. Besides, her babies were due soon and I wanted to see her before that event eclipsed everything else for several months. I wanted to discuss one more area with her. So on a rare, quiet afternoon just after Labor Day I picked up the phone.

"Hey, girl, how are you? I've been thinking about you a lot lately. How are things going? How are you feeling these days?"

"Oh, Katie, I'm a mess! Pregnancy is for the birds, especially if you're carrying twins. I'm as big as a house. I can't sleep; I can hardly move, I feel like a blimp!"

"Oh, honey, I know how you feel. How much longer do you have?"

"I'm not due for another month, but my OB doesn't want me to go longer than a few more weeks. I don't know if I can even go that long. I think I might explode."

"The one thing you *can* count on is that just another few weeks and this part will be all over."

"Yeah, and then comes the part about no sleep and doing nothing but baby care from morning 'til night. I'm not exactly looking forward to that either, I want you to know!"

"Sounds like you could use a little pampering before your life changes forever. Can I take you out to lunch? How would you like to go to Jimmy's on the Square for a fancy ladies' lunch, just us two?"

"Oh, Katie, really? Are you sure? That's a lot of money. But before you change your mind, yes, I'd love to come. It'll probably be the only time in my life that I'll get a chance to go there so I'll come, waddles and all."

"Wonderful. I'd love to treat you, honey."

"But, Katie, wait—what'll I wear?! I've been wearing Jim's sweats for the past month, and even they don't fit too well now. Everything's stretching and popping to the point where I look like the original Michelin man. And we sure don't have it in our budget to go out and buy me a whole new outfit! Maybe we should just forget it. . ."

"No way, girl. I'll dig around and see what I can find that will fit you. I'll come a little early to help you get all dolled up. Now, what day?"

*   *   *   *   *   *

Early the following week I drove to Theresa and Jim's apartment. Theresa opened the back door for me but I couldn't get in past her. She had to waddle all the way back to her bedroom before she could turn around and give me a hug. She was right; she was as big as a house. Poor girl!

Jim had taken Addie to Jeannyne's house for the day on his way to work so we took our time getting Theresa prettied up. It had been weeks since she'd put on make-up or done any more than run a comb through her hair. I'd brought her one of my old maternity dresses; a green jersey one that stretched tight over her huge belly but nonetheless complemented her shape and brought out the green in her eyes. We curled her hair and I put it up in a high ponytail, tying it with a pink ribbon. I'd bought her a new pair of hot pink flip-flops to go with the outfit—something she could slip into without having to bend over.

When the makeover was complete I snapped a picture of her and sent it to Jeannyne, Craig and Jim. She looked gorgeous.

We got to Jimmy's on the Square after the noon rush was over so we had plenty of space and time to sit and talk. We both ordered quiche and salad and split a cheesecake for dessert.

"Okay, lovely Mama, are you ready for one more teaching before you go into hibernation when the twins come?"

"Can you reach into my bag for me? My notebook and pen are in there, but there's no way I can bend over that far." She rolled her eyes at her helpless condition.

"Sure. Here they are. Now, we've covered all but the last section of what we said we'd discuss about raising an older child. Actually, this last section is important for kids of all ages. I call it GIGO: garbage in, garbage out.

"You've heard the phrase, I'm sure, 'We are what we eat'? Well, I'd expand that to say, 'We are what we eat, see and hear.' Consequently, as you're raising these children of yours be careful not only about what they eat but also about what they see and hear."

Theresa had turned herself sideways to the table and was jotting notes as I spoke. "I'm with you so far; keep going."

"Let's start with eating, then. Think for a minute about your attitude about eating. Give me a quick synopsis of how you look at food."

"Well, I know we're supposed to eat right and all and I'm really trying to cut out fast food from our diet for financial reasons if nothing else! I try to limit the amount of junk food the kids eat. Why, what are you getting at?"

"Think of it this way. As a mom, one of the main ways in which you take care of your family involves food. You can affect your family's health, their moods, and even the kids' grades as they get into school through what you feed them. In these childhood years, you're establishing eating patterns—emotional as well as physical— that will affect them for a lifetime. Craig's mom used to feed him bread and butter sandwiches when he was little so even to this day, bread and butter signifies comfort and care to him."

"What am I supposed to do to give them good eating habits? Keep it simple, will you? As you might have noticed, I'm about to have twins and can't handle anything terribly complicated."

"Okay, here's my main point. Educate yourself all you can. It will be a life-long process so don't worry about trying to do it all at once. But just get in the habit of reading nutritional labels, of thinking about good nutrition, and of making a conscious effort to provide your family with healthy foods ."

"Give me some specifics."

"As a rule of thumb, make your meals colorful. Have fruit with your breakfast and at least two bright colored fruits or vegetables at lunch and dinner. For lunches, along with their sandwiches or macaroni and cheese, you could offer AdaLayne and Travis baby carrots and sliced red and yellow bell peppers—sweeter than the green ones—tomatoes and dark green lettuce, or peas and carrots.

"For suppers, try spinach and winter squash as side dishes, sweet potatoes and broccoli, or green beans and sliced tomatoes. Experiment with different kinds of vegetables. Try slicing zucchini squash thin, drizzling it with olive oil and roasting it. Or dot cabbage with butter, sprinkle with salt and pepper, wrap it in tinfoil and roast it.

"Buy fruit and vegetables in season. They're fresher then than if you buy them canned or even frozen. And canned fruit usually contains a lot of sugar as a preservative, something you don't want to add to your kids' diet.

"Watch for ways you can add a vegetable here or there. Serve carrot sticks with your kids' sandwiches instead of chips or give them fruit for breakfast along with their cereal. Offer them cut up raw veggies with a little ranch dip for a snack instead of a cookie. If some of the stronger tasting vegetables like spinach or kale don't appeal, chop them up fine and put them in spaghetti sauce, vegetable soup, or stews.

"I don't even know what kale is, let alone how to use it!" she put down her pen and looked at me in bewilderment, shaking her head.

"It's a leafy green vegetable kind of like spinach that's loaded with calcium. You can chop it up and put it in coleslaw or spaghetti sauce or soup. Broccoli's got a lot of calcium in it too, by the way.

"There are all kinds of ways to sneak vegetables into food without your kids knowing about it. If you're making waffles or muffins you can add pureed pumpkin from a can for some extra nutrients. Or nuts and raisins. If you make them oatmeal in the morning add raisins, dried cranberries, chopped apples, or wheat germ. The trick is to always be on the lookout for ways to increase your family's nutritional health by adding extra fruits and vegetables."

"Isn't all this kind of expensive?" she asked, looking at me with narrowed eyes.

"It might be, in the short run. But when you think about the doctor and dentist's bills you'll avoid, it turns out to be a good investment."

"I'll keep that in mind as I balance a baby on each hip and whip up a batch of homemade vegetable soup, I promise!"

"You don't have to put all this into practice immediately, girl. These are just things for you to think about as you go along. Always think healthy. Use whole wheat bread instead of white. I know whole wheat bread is about three times more expensive, but think of all the nutrients your children are getting from it that they won't get from highly processed, fiber-free white bread made with bleached flour. And while we're on the subject of baked goods, you might as well decide now not to buy pre-packaged muffins, cookies, cupcakes or pop tarts. They're all loaded with sugar, preservatives and saturated fat—which is the worst kind. If you really want to give your children muffins as a treat once in a while, bake your own and put nuts and raisins in them."

Theresa laid her pen down and looked at me. "Yeah, right. Like that'll ever happen. I don't think I've ever baked muffins in my whole life."

"I bet you're doing all kinds of things you've never done in your whole life. Give me a call and I'll come bake with you one day."

She just rolled her eyes and shook her head wearily.

"Here's another way to guard your kids' health: watch their body shape. If they begin to develop a spare tire around their middle, nip it in the bud as quickly as possible because fat cells, once created, never disappear. Actually, fat around the middle is a bad sign for all of us no matter what our age. It's called visceral fat and it's the worst kind for our organs and heart.

"Because, remember, you're establishing in your children lifetime attitudes towards food and eating right in these early years. What you feed them now will become normal for them as they grow older."

"So, on the off chance that I should see just a smidge of belly fat," she said, patting her own tight belly and looking up at me, "what do I do about it, before we all fall over dead?"

"Check out your habits. It's our habits that can make or break us, not the occasional treat or lapse. What are you feeding your family in general? How much sugar and fat creeps into your diet on a daily basis? How much physical exercise do you and your family get? Do you encourage outdoor play? Do you take walks as a family?

"And here's another tip. Watch what you drink. Sodas are full of calories and even the artificially sweetened ones contain chemicals that neither you nor your kids need. Interestingly enough, fruit juices have about as much sugar content as soda does so don't let your child drink excessive amounts of it. And *never* leave a young baby alone in his crib, sucking on a bottle of fruit juice or even milk, for that matter. Not only could they choke if left alone like that but also having a steady wash of milk or juice on their teeth is a great way to give them cavities. Give them water instead."

"I'm gonna have to get up and walk around here in a minute; my legs are cramping. Can you condense all this down to a few rules of thumb for me? Something I can remember?"

"Sure. Here are four quick things to remember.

1) *Avoid white stuff*, especially if it's processed. Try to limit white flour, white sugar, white rice, and white potatoes. I'm not saying you can never eat these things; just remember they're full of pretty empty carbohydrates which turn into sugar in your body. It's that excess sugar which contributes to unnecessary weight gain if you're not careful.

2) *Read nutritional labels.* Try to avoid or use sparingly foods that have sugar in the first five ingredients. Anything that ends in '*-ose*' is a form of sugar. Food manufacturers often divide sugar into its different compounds—all words that end in '*-ose*', like sucrose, fructose, glucose, etc—so it doesn't look so bad, but don't be fooled, as far as your body's concerned it's still sugar. And if you can't under-stand the majority of the ingredients, don't buy it. If you have no idea what's in it, why should you eat it or feed it to your family?

3) *Eat food as close to its original form as possible.* Food does not need to be sweetened and breaded and covered with cheesy sauce to be good and all those added extras

just pack on the pounds. Besides, when you feed your children food like that, you're just training them to shy away from the real thing.

4) And last, *move, move, move.* Limit time on the computer or in front of the TV and get out and move! Make activity a way of life, because every little bit helps."

"Speaking of moving," Theresa said, laying down her pen and stretching a little, "I have to get up and walk around for a bit. I'm losing feeling in my legs, below the bulge. Wanna walk a little? Do you have time?"

"Sure. We can go outside. It's a glorious day and a little walk would do us both good. You mind if I finish up with my thoughts while we walk?"

"Fire away. I just can't write anything down. Maybe it's better if I keep it in my head, anyway. I'm not going to have any time in the next few months to look at my notes, that's for sure!"

"Okay. I'll try to make it brief. I need to pay—"

"And I need to go to the bathroom."

"—so I'll see you out front."

Ten minutes later, I found her sitting on a bench in front of the restaurant, looking hot, awkward and uncomfortable with her belly resting on her knees.

"Come on, girl, let's get some walking in while we can. I have a feeling you don't have much longer."

"Gimme a hand up, will you?"

"Always, my dear. Always." Smiling, I took her outstretched arm and heaved. Up she came, like a majestic ship righting itself after a squall.

"Now that the beached whale is up and moving, you can talk. I think I can walk and listen at the same time. No guarantees, but I'll try."

"Alright. Here are some more tidbits for you. First, as you remember, all of us are made up of three parts—"

"Even I can remember that: we're body, soul, and spirit. The body's obvious, the soul is our mind, our will and our emotions, and the spirit is the part that connects us to God. There, how'd I do?" She grinned over at me.

"Way to go, girl! You have been taking all this in. I'm impressed."

"Seriously, Jim and I do talk about this stuff in the evenings some-times. I get out my notes and we go over what you and Craig have taught us. I don't want you to think it all goes in one ear and out the other."

"Well, I'm glad to hear that. As you know, I think you have a tre-mendous gift for teaching. I bet some day you'll be passing all this along to some other young woman."

"If I do, I just hope she isn't in as bad a shape as I was when I first came to your house! Either that, or I hope I can be as patient with her as you've been with me."

"Oh, girl, it hasn't been hard to be patient with you! We-e-ll, maybe once or twice it was, right there at the beginning, but from then on it hasn't been. You've been like a baby bird with its mouth open."

"So fill me up one last time, Mama bird," she said, leaning on me heavily as we slowly navigated the steps out of Jimmy's courtyard.

"Okay. About body, soul and spirit: you need to exercise, care for, and develop each one. So let's talk for a moment about what we put into our souls and spirits: pretty much anything we see or hear.

"Remember that Satan, our spiritual enemy, has a *huge* influence in the things we watch—movies, TV, DVDs—as well as the things we read. So be careful about what you let your children see, listen to and read. Here's an example of what I mean. There's a well-known series of books about a bear family that is popular with young children. The only problem with these books is that the dad is always messing up and doing something stupid, exemplifying the saying that I've many mothers use, 'I have four kids: my three children and my husband.' How far removed is that from the Biblical standard of the father being the head of the household, the provider and protector, the one to honor and obey?"

"I think I see what you're getting at. . ." Theresa said, her voice quiet.

"Think about it for a moment. Wouldn't Satan just love to ridicule and demean men in the guise of harmless children's literature? People may say when we object to books like these, 'Oh, it's just a *children's book*, for heaven's sake! Don't be such a *stick-in-the-mud*'. But that's exactly the point: little children don't question what they read. They don't have critical thinking skills yet, and Satan knows that children are gullible enough to receive his destructive messages when they're wrapped in stories. A spoonful of sugar makes the medicine go down."

"Well, *this* is great news! How am I supposed to tell what's good and what's bad for my children to read or watch? Now I have to be media police along with everything else? I'm getting exhausted just thinking about all this, Katie!"

"Don't think you have to do it all on your own, Theresa," I said, taking her arm and guiding her around a broken place in the sidewalk. "God will help you. Sharpen your own understanding of what God considers right and wrong by reading the Bible and spending a little time with Him each day. He'll show you.

"Here's another example of what I mean, this time from a movie. A popular movie out not too long ago was advertised as a good family film so we watched it. Well, at least it gave us a lot to talk about as a family! It was a prime example of how Satan slips his message in virtually unnoticed."

We turned right and walked down a side street where there was more shade. Theresa was sweating and slowing down. I looked for a place for us to sit.

"In this movie, not only was the man the clueless one and the woman the calm, cool and competent one but even more inappropriately, it was the little girl who really knew what was going on. She was the one who told the helpless dad where the daycare was and what to fix for supper. *She* certainly had it all together even if he didn't!

"In addition, references to inappropriate drinking, to living together without the benefit of marriage and to lecherous behavior were slipped in here and there, all as perfectly acceptable lifestyles. Interesting 'family fare'!"

"Come on, Katie, all that stuff's pretty common. We don't live in the last century, you know."

She stopped, breathing heavily, and leaned against the side of a building for a minute. I watched her closely, trying not to look too concerned.

"And that's just what I'm talking about. The culture around us *is* changing and it says that there's no problem with all the things I just mentioned; they're all are fine; no problem. But, for one who is trying to follow Jesus, some things—like the ten Commandments—are *not* supposed to change. It still says that if you honor your father and your mother it will go well with you **(Deut. 5:16)**. In my book, putting a father down and portraying him as a weak and childish character is not honoring him. Portraying the children as wiser than the parents is just plain upside down. Kids don't need encouragement to be rebellious and sassy know-it-alls; that comes pretty naturally. On the contrary, they need to be trained to be respectful and obedient."

"Katie, you mind if we just rest here for a minute or two? My legs don't seem to want to walk much farther."

"Of course, honey. You want me to get the car?"

"No, just stay here with me. You can go on talking. I just need to rest a minute, that's all." She lowered herself onto a low brick wall that ran along the edge of the building and leaned back heavily. Closing her eyes, she began to lightly massage her massive abdomen: up, down and around. I remembered just how soothing that felt.

"Keep talking, please. It makes me feel safe and loved when you talk."

Oh, girl, I'll talk all night if that's how it makes you feel!

I glanced at her, my brow furrowed and sat down next to her. Maybe my talking would keep her mind off her discomfort.

"So how do we train ourselves and our children to be able to spot Satan's counterfeit and evil values? The same way bank tellers are trained to spot counterfeit money: they train themselves to recognize the real thing by looking at genuine money for hours at a time. We need to do the same by reading the Scriptures and learning to recognize truth when we see it. Then we need to teach it to our kids. Make it fun for them. We used to use a book that had verses for kids to memorize for every letter in the alphabet. We'd work on it a little each day until they had all the verses memorized. I'd give them rewards and prizes as we went along to keep them motivated."

I looked at Theresa. She was listening, but seemed to be almost in a trance, massaging her belly up, down, and around. I went on just to keep her calm.

"Read them books that have characters and values you agree with and that are about people you'd like to have in your own house as a guest. Talk about what God is doing for your family. Let them know that God is working behind the scenes at all times on their behalf. Always remember that you are training and raising a child to love and serve God with all his might, all his days."

I looked over at her. She was leaning her head on the wall behind us with her eyes closed, but her nostrils flared with every breath and her lips were pressed together tightly.

"I think I'd better go get the car, sweetie. Think you'll be okay here by yourself for a few minutes?"

"Yeah, I'm fine. Only, Katie, don't dawdle, okay?"

Believe me; I didn't.

*   *   *   *   *   *

I pushed the speed limit and got her home in record time. There wasn't room for the two of us side by side on the rickety stairs to her apartment so we made it up with me pushing from the back and her pulling herself up by the railing, panting and resting on each step. I propelled her down the hall to her bedroom, slipped her dress over her head and helped her under the covers. Lying down, she seemed to calm down, her breathing slowing and her face relaxing. I called Jim to let him know what was going on, Craig to let him know that I might be late for dinner, and Jeannyne to let her know that she might need to keep AdaLayne for the night. Then I sat next to her on the bed with my hand on her shoulder, praying for her. She was sleeping peacefully by the time Jim arrived home, so I slipped out. This was their time.

CHAPTER 34

Garbage In, Garbage Out

Questions for Discussion

§

1. Have you ever given much thought to what you eat? Have you ever considered the effect your eating habits have on your moods, your health, and even your school grades (or those of your children)?

2. What kinds of foods did you grow up with? What kinds of foods are your comfort foods? Different areas of the country and different ethnicities have different foods they consider to be their own. Do you come from an area or an ethnic group that eats a particular kind of food?

3. How healthy do you consider your current eating habits to be? Considering the rise in this country of diabetes and obesity (both diseases directly linked to what we eat), how important do you think it is to cultivate healthy eating habits?

4. Have you ever read the nutritional labels on the back of all packaged foods produced in the U.S.? Those labels contain a wealth of information that can be very helpful to anyone trying to eat in a healthy way.

5. Similarly, have you ever considered what goes into your eyes and ears and how that affects your moods? Music is an especially powerful tool as it goes into our brains in a different way than the spoken word does. Satan knows this and uses music for his purposes whenever he can. What do you think is the difference between music that glorifies God and music that glorifies Satan?

6. Think about your favorite movie. What kinds of messages does it portray about parents, lifestyle, and attitudes?

7. Discuss ways in which you can control what goes into your—or your children's—eyes, ears, and stomach.

CHAPTER 35

And So It Goes...

§

Jim texted me early the next morning that they were headed for the hospital. I prayed for them off and on all day while I waited eagerly for the next call. After supper, I made a cup of tea and sat up with a book, determined to wait up until I heard something. A text finally arrived around midnight: "Twins arrived 11:47. Beautiful! James Craigson, Katharine Theresa. Babes, mom all fine. Come see us when u can." I mumbled a grateful prayer of thanks and shuffled off to bed, where Craig already lay snoring.

* * * * * *

I went to see them the next day. Theresa sat in the bed, glowing, holding two tiny, tightly wrapped bundles, one in a blue blanket and one in a pink.

"We're going to call them Jamie and KT. Aren't they beautiful?"

"They're gorgeous, sweetie. How are you feeling? How was labor?"

"Fine, fine, and fine. Actually, labor was a real drag this time around. After last time's twenty minute experience, I thought that's how all labor went. Boy, was I wrong! This lasted all day, with *hard* contractions. I wasn't sure I was going to make it, a time or two. But every time I thought I was going to die, Jim was right there, rubbing my back, telling me I was doing great, keeping me going. So we both finally made it. He just left to go get Addie."

*   *   *   *   *   *

Over the next three months, I went over to Theresa's one day a week to give her a hand. I'd take Addie out for walks or take the twins out so she could spend some time with just Addie. Once or twice, she brought all three of them to our house on a Saturday morning so she and Jim could get out for a while.

I could tell things were getting tight in their apartment as the twins grew too big to sleep in a bassinet next to Jim and Theresa's bed. They didn't want to put them in with AdaLayne since they were still waking up several times a night and the room they saved for Travis when he came to visit was little more than a closet. Something had to change, so I wasn't surprised when Theresa told me that Jim was putting out feelers for a better-paying job. However, I was strangely unprepared for the phone call when it came, just before Christmas. I hadn't been over to help for a few weeks as the Christmas crunch had arrived at our house, complete with science projects due, basketball tournaments and Christmas plays and concerts at the high school and junior high.

"Katie, are you sitting down?"

"Good grief, girl! What's up? Don't scare me like that. What's going on? Everything okay?"

"Well, yes and no. Yes: Jim found a really good job. No: we're moving."

"Where to? When?"

"Seattle. Just after Christmas." Her voice quavered, just a bit. She sniffed and cleared her throat loudly.

"Like in a month or two?"

"Like in two weeks. The moving van comes for our stuff, such as it is, the day after Christmas. We follow the next day, driving all the way to Seattle. I can hardly believe it."

"My gosh, girl. When did all this happen?"

"Jim's been talking with some people out there, and they've offered him a really good job in the airline industry; one he can't turn down.

371

It'll be good for our family and all, but. . ." her voice drifted off and I hurried to fill the silence.

"Can I help you? What can I do? You need me to watch the kids so you can pack? I mean, this is all so—"

"Sudden. I know. I'm still pinching myself. Um, yeah, if you want to watch the kids, that'd be great. I kind of don't know where to start, but I guess if the kids were out from under my feet for a morning, I could think straight enough to start packing stuff up. Yeah, watching them for a while would be super. Thanks so much, Katie. What day's good for you?"

Two days later, she arrived at eight in the morning. She walked into the house with Jamie in one arm, KT in the other and a huge diaper bag hanging off her shoulder. Addie, suddenly shy, hid behind her mother's legs. Wearing sweats and an old hoodie, Theresa looked worn and tired, her hair flat and limp, no make-up and her birthmark blazing red on her neck. Heading straight for the family room, she laid both snowsuit-clad infants on the floor and turned to me, throwing her arms around my neck and laying her head on my shoulder. Silently, she began to weep, her thin shoulders shaking.

"Katie, I don't know if I can do this. I don't know if I *want* to do this," she mumbled into my hair. I stood quietly and stroked her back as her sobs subsided slowly. I put both arms around her and rocked her ever so slightly. I could almost feel her going limp in my arms.

*   *   *   *   *   *

The day after Christmas, the moving van arrived and in two hours, the men had packed up all of Jim and Theresa's earthly possessions. We invited them to spend their last night at our house, which they gratefully accepted. The next morning, after one last homemade waffle breakfast, we all hugged and said our good-byes and gathered in a circle for a quick prayer before they set off. Then they were buckling the kids into their car seats and with a final wave out the window, were off down the road. I felt a huge emptiness in my gut as I waved until they were out of sight. The rest of the day, I was restless and irritable, not knowing quite what to do with myself.

Theresa called a few days later to let me know they'd arrived safely and had found a large apartment to rent until they could find a house to buy, "maybe by next summer." I called her in March, just to see how they were doing, and she sounded busy but happy. The twins were scooting everywhere and Addie was registered for nursery school in the fall. Travis was going to spend the summer with them and maybe even live with them for the school year. I told her I loved her, gave her a brief run-down of our family news and hung up.

Our school year raced by, and before I knew it, the college kids were home, looking for jobs, and the house was full once again. I relished that summer, knowing that it might be the last one we'd all be home together.

Theresa called near the end of the summer, just to catch up. The twins were crawling; Addie was excited about going to school in a few weeks; Jim loved his new job; Travis had spent the summer and had decided to spend the school year with them as well, and best of all, they'd found a church to go to and were beginning to get involved there as a family. They were still looking for a house to buy or rent, but the apartment was big enough for now. She sounded happy and content. I rejoiced.

Fall flew by with three in college and three in high school. I thought of Theresa often, usually on the run, and I'd send up quick little prayers for her. Christmas arrived, and with it a Christmas card from Seattle. I eagerly opened it, to find a photograph of Jim and Theresa and their family. Travis stood almost as tall as his dad, obviously in full adolescent bloom, five year old Addie smiled wide enough to show a gap where her front tooth should have been and the twins hung on Jim, KT on his shoulders and Jamie hanging off an arm. Theresa stood next to Travis, with a baby bulge clearly showing. I called her the next day.

"So what's this beautiful little bulge I see on your front?" I asked and almost added, 'and why haven't I heard about this before?' but realized things had changed, so I kept quiet.

"Oh jeesh, Katie, can you believe it? Another baby? I've been having a pretty hard time believing it myself, let alone telling you about it. This wasn't exactly planned you know. I thought four was plenty!"

"I know the feeling, girl. Believe me; I do. How far along are you and how are you feeling?"

*   *   *   *   *   *

I carried Theresa in my heart all that winter, and into the spring, but we didn't talk much. Her life was full, and so was mine. In the middle of April, I received a birth announcement for little Joseph Adair Schipper, 9 lbs. 3 0z. 22 in. long, born April 9. I called her that night, and we had a long talk, catching up. I sensed she was firmly settled into her new life and although tired, was still on top of things and able to cope. I couldn't help but think of her after her first childbirth, and the time I'd found her curled up on the couch, miserable and alone.

We received Christmas cards regularly after that, each one with a loving and personal note, catching me up on all the kids' doings. Travis decided to live with them permanently and adored his little brothers and sisters, who, in turn, idolized him. Jim advanced regularly in his work, and Theresa even found time to start going back to school at night to finish her nursing degree.

Just before the end of his senior year of college, Jeff brought home a lovely young woman to visit and they announced their intentions to get engaged that summer. We were surprised, not having heard him mention her, but Jeff hadn't been telling us a whole lot lately. Not that there was anything wrong; he was just beginning to live his own life and didn't feel the need to check in as often as he used to. By the summer after that, they were married in a lovely, simple ceremony at her folks' house in another state. Our whole family attended, all of the siblings from both sides of the family standing in as bridesmaids and groomsmen.

They hadn't been married more than a few months when Liz came home from college with a young man. At least this time we'd heard her talking about him for a while and were more than delighted to meet him. Before we knew it, another wedding was in the works and Jeff and Abigail announced that they were expecting.

For the next five years, our lives were a blur of high school and college graduations, one a year for a while, with babies and weddings thrown in there as well. I decided to go back to school and get my teaching degree, ironically enough, I thought, now that all our kids were out of school. Craig supported me enthusiastically, and I loved the mental stimulation of the academic world.

*   *   *   *   *   *

It was Christmas again and I brought the mail in as I came home from school. On the top of the pile was an envelope from Seattle; still my favorite Christmas card, I thought to myself as I ripped it open. As usual, there was a photo of Jim and Theresa and their growing family; Travis sporting a beard, AdaLayne as a lovely young junior higher, the twins gangly and skinny at seven, and little Joey a sturdy five year old. I flipped it over to read Theresa's update on the back.

"Dear Katie,

I just wanted you to be the first to know that I have actually written a book, just like you used to tell me I would. It's dedicated to you since it's all about everything you ever taught me. I have been teaching a class for young women at our church for some time on all these topics—yes, I use the material straight from the notes I took from our talks—and I always tell people about you so I thought I'd finally put it all in book form and get it published. However, since it's really your book, I wanted you to know about it first. It should be out in the spring and I will send you a copy as soon as it is.

I love you and am eternally grateful for all you've done for me. People here think I'm quite the expert on motherhood and Christian womanhood. Ha! Little do they really know. Maybe some day you can come out here and I'll introduce you to the women I teach and they can see who the <u>real</u> expert is.

Until then, I remain always, your 'daughter'.

Love forever, Theresa."

I couldn't help but cry, just a little, standing there in the cold air by the mailbox.

Well, thank You, Lord.

Afterword

§

L est it appear that I believe that only a stay-at-home mother can do a good job of raising a family—even though that was the only way *I* knew how to do it and I am still amazed at those women who seem to be able to run a household, give their children love and care *and* work full-time outside the home—let me offer this letter, written by a mom of two small boys who has a full-time job outside her family.

"To my boys, both of you.

I feel like this summer is slipping by like sand through my fingers. So, I wanted to write to you both to let you know just how much I am enjoying watching you grow, enjoy life and be the boys that God is creating you to be.

I am having so much fun being your mom. This is an incredible, exhausting journey. I hope both of you become dads some day. In fact, I pray for both of your wives, wherever they are, that they would be women who know God's grace. I pray that you both have kids, and are able to experience the joy that comes along with being a parent.

This summer has had so many moments that I just want to hold in my heart forever. . .

The hot air balloon race last weekend—how fun was that!!!?? Joshua, you'd asked me a few times if we could go up in a hot air balloon, especially after watching Curious George take a hot air balloon ride. I'd always said no, it was too dangerous for a little boy, but that tethered balloon was the way to go! Stevie, you didn't really like it at first, did you? The man who was running the balloon asked if anyone needed to get off, and out of 3 year old terror, you cried, 'Me needs to get off!' Then, as soon as we got to the ground, you said, "I gink I didn't need to get off. I gink I didn't." I loved it!

We had a blast on vacation in Traverse City with your grandparents. Wasn't it fun to go to the sand dunes? We ran with abandon, three generations whooping and hollering, down a steep, sandy, soft mountain of sand and ended up at a rocky Lake Michigan shore, where we all stood and threw rocks in the water. Then you two boys, your grandmother and I climbed all the way back up the dune again!

You both loved the train ride where the conductor let you pull the whistle. Joshua, you pulled it just a wee bit timidly, but Stevie, you cranked on it long and loud. I hopped on the train with you at the last minute even though you could have gone by yourselves, but geez, these little steps—all part of letting you go—are hard for a mom. But I have no choice; you're growing up, guys.

Joshua, I loved watching you—with your orange hat on backwards—try out for soccer this summer and try your hardest. Be sure and be thankful for the accolades you receive: be humble and teachable.

Both of you like sleeping in the same room which makes Daddy and me happy. We want you guys to be buddies with each other—yeah, there are days when you don't get along and there may be life stages where you're interested in different things or maybe you'll be interested in too much of the same things and need some space—but either way, we hope and pray for lifelong friendship between you guys.

I've been working full-time for the past year, and Daddy is part-time right now. He's home with you a lot more, and boy am I thankful for all the stuff he does to keep this home running. You guys have a wonderful Daddy. I hope you can both be like him some day.

Life could change for us soon. We hope to have another baby and we may be moving too. But last night, as the three of us were riding our bikes—Stevie on your trike, Joshua on your bike with the training wheels and me on my bright yellow bike—with the last vestiges of sunlight shooting out from behind the trees, I thought, 'This is just perfect. I don't want to wish away these days. Life is very good right now.'

And it is. I love you both. I'm SO glad I get to be your mom."

So, my prayer is that each of you who reads this book, as you work your way through the motherhood years with God's help and direction, will be able to say the same thing to your child or children: I'm SO glad I get to be your mom.

Kitty Block

For questions, advice, or information about ordering more copies
of this book,
please visit my website:
kittyblock.net

CPSIA information can be obtained at www.ICGtesting.com
Printed in the USA
LVOW070441211212

312659LV00001B/1/P